"Holy Cripes! My Mac's Busted!!!"

Quick Fixes for a Funky Mac

Although I'd like to believe you purchased this book because of my winning smile and sophisticated air, I realize that many of you clutch this tome in a state of sheer panic. Your Mac is on the fritz; you've neglected to back up the important documents on your hard drive; and you pray that within these pages, you'll find the solution to your Mac's woes. Relax. I've placed these emergency pages at the beginning of the book solely for your salvation. This is the paramedic portion of *Mac 911*—the section designed to get your Mac back on its little plastic feet without a lot of blather about the whys and wherefores of Mac troubleshooting and repair. Take a couple of deep breaths, and let's get started.

Your Mac Won't Start Up

Sometimes when your Mac won't start up, it offers you a helpful hint as to why: a strange beep, maybe. But even if you Mac doesn't do anything when you try to start it up, that is still a good clue.

UH-OH: You switch on your Mac, and nothing happens—no lights, no sound, no nothing.

Although it's tempting to throw up your arms in despair and simply proclaim your Mac to be "broken," a completely kaput Mac is a rare Mac indeed. Look first to the obvious.

Treatment 1: Check power connections.

Every Mac user on earth has run into this issue, so put aside your chagrin and count your blessings if your problem is as simple as a power cord that's come loose. If the connection between your power source and Mac seems solid, double-check the power strips the Mac is plugged into; they should all be switched on. Also, if the power outlet connected to your Mac is controlled by a wall switch, make sure that the switch is in the on position. If all else fails, swap in a new power cord.

Treatment 2: Switch different.

Push the Power button on the Mac itself rather than the one on the keyboard (if, indeed, your keyboard has a Power button). If the Mac starts up with this Power key, you have a bad connection between your keyboard and the Mac. Make sure that the keyboard is plugged into the Mac properly. If it's a USB Mac, be sure that the keyboard is plugged directly into the Mac rather than into a USB hub. If your Mac has an ADB keyboard, replace the ADB cable.

Treatment 3: Check the battery.

If you have a PowerBook or iBook, and you're attempting to run on battery power, use the power adapter instead. Your battery may be dead.

The external batteries on PowerBooks and iBooks are not the only batteries you need to be concerned about. Macs also carry internal batteries. If your Mac's internal battery poops out, you may be unable to boot your Mac. To replace your battery, open the Mac (with the power *off!*), remove the thing that looks like a battery (it *is* one), and take it to a local computer or electronics shop for replacement.

Treatment 4: Check the monitor.
New Mac models, such as the ill-fated Power Mac G4 Cube, are amazingly quiet. Unbeknownst to you, the Mac may be switched on, but the monitor switched off. Push the monitor's Power button to find out.

Treatment 5: Call Apple.
If these do-it-yourself solutions don't work, your Mac may be beyond the help you and I can provide (of course, you might want to read the rest of the book before you give up). Dry those tears, pick up the phone, and give Apple's support line a call at (800) 275-2273 during normal business hours on the Pacific Coast.

Treatment 6: Take it to the shop.
The technician you speak with at Apple may recommend that you take your Mac to a local Apple Authorized Service Provider for repair. This advice is rarely given lightly. If you've tried everything else, save yourself some frustration, bite the bullet, and take it in.

UH-OH: You switch on your Mac and see the icon of a frowning Mac or hear odd beeps, chords, or sound effects.

The Mac runs a series of hardware tests when you start up the machine. If these tests fail, you may see the infamous "Sad Mac" icon, hear error tones, or both. These tones may be a chord, the sound of a car crashing, the smash of broken glass, or a series of unfamiliar beeps.

Treatment 1: Check your RAM.
Have you just changed the RAM in your Mac or moved the Mac from one place to another? More often than not, error tones are the result of a RAM module that's not seated properly or that's incompatible with your Mac. If you've installed new RAM and hear unusual tones, remove the new RAM and try starting your Mac again. If the Mac starts properly without the RAM, switch off the Mac and reseat the RAM module.

If, on restarting, you continue to hear error tones, switch off the Mac, open its case, and look for a small round black or red button near the internal battery. This button is called the *Cuda button* (see Chapter 2 for more information). Press this button, reassemble your Mac, and restart with the new RAM module in place. If the Mac remains obstinate, and you still hear these ominous tones, report your difficulties to the vendor who sold you the RAM.

If you have an iMac, of course, cracking the case may seem to be completely beyond your ken. Don't worry—I show you how to break it open in Chapter 7.

Treatment 2: Check other installed cards.

It's possible that another kind of add-in circuit board is causing the problem. Try reseating any AGP, PCI, PDS, or NuBus cards in your Mac.

Treatment 3: Try a different startup disk.

Although this situation is rare, error tones can occur if your startup drive is under the weather. Try booting your Mac with the System software disk that it shipped with. Macs produced in the past several years shipped with a System software CD (sometimes called the Software Install CD). To start up from this CD, insert it and hold down the C key until the Mac's welcome screen appears. If the C-key trick doesn't work, try pressing Command-Shift-Option-Delete. This key combination tells the Mac to try to boot from a device other than the startup disk.

Treatment 4: Think back.

Have you changed anything since you last used your Mac—added a new PCI card or peripheral, for example? If so, you've found the likely culprit. Undo your recent actions, and try booting your Mac again. If the Mac starts up properly, you'll need to troubleshoot this new acquisition. (Tips on troubleshooting appear in subsequent chapters.)

Treatment 5: Call Apple.

As I mentioned earlier, a call to Apple may be the right solution when you're otherwise stumped.

Treatment 6: Take it to the shop.
Rarely, those hardware tests can indicate a more serious problem: a dead motherboard, bad SCSI controller, or malfunctioning ROM chip, for example. If you can't find a way around these errors, take your Mac to your local Mac repair emporium to have it eyeballed by a qualified technician.

UH-OH: You see a blinking folder or disk icon, and the Mac refuses to start up.
This blinking icon is the Mac's way of telling you that it can't find the System software it needs to start up.

Treatment 1: Make sure the drive is bootable.
Not all hard drives are bootable on all Macs. You can't boot a Blue & White Power Mac G3 or a Power Mac G4 (PCI Graphics) from a FireWire drive, for example. Neither can you boot from all USB drives. If you've been able to boot from the drive in the past, you've got a problem. If the drive is new, and you have no other bootable drive attached to your Mac, check the documentation to be sure you can use it to start up your Mac.

Treatment 2: Unplug your peripherals.
Add-on hardware can cause this problem sometimes. Remove any external devices save your monitor, keyboard, and mouse (and your external hard drive, if you use it to boot your Mac). If you do boot your Mac from an external hard drive, ensure that its cables are seated properly. And if that external drive is a SCSI device, be sure that its SCSI ID isn't set to a number that's likely to conflict with any other SCSI devices attached to your Mac. SCSI ID 0 normally is reserved for the Mac's internal drive, SCSI ID 3 for the CD-ROM drive, and SCSI ID 7 for the Mac itself.

Treatment 3: Boot from your system/repair disk.
If your Mac won't boot from the System Folder that you swear is on your startup drive, force it to boot from another disk. If you have a Mac old enough to have shipped without a CD-ROM drive, rummage through your possessions until you find a floppy disk capable of booting your Mac. You can start up floppy-friendly Macs with the Disk Tools floppy disk that shipped with early Macs. More-recent Macs ship with a CD-ROM that can be used as a startup disk. To boot from a CD-ROM, hold down the C key

on the Mac's keyboard after pressing the Mac's Power button. If the C-key trick doesn't work, try pressing Command-Shift-Option-Delete. This key combination tells the Mac to try to boot from a device other than the startup disk.

When you've booted from that System disk successfully, run Apple's Disk First Aid to diagnose and (possibly) repair the drive. If you have a more-robust diagnostic/repair utility—such as Alsoft's Disk Warrior, Micromat's TechTool Pro, or Symantec's Norton Utilities—boot from your repair disk and then diagnose the drive.

Treatment 4: Check for a valid System Folder.

After booting from your System/repair disk, open your hard-disk icon, and scroll down until you find the drive's System Folder, which should sport the icon of a smiling Mac. If not, this System Folder is not *blessed* (meaning that the Mac doesn't recognize it as the real deal and, therefore, won't use it to boot your computer). To bless the folder, open it, drag the System file to the desktop, close the System Folder, drag the System file back to the System Folder, open and close the System Folder, and pray that the "blessed" icon appears. If it does, try rebooting your Mac.

Treatment 5: Toss stuff.

Corrupted preferences files sometimes cause a System Folder to go unrecognized. Open the Preferences folder inside the System Folder, locate the Finder Preferences file, and drag it to the Trash. Then reboot the Mac.

Treatment 6: Zap your PRAM.

Parameter RAM (lovingly referred to as PRAM—pronounced "pea-ram") holds certain software settings (including date and time, AppleTalk's on/off state, and startup-disk information) in a bit of carefully maintained RAM on the Mac's motherboard. PRAM can get munged up occasionally, and when it does, trouble results—including a Mac that won't boot properly. To flush—or *zap*—this parameter RAM, hold down the Command-Option-P-R keys at startup. When the Mac starts a second time, let go of these keys.

Treatment 7: Perform a clean install.

If the drive appears to work but its System Folder refuses to boot your Mac, perform a clean install of your System software. To learn how to do so, see Chapter 2.

UH-OH: **The Mac makes all the right sounds and its power light comes on, but the screen remains dark.**

This retrograde-inversion of the classic "all the lights are on, but nobody's home" conundrum is rarely a serious problem.

Treatment 1: Check the monitor's power switch.

Is the monitor plugged in? Is it switched on?

Treatment 2: Check the brightness control.

PowerBook and iBook users often turn down the screen brightness to save battery power. If your Mac or monitor has a brightness control, turn it up.

Treatment 3: Check your monitor cable.

Perhaps the heft of the darned things is the problem, but monitor cables have an annoying way of coming loose. Make sure that yours is plugged in properly. Monitor cables that are partly plugged in can cause your monitor to display odd colors—lots of green or pink, for example.

Treatment 4: Check your video card.

Though they're not as prone to becoming unseated as the monitor cable is, graphics cards can come loose—particularly if they're not bolted to the case securely with the screw provided for that particular purpose.

Treatment 5: Swap in a new monitor.

Now that computers are as common as coffeemakers, borrowing another monitor shouldn't be difficult. If the borrowed monitor displays the Mac's video signal properly, you may need a new monitor. Note: Monitor repairs can be expensive. Before committing to a costly repair, price new monitors. It may be cheaper simply to buy a new one.

MAC 911: THE EMERGENCY PAGES

UH-OH: Your Mac running Mac OS 9.x or earlier begins to start up and then abruptly stops.

Such startup problems usually can be traced to an extension or hardware conflict. Extensions—the bits of computer code that add functionality to the Mac's operating system—occasionally conflict with one another. When they do, all kinds of h-e-double-toothpicks can ensue—including a Mac that freezes during the startup process. SCSI and USB conflicts can have the same effect.

Treatment 1: Hold down the Shift key at startup.

Holding down the Shift key at startup disables extensions, most control panels, and all items in the Startup Items folder. If your Mac boots properly with the Shift key down, you have an extension conflict. To learn how to deal with extension conflicts, see Chapter 3.

Treatment 2: Unplug your peripherals.

The hardware devices attached to your Mac—printers, removable media drives, scanners, MP3 players, whatever—can also come into conflict and keep your Mac from booting as it should. Try stripping your Mac of everything but the keyboard, mouse, and monitor.

Treatment 3: Zap your PRAM.

Rather than give you the impression that I'm padding my page count by parroting the same information over and over, I'll simply suggest that you flip back a couple pages to learn how to do this.

Treatment 4: Boot from your system/repair disk.

The reason for taking this action is similar to the reason stated earlier in this chapter: your Mac's hard drive may be so confused that even with extensions disabled, peripherals peeled away, and PRAM zapped, it can't summon the gumption to boot your computer.

UH-OH: You've booted your Mac from your System/ repair disk, and your hard drive is nowhere to be seen.

Few things are more distressing than finally booting your Mac from an emergency disk only to discover that your hard drive is missing in action.

Treatment 1: Run Disk First Aid or another disk-repair utility.

You'll find a copy of Apple's diagnostic/repair utility on the System disk that shipped with your Mac. Launch this utility, and pray that it recognizes your hard drive. If so, attempt to repair it. If Disk First Aid fails to find the drive, and you have a more robust diagnostic/repair utility—such as Disk Warrior, TechTool Pro, Norton Utilities, or the Apple Hardware Test CD (a CD that ships with some late-model Macs)—boot your Mac from that utility disk, and run the utility in the hope that it will recognize and repair your drive.

Treatment 2: Run Drive Setup.

If your diagnostic/repair utility fails to find your drive, launch Drive Setup (also on your System disk) and see whether it can see the drive. If the drive appears in the list of available drives, attempt to mount it by selecting the drive and choosing Mount Volumes from Drive Setup's Functions menu.

Treatment 3: Unplug your peripherals.

Unplug any external peripheral cables, excluding those attached to your keyboard and monitor. If you have two or more internal hard drives, disconnect cables to all but the startup drive. If the Mac boots from the drive, you have a hardware conflict that I'll deal with in "Peripheral Problems" in Chapter 2.

Treatment 4: Check your cables.

Be sure that any data and power cables running to your start up drive are seated securely.

Treatment 5 (next-to-last-ditch effort): Give your hard drive a tiny tap.

Troubleshooting experts blanch when you offer this recommendation, but it works occasionally. If all else fails, try giving your hard drive a tiny jolt with the heel of your palm—and *please,* do this with the Mac and hard drive switched off! Hard drives can get gunked up to the point where their platters won't spin or their drive arms refuse to flit across the drive platters to read and write data. A gently jolt sometimes convinces them to work again. Note: This operation is a next-to-last resort, for a very good reason. Banging a hard drive can seriously mess with its well-being. Perform this operation only if you see no other way out (and are resigned to losing everything on your disk anyway). And as frustrating as a dead drive may be, don't do this when you're angry.

If this treatment works and you're able to boot from the drive, *immediately* back up everything on the drive—you're living on borrowed time—and replace it. A drive this badly gunked is not one that you ever want to rely on again.

Treatment 6 (last-ditch effort): Call DriveSavers.

DriveSavers (www.drivesavers.com; 800 440-1904) is a wonderful company that will charge you a small fortune ($700 and up) to recover data from a drive that appears to be hopelessly trashed. If you've neglected to back up your data, and that data is worth more to you than one (1) arm and one (1) leg, give these good people a call.

Your Mac Will Start Up, but...

I don't want to give away the plot of the rest of this book, but a few just-after-startup annoyances are so vexing that I'd feel like a heel if I forced you to scamper to the book's index to find assistance.

UH-OH: Your Mac running Mac OS 9.2 or earlier starts up, but only long enough to display an error message before it crashes.

Technically, your Mac has booted successfully, but how helpful is that if, after displaying the desktop for a split-second, your Mac goes kablooey?

Treatment 1: Press Command-Control-Power or the Reset button.

If your Mac won't respond to keyboard or mouse input, it's frozen. To take some of the chill off your Mac, you must force it to restart. One way to restart is to press Command-Control-Power key at the same time. If you Mac doesn't respond to this key combination, press the Reset button on your Mac (a button with a left-pointing triangle).

Treatment 2: Hold down the Shift key at startup.

Yup, it's our old friend Mr. Extension Conflict again. If your Mac behaves after disabling extensions, you'll need to ferret out the troublesome extension or extensions.

Treatment 3: Hold down the spacebar at startup.

If disabling extensions by holding down the Shift key at startup made your Mac a more contented computer, see whether a third-party extension is the cause of your problems. Holding down the spacebar brings up the Extensions Manager as your Mac boots up. When the Extensions Manager window appears, select Mac OS 9.2 Base (or whichever version of the Mac OS you're using) from the Selected Set pop-up menu and restart. If all goes well, reopen Extensions Manager (you can find it in the Control Panels hierarchical menu), select Mac OS 9.2 All (or, again, whichever version of the Mac OS you're using), and restart. If things seem to be hunky-dory, a third-party extension or control panel is the likely culprit.

Treatment 4: Undo your handiwork.

Have you just installed a new piece of software or a peripheral that requires its own special software? If so, restart your Mac by holding down the spacebar at startup to bring up the Extensions Manager. When the Extensions Manager window appears, look for any extensions and control panels related to the item you just installed. If you just installed a new Acme Super-Duper Mouse, for example, and that mouse required you to install the Acme Super-Duper MousePlay extension, locate that extension, and turn it off.

Treatment 5: Benefit from the kindness of strangers.

Casady & Greene (www.casadyg.com) makes a utility that I wouldn't live without: Conflict Catcher. Conflict Catcher earns its daily dollar by locating conflicting extensions and control panels. I think it's worth every penny of the $80 suggested retail price. But why take my word for it when you can download a fully functional demo and see for yourself?

UH-OH: My Mac doesn't recognize such-and-such USB device (printer, removable-media drive, scanner, three-speed blender...).

USB was supposed to put an end to hardware conflicts. It doesn't.

Treatment 1: Search for updated drivers.

USB drivers are updated routinely when folks like you discover these annoying conflicts. Check the peripheral maker's Web site for driver updates, and install any that you find.

Treatment 2: Run Software Update.

The Software Update application included with both Mac OS 9.x and Mac OS X exists solely to keep your Apple software up to date. Apple is also responsible for its share of USB drivers, and Software Update may be able to outfit your Mac with drivers that are more up to date.

Treatment 3: Juggle peripherals.

Certain USB peripherals just don't get along—Zip drives and some printers, for example. Pull the plug on a peripheral, and restart to see whether there's a conflict between that peripheral and another.

Treatment 4: Give 'em enough juice.

Some USB peripherals require more power than an unpowered USB hub or the USB port on your Mac's keyboard can provide. Give a powered USB hub a try.

UH-OH: You've installed Mac OS X, yet you either can't boot or your Mac always starts up with Mac OS 9.

Mac OS X should boot if you've selected it in the Startup Disk control panel, but sometimes, it just won't.

Treatment 1: Be sure that Mac OS X is selected in the Startup Disk control panel (Mac OS 9) or in the Startup Disk System Preferences (Mac OS X).

An obvious suggestion, I know, but double-check anyway.

Treatment 2: On recent-model Macs, hold down the Option key at startup, and select the Mac OS X partition in the resulting screen.

"New world" Macs—Power Mac G4s, iBooks, and recent PowerBooks and iMacs—allow you to select a startup disk by holding down the Option key when you start up your Mac. Note: This treatment is a quick fix only. If the Mac believes that it's supposed to boot into Mac OS 9 instead of Mac OS X, it will do just that the next time you restart.

Treatment 3: Insert your Mac OS X CD, restart with the C key held down, and run Disk Utility.

Apple combines Disk First Aid and Drive Setup in a single Mac OS X utility called Disk Utility. When the Mac OS X CD boots into the Mac OS X installer, select Open Disk Utility from the Installer menu, click the First Aid tab, select your Mac OS X drive, and click the Verify button to see what's what. If Disk Utility finds a problem that it can fix, click the Repair button.

Treatment 4: Run a third-party troubleshooting utility.

Current versions of Disk Warrior, TechTool Pro, and Norton Utilities can diagnose and repair Mac OS X volumes. Boot from your troubleshooting utility's CD and examine (and, if necessary, repair) your Mac OS X volume.

Treatment 5: Reinstall Mac OS X.

As I write this chapter in late 2001, we're in the infant days of Mac OS X. Many parts of the new OS are unfinished, and an unfinished operating system sometimes does odd things. Rather than spend hours troubleshooting unusual Mac OS X behavior, I'd simply reinstall the sucker.

MAC 911: THE EMERGENCY PAGES

UH-OH: Mac OS X displays a spinning beach ball and you can't seem to make anything happen.

Applications in Mac OS X can freeze just as they can in Mac OS 9.2 and earlier.

Treatment 1: Force Quit.

Click any application in the Dock to open it and then select Force Quit from the Apple menu. In the dialog box that appears, select the frozen application (the one in which you see the omnipresent beach ball), and press the Force Quit button. You can Force Quit the Finder too. Just select it and click the Relaunch button.

Treatment 2: Quit from Process Viewer.

The Process Viewer application also allows you to Force Quit applications and background processes. It's possible that the thing that hangs up your Mac is not an application at all but rather a background process such as the Dock. If the regular ol' Force Quit rigmarole doesn't seem to work and you can open Process Viewer, try quitting applications from there.

UH-OH: Mac OS X displays a completely indecipherable string of text and then nothing happens.

Your Mac has just crashed (or "panicked," in the parlance of Mac OS X).

Treatment 1: Reboot your Mac.

There's nothing else for it. A panicked Mac is one that won't work again until you reboot. Press Command-Control-Power key or the Mac's Reset button.

Treatment 2: See Treatment 1.

UH-OH: Your Mac running Mac OS X continues to panic after each restart.

Panics generally happen just once and then go away. When they don't, something's wrong.

Treatment 1: Check your hardware.

Peripherals attached to your Mac may be in conflict with one another. Detach all peripherals save your keyboard, mouse, and monitor and reboot. If your Mac boots and stays alive with no problem, troubleshoot your hardware.

Treatment 2: Try to remember.

What were you doing before the problem occurred? Did you move files or install new software? If so, try to undo what you did by booting into Mac OS 9.2 or earlier and putting your Mac OS X volume back the way it was before you made the changes that caused this problem. Unlike with earlier versions of the Macintosh operating systems, Mac OS X is very finicky about where certain files and folders are located. If you move them, the Mac may act up.

Treatment 3: Reinstall Mac OS X.

It may be broken beyond repair.

MAC 911

Christopher Breen

Mac 911
Christopher Breen

Peachpit Press
1249 Eighth Street
Berkeley, CA 94710
510/524-2178
800/283-9444
510/524-2221 (fax)

Find us on the World Wide Web at www.peachpit.com
To report errors, please send a note to errata@peachpit.com

Peachpit Press is a division of Pearson Education

Copyright © 2002 by Christopher Breen

Editor: Clifford Colby
Production coordinator: Connie Jeung-Mills
Copyeditor: Kathy Simpson
Compositor: Owen Wolfson
Indexer: Joy Dean Lee
Cover design: Mimi Heft

Notice of rights
All rights reserved. No part of this book may be reproduced or transmitted in any form by any means, electronic, mechanical, photocopying, recording, or otherwise, without the prior written permission of the publisher. For information on getting permission for reprints and excerpts, contact permissions@peachpit.com.

Notice of liability
The information in this book is distributed on an "As Is" basis, without warranty. While every precaution has been taken in the preparation of the book, neither the author nor Peachpit Press shall have any liability to any person or entity with respect to any loss or damage caused or alleged to be caused directly or indirectly by the instructions contained in this book or by the computer software and hardware products described in it.

Trademarks
Mac 911 is a copyright of *Macworld*.

Throughout this book, trademarks are used. Rather than put a trademark symbol in every occurrence of a trademarked name, we state that we are using the names in an editorial fashion only and to the benefit of the trademark owner with no intention of infringement of the trademark.

ISBN 0-201-77339-2
9 8 7 6 5 4 3 2 1

Printed and bound in the United States of America

To Claire

Acknowledgements

It seems to me that there are three distinct groups of people who help you get through this book-scribbling process:

Those who actively help you give birth to the thing.

Those who stay out of your way and pick up the slack so you have enough time to complete the job.

Those who, just by their existence, inspire you to do it at all.

With this in mind, I'd like to incline my noggin in a most grateful way to:

Group 1: The folks at Peachpit Press who took what can only be described as an amorphous proposal (followed up by the barest of outlines) and still signed on the dotted line. This book's editor, Cliff Colby, who A) listened to that first proposal without once interrupting "You're kidding, right?" B) never uttered the phrase "You realize the book is due in a month, yes?" even when it seemed I'd badly slipped the schedule; and C) was as thoughtful and thorough as any author could wish. Mac Publishing's Big Cheese, Colin Crawford, who generously granted me permission to use the title of my *Macworld* column, "Mac 911," for this book.

Group 2: My wife, Claire, who managed to set up a new house, refinance same, scout out a new community, haul in salt and cartridges, and act as primary parent to our child, Adelaide Rose, while I clacked on heedlessly in the basement. My *Macworld* editors (Jennifer Berger, Linda Comer, Scholle Sawyer-McFarland, Lisa Schmeiser, Jason Snell, Terri Stone, and in particular, Nancy Peterson) who graciously shuffled assignments to accommodate my schedule. The boys of System 9—Ed Bangert, Hobey Landreth, Kevin Mullane, Pat Reilly, and Steve Smith—who covered for me when I couldn't make a gig.

Group 3: And the following just because of what they do (or have done): Patty Ames, Henry Bortman, Jim Bradbury, Ullysis Bravo, Shelly Brisbin, Cys Bronner (and Dave), George Clark, Fred Davis, Kristina DeNike, Philip Dyer, Cheryl England, Adam and Tonya Engst, Bart Farkas, Tara Gibb, Andy Gore, Nancy Groth, Ilene Hoffman, the Holmes Bros. (Chris, Joe, and Tim), Trish Huffman, Andy Ihnatko, Russ Ito, Susan Janus, Shawn King, Ted Landau, Leo Laporte, Brett Larson, Rick LePage, Bob LeVitus, Chris Lombardi, the Loyola Boys (Gil and Roman), Jeffy Milstead, Rik Myslewski, Michael Penwarden, Pam Pfiffner, David Pogue, Jim Shatz-Akin, Michael Swaine, Tim Warner, Johnny Wilson, and Jon Zilber.

And of course, thanks to Apple Computer for indirectly making it possible for me to put bread on the table during the past several years. We have our little spats from time to time, but no one does it better.

Table of Contents

MAC 911: THE EMERGENCY PAGES — ER1

Quick Fixes for a Funky Mac ER1
   Your Mac Won't Start Up ER2
   Your Mac Will Start Up, but. ER10

INTRODUCTION — xi

CHAPTER 1: THE WAY OF THE (MAC) WORLD
How the Mac Works — 1

   Dumb as a Stick and Twice as Thick. 2
   Information Management 4
Let's Get Organized (Mac OS 9.2 and Earlier) 6
   The Desktop. 6
   The System Folder 7
   Extensions and Control Panels. 8
   Preference Files 8
   Startup Items/Shutdown Items Folders 9
Let's Get Organized (Mac OS X) 9
   A Familiar Interface. 10
   File Placement 10
   The End of Extensions. 10
   Preference Files. 11
   No More Big Crashes 11
   The Unfinished OS 11
What It All Means 12

CHAPTER 2: I CAN'T GET STARTED!
Making Your Mac Get Up and Go   17

    The Lifeless Mac.................................18
    The Sad Mac...................................26
    The Questioning Mac.............................31

CHAPTER 3: FINDER MISHAPS
Crashes, Freezes, and Other Finder Funk   45

Common Causes of Finder Funk......................46
Extension Conflicts...............................47
    The Story of the Extensible Mac OS 47
    Preventing Extension Conflicts....................49
    Extension Management 50
    Troubleshooting Extension Conflicts................55
    Dealing with Things 60
Hardware Conflicts..............................61
    SCSI Conflicts.................................61
    USB Conflicts.................................61
    Bad RAM....................................64
File or Application Corruption......................65
    The Confused Desktop 65
    The Usual Suspects.............................67
    Diagnostic and Repair Utilities....................69
    Buggy Software 73
Something Else.................................75
Fixing the Darned Mac...........................77
    Reinstall Troublesome Applications 77
    Perform a Clean Install of Your System Software 77
    Reformat the Drive and Begin Again 78

CHAPTER 4: AND OTHER STUFF
Common Conundrums of a Well-Meaning Mac   79

Applications Gone Bad............................80
    Bugs..80
    Conflicts.....................................81
    Memory Allocation 82
    Preferences Files...............................86
    Corruption 88

Printing Problems 90
    Check Connections 91
    Check the Chooser 91
    Printer Troubleshooting 92
Modem Problems 93
    No Connection 93
    Slow and Dropped Connections 94
Performance Issues 96
    Trim Extensions and Control Panels 96
    Use Real RAM Rather Than Virtual Memory 98
    Disable the Mac's Startup Memory Test 98
    Increase the Disk Cache 99
    Decrease Color Depth 99
    Choose a Startup Disk 100
    Rebuild the Desktop 100
    Optimize Your Hard Drive 100
    Upgrade Your Mac 100
    Buy a New Mac 100

CHAPTER 5: TOOLS AND TECHNIQUES: CLASSIC MAC OS
The Ways and Means to Keep Your Mac OS 9 (and Earlier) Mac on the Straight and Narrow   101

Diagnostic Tools 102
    Disk First Aid 102
    Disk Warrior 106
    TechTool Pro 109
    Norton Utilities for Macintosh 117
Extension Management 124
    Extensions Manager 124
    Conflict Catcher 128
Backup Utilities 131
    CopyAgent 131
    Retrospect Desktop and Retrospect Express 132
Antivirus Utilities 133
    What to Look For 135
    The Players 137
Firewall Utilities 139
    Hardware Firewalls 140
    Software Firewalls 142

CHAPTER 6: MAC OS X
Troubleshooting with "Trouble-Free" Mac OS 143

The X Advantage 144
Where X Has No Influence 146
Not Quite Bulletproof 146
Be Prepared 147
    Get Religion; Back up Your Data! 147
    Quarantine Mac OS X 148
    Create an Mac OS 9.2 Volume 148
Mac OS X Problems 149
    Your Mac Won't Boot 149
    The Login Window Appears, But Your Username
        Is Nowhere to Be Seen 154
    Your Mac "Freezes" 158
    Your Mac Panics 162
    You've Lost Your Password 163
    Device X Doesn't Seem to Work with Your Mac 164
    The Mail App Won't... 165
    Application X Got Weird! 165

CHAPTER 7: MORE !!! FOR LESS $$$
Upgrading Your Mac 167

    Upgrade Options 168
Upgrading Your RAM 171
    Purchasing RAM 172
    Installing RAM 174
Upgrading Your Hard Drive 178
    Types of Hard Drives 178
    What to Look for in a Drive 181
    Installing the Hard Drive 182
    iMac 184
    The Tray-Loading iMac 184
    The Slot-Loading iMac 190
    PowerBook and iBook 193
Upgrading Your Processor 194
    Types of Processor Upgrades 194
    Installing a New Processor 196
Upgrading Your Graphics Card 198

Adding Other Cards and Adapters 200
   Add a Sound Input Device 200
   Add an ADB Device 201
   Add a Serial Port................................. 201
   Add a Network Printer 202
   Add a SCSI Device 203

CHAPTER 8: SHARE AND SHARE ALIKE
The Networked Mac   205

A Little History. 206
Making Connections 207
   Coming to Terms 207
   Typical Physical Connections 209
Software Setup: Mac OS 9.2 and Earlier 211
   Configure AppleTalk 211
   Selecting Volumes and Files....................... 211
   Turn on Sharing 214
   Accessing the Network 215
   Adding AirPort 217
   Configuration..................................... 218
   Adding a Router 222
Software Setup: Mac OS X 224
   Turn on Sharing 224
   Switch on AppleTalk 225
   Add Users 226
   Assign Privileges 229
   Logging On 230
Practical Networking Projects 232
   The Backup Server 233
   The Wireless MP3 Jukebox 240

CHAPTER 9: DIGITAL HUBBUB
Music, Movies, and More on Your Mac   243

Recording LPs and Cassettes on Your Mac 244
   Hardware Connections 244
   Software and Recording 246
   Burning 251
Make a Video CD.................................. 253

Make a Slide Show..255
    The (Probably) Free Solutions................................256
    The Not Free (But Very Cool) Solution.......................260
Make a Custom Mac OS X Screen Saver...........................262
Make Better iMovies...264
    As You Shoot...264
    As You Edit..265
    Exporting iMovies..267
QuickTime Player Pro Tips...272
    MIDI to Audio..272
    Multiple Audio Tracks..272
    Play It Backward...273
    Add Effects..274
    Add Annotations...275

APPENDIX A: HELPFUL RESOURCES — 277

Apple Computer..278
Other Resources..282

APPENDIX B: TIPS AND TRICKS — 287

Mac OS 9.2 and Earlier..288
Mac OS X..297

APPENDIX C: 10 SUREFIRE WAYS TO BECOME WILDLY UNPOPULAR ON THE WEB — 301

INDEX — 307

Introduction

Our story begins a little more than two years ago at the East Coast edition of Macworld Expo, the Mac-centric convention that convenes twice a year in San Francisco and New York, respectively. The show floor had recently closed for the day, and in typical postshow fashion, I made my way to the nearest Mac-vendor party and began packing as many mini-quiches into my gaping gob as the generosity of my host would allow.

'Round about quiche 17, a hand encroached from the left. Just as I was about to slap it away and slide the remaining pastries into the plastic-lined pocket I devised for such occasions, the hand's owner spoke.

"Chris, how are you?"

"Mmmmbffhhff!" I responded through hors d'oeuvre-stuffed cheeks.

Mistaking my crummy ejaculation and look of glutinous embarrassment for lack of recognition, my questioner offered her hand and said, "Marjorie Baer, from Peachpit Press."

After a good deal of swallowing, I finally managed to choke out, "Of course, Marjorie. Great to see you."

We chatted over the Mac news of the day, and then my canapé companion uttered the seven fateful words that have brought you and me together: "You should write a book for us."

Having spent the better part of my life saying exactly the wrong thing at the most inappropriate moment, I couldn't help but reply, "What a wonderful thought! As a matter of fact, I've been kicking around an idea for a book. I'd like to take the Macintosh knowledge I've accumulated over the past decade or so and shove it all into a lengthy tome entitled *Chris Breen's Massive Macintosh Brain Dump.* The cover will feature a large, inflatable gray brain that throbs and pulses (or do you think simple embossing would be more tasteful?). I haven't conceived all the book's elements, of course, but a QuickTime VR pop-up page is a must, and surely the book would benefit from a scratch-'n'-sniff troubleshooting section."

Without missing a beat, Marjorie smiled, replied, "Works for me. Here's my card," and left me to inhale what remained of the shrimp platter.

"Now that," I mused as I propelled the hindquarters of a seagoing decapod down my gullet, "is an outfit I can work with."

Who I Am

Oh, I'm sorry. I seem to have launched into a story about my personal life without introducing myself properly.

I'm your host, Chris Breen. I've been writing about computers since the latter days of the Reagan administration for such publications as *Macworld, MacUser, MacWEEK, PCWorld, Access Magazine, Computer Gaming World,* and *Inside Mac Games.* I've contributed to four editions of Peachpit Press's venerable *Macintosh Bible,* and I cowrote *The Macintosh Bible to Games* (Peachpit Press) and *My iMac* (Hungry Minds).

I currently spend much of my time writing for *Macworld* magazine. Specifically, I pen "Mac 911" (my, now, there's a catchy title!), *Macworld*'s monthly tips and troubleshooting column. In addition to the column, my name is often tacked onto features, how-to articles, and reviews. I also write Macworld Daily Tips (www.macworld.com/newsletters), a Mac tips newsletter sent to subscribers each business day. And my video visage appears each month as host of the CD-ROM bundled with newsstand copies of *Macworld* (as well as within "Breen's Bungalow," a video tutorial that appears on the disc and on

Macworld's Web site each month). You may also see me in video form on the compucentric cable channel TechTV, where I occasionally appear as a guest on the "Call for Help" and "Screen Savers" programs.

Before writing for *Macworld*, I was a contributing editor for the dear, departed *MacUser* magazine, where, with the lovely and talented Bob LeVitus, I cowrote *MacUser*'s wildly popular troubleshooting column, "Help Folder."

In other words, I've spent the better part of 13 years planted in front of various Macintosh computers, trying to understand how they perform their magic and—when they fail to produce the expected rabbit from the requisite hat—what hinders them. Having scrutinized, diagnosed, repaired, upgraded, nursed, and cursed countless Macs and written more than a million words recounting my experiences in numerous publications, online, and on TV, I think I have a pretty good handle on what makes a Mac tick.

What This Is

A glance at the cover and a flip through these pages reveals that I've abandoned the more flamboyant elements of my original book proposal. Instead of *Chris Breen's Massive Macintosh Brain Dump*, this book is titled simply *Mac 911*. And sorry—unless some horrible mix-up occurred at the printing house, you'll find no pages that pop up, and the aroma that greets your nostrils should be composed of nothing more than a pleasing mélange of wood pulp and ink.

What hasn't changed, however, is the basic notion behind the book. I wanted to produce a book that was not only helpful in regard to keeping a Mac up and running but also one that provided a hint or two about what useful things you might do with the Mac after it's ticking along on all cylinders.

Having read through these pages more times than I care to recount, I think that I may have succeeded. I hope you agree.

Who This Is For

Mac 911 is for just about every Mac user—from the newest of the newbies on up to crusty old veterans. If you've just unpacked your first Macintosh, however, and the *terms point, click, drag, menu,* and *icon* are foreign to you, I suggest that you pick up a copy of Robin Williams's *The Little Mac Book* (Peachpit Press) before reading further. I've made every effort to write a book that my mother can understand (and believe me, Mom's no computer whiz), but you'll get far more use out of *Mac 911* if you know your way around the Mac.

Mac 911 is also appropriate for those who are using Mac OS 9.2 and earlier (the old Macintosh operating system we're all familiar with) or Mac OS X (the brand-new Macintosh operating system that far fewer people are familiar with). As I write this introduction at the close of 2001, the Mac community is at a crossroads. Most Mac users continue to run the old Mac OS for their everyday computing chores but Mac OS X is quickly becoming a viable everyday operating system as well—particularly with the Mac OS X 10.1 update and such staples as Microsoft Office coming to the Mac in Mac OS X-native form. Although many of the tips and techniques I discuss work with both the old and new Mac OS, I speak specifically about one or the other when appropriate. Those looking for Mac OS X troubleshooting information will find it in a chapter devoted specifically to that subject.

As the title hints, a goodly portion of *Mac 911* is intended to be helpful to those who are having trouble with their Macs. But as much as I'd love to lay claim to writing the ultimate guide on the subject, this is not the most comprehensive Macintosh troubleshooting book on the planet. That honor goes to Ted Landau's wonderful *Sad Macs, Bombs, and Other Disasters* (Peachpit Press). No person is more knowledgeable about Mac troubleshooting than Ted, and no troubleshooting book is more comprehensive than *Sad Macs*. If your interest in Mac troubleshooting and repair goes beyond the limits of this book, you must own a copy of *Sad Macs*. (Also, Ted's a really good guy who turns the most endearing shade of red when he laughs.)

How This Book Is Organized

The first portion of *Mac 911* deals with the misbehaving Mac: troubleshooting and repair. Throughout this section of the book, I do my best to convey how a Mac works and what's likely to keep it from performing at its full potential. As I explain at greater length elsewhere, my goal is to teach you to think like a Mac—to become generally familiar with the way it goes about its business. After you gain this understanding, you can more easily intuit where a problem lies. The advantage in teaching you to fish rather than plunking a plate of pike before your puss is that there's a greater likelihood that you'll be able to use the knowledge you've gained here to solve problems not specifically mentioned within these pages. In short, I want to help sharpen your detective skills so that you can find the bad guys on your own.

And although it's wonderful to preside over a Mac that runs properly, a computer that does little more than comport itself in an agreeable manner is a pretty dull appliance. In addition to keeping your Mac on the straight and narrow, I intend to help you create a Mac that's useful and fun to work with. That's where the second section of *Mac 911* comes in. In part *deux*, I present you a series of projects—the kind of projects that beginning and intermediate Mac users shy away from, for fear that such tasks as upgrading a Mac or creating a network are too complicated. They're not, honestly.

Then there's part three, which is the most obvious remnant of the brain-dump idea. Here, I present some of my favorite Mac tips and tricks, a list of useful resources, and a couple of bits that just didn't seem to fit elsewhere. I think that you'll find it helpful (or at least amusing).

Speaking of amusement, I should issue a warning before closing this introduction:

I have a sense of humor, and I'm not afraid to use it. I'm deadly serious about this book being useful, but if I have the opportunity to make my point with a smile, I won't hesitate.

Have no fear. No animals were harmed, nor information sacrificed, for the sake of a joke.

Thanks for joining me. Now let's get to it.

The Way of the (Mac) World

How the Mac Works

Although the title of this chapter appears to convey a subliminal message to purchase a copy of the magazine I routinely write for (buy *Macworld!* buy *Macworld!* buy *Macworld!*), I assure you that I have a loftier goal in mind. You may recall that in this book's introduction, I mentioned that if I could impart a sense of how the Mac functions, you'd be better equipped to troubleshoot and repair it should something go wrong. That's essentially what I'm after in this chapter. If I do my job properly, a little internal light will blink on, and when it does, you'll emit a satisfying, "Oh, *now* I get it!"

The following is by no means a comprehensive rundown on all the Mac's hardware and operating-system functions. The point isn't to burden you with useless technical detail but to provide you a solid sense of what makes a Mac tick. It's a little like showing you how a blender works. If you understand that the blender needs power to do its job, and nothing happens when you flick the switch, you're likely to suspect an electrical problem. Likewise, if smoke billows from the blender's bottom, and you're sympathetic to the delicate relationship between the motor and rotor, you'll have better luck pinpointing the problem.

A couple of words of warning before you begin:

Warning 1: This chapter is not intended to be a replacement for Robin Williams's lovely *The Little Mac Book* or any other treatise that teaches you how to drive your Macintosh. My intent is not to tell you how to operate your Mac—shove the mouse around in a productive way or provide you umpteen different ways to open a file. Rather, I want to help you better comprehend your Mac's little digital brain—to more clearly understand how it thinks. That said, I will use this chapter to define some terms that I casually toss about in the rest of the book. You've been warned. If you blip over this chapter and later wonder what the heck I'm talking about, don't blame me.

Warning 2: When I write about Mac basics, I think of exactly one person as my audience: my mother. Mom did a wonderful job of rearing me and my two sisters, but when it comes to computers and other electronic doodads, she has a tendency to become thoroughly confused. For this reason, I will occasionally delve into some pretty basic areas. I don't mean to be remedial (and certainly not patronizing), but Mom sometimes needs these things broken down into tiny, digestible pieces.

Enough of the warnings. Let's get to it.

Dumb as a Stick and Twice as Thick

I'll start by talking about computers in general. The innards of today's desktop computers include, among other things, the central processing unit (CPU), random-access memory (RAM), read-only memory (ROM), and the hard drive. Here's what they do.

The CPU

The *CPU* is the computer's brain—the big computer chip that makes most of the calculations that allow the computer to perform so many wondrous tricks. Unlike the human brain (or a carp's brain, for that matter), the CPU isn't capable of making decisions or being proactive; it simply does what it's told to do. Although this quality is an admirable one in football players and toddlers, it's not the kind of thing to gloss up an otherwise dull résumé. No, what makes the CPU so spectacular is that it does what it's supposed to do at incredible speed.

Any CPU worth its salt carries on with nary a flinch when asked to execute thousands of instructions in the blink of an eye.

When you hear people talking about a 680x0 processor or a PowerPC G3 or G4 chip (or even, Lord help us, a Pentium processor), they're talking about the computer's CPU. A CPU's speed is rated in megahertz (MHz) and gigahertz (GHz), much as a stereo amplifier is rated in watts or an electric guitar's output is rated in decibels. Generally speaking, the higher megahertz and gigahertz rating a *specific processor* has, the faster it is. I emphasize *specific processor* because you can't compare the ratings of two CPU architectures, such as a PowerPC G4 and Pentium III processor. It's an apples-and-oranges comparison, so megahertz mean nothing in such cases.

RAM

RAM is made up of one or more small circuit boards that contain memory chips. In these memory chips, the computer stores short-term information. RAM is a little like your own short-term memory—a place where you store messages such as "Don't forget to pick up the milk" that you can forget quickly when something more important grabs your attention. When you switch off your computer, any information stored in RAM vanishes.

ROM

ROM is a set of instructions permanently stored in a chip. On a Mac, these instructions include components of the Mac OS and information the Mac needs to start up. In earlier Macs, oodles of information was stored in ROM. On more recent Macs (the iMac and beyond), Apple included a much smaller ROM chip that contained a far more limited set of instructions. In its place, Apple created a software architecture scheme, code-named NewWorld. This NewWorld architecture places many of the old ROM commands in software. When this software loads at startup, the ROM instructions are copied to RAM. The advantage of ROM-in-RAM is that the Mac performs better because a RAM chip is faster than a ROM chip. The disadvantage is that ROM-in-RAM consumes about 3 MB of RAM.

Hard drive

The *hard drive* is a metal box containing magnetic platters that hold information you want to keep long-term. In some households, you might compare the hard drive to a bookshelf that holds a family's reference library, scrapbooks, and photo albums. (In my house, that place would be the floor of my office and the three overflowing cardboard boxes shoved over in the corner.) Information is written to and retrieved from the hard drive by a read/write head mounted on an arm that travels over the hard drive's surface (a bit like a phonograph's needle and tone arm, if you're familiar with such ancient technology). The computer's operating system and all its programs are stored on the hard drive. A read-only disc (such as a CD-ROM) works much the same way as a hard drive. The difference is that data can only be read from the disc, not written to it.

And the rest

If you've had occasion to open your Mac, you know that you'll find a lot more inside than just the preceding three things. In addition to the CPU, RAM, and hard drive, a Mac contains all kinds of ancillary computer chips that manage such chores as displaying video on the monitor, directing traffic to and from internal and external devices, and handling connections to the Internet. A Mac also has important peripheral devices, such as the monitor (sometimes built into the case, as is the case with the iMac), CD-ROM drive, input devices (such as the keyboard and mouse), and all the other doodads (digital cameras, MP3 players, joysticks, digital camcorders, and removable media drives) that make your computer more productive and fun to use.

Information Management

Information moves around a Mac in this way: When the Mac starts up, it looks to the ROM chip for instructions on how to start up. During this process, the Mac runs a series of hardware tests to make sure that everything is ready to go; it checks to make sure that functioning RAM chips are in place and that the processor works, for example. The ROM-in-RAM process then kicks in, with more startup instructions and portions of the Mac OS being loaded into RAM.

Next, the Mac searches for a valid startup drive, first attempting to boot from the disk chosen in the Startup Disk control panel. This drive may be your internal hard drive or, barring that, any other attached drive with a kosher System Folder (including a CD-ROM). When it finds the desired startup disk (or another disk with a bootable system, if your chosen disk isn't capable of booting the Mac), it proceeds to load the system and—under Mac OS 9.2 and earlier—such add-ons as extensions and control panels from the hard drive into RAM. During this startup process, the Mac also communicates with any hardware devices attached to the computer, such as your printer or scanner. When the Mac is completely up and running, any items stored in the Startup Items folder are launched.

When you open an application, the Mac locates the application on the hard drive and directs the hard drive's read/write head to that location. That application is then copied from the hard drive into RAM. If you don't have enough RAM to hold that program, you generally won't be allowed to open that program. (Well, technically, you can do this by using *virtual memory*—a memory scheme that lets you use the hard drive as RAM).

Applications are loaded into RAM rather than run directly from the hard drive, and you should thank the stars above that they are. Data moves much more quickly in and out of RAM than it does on and off a hard drive.

When an application is loaded into RAM, the CPU follows the instructions written in the application. Such instructions may include "Produce the picture of a tiny robot that says 'mleep, mleep, mleep'" or "Produce an open window and these six toolbars." Opening a document within that application works much the same way. The Mac tells the hard drive where to find the file, the file is sucked into RAM, and the application tells the CPU something like "Align the included numbers in a column, add them up, and tell me how broke I am." When you save the file, the file is moved from RAM and written, in its current state, to the hard drive.

Let's Get Organized (Mac OS 9.2 and Earlier)

So much for how the Mac shifts data from the hard drive to RAM to the CPU and transforms it into information you can understand. This section talks about how Mac OS 9.2 and earlier organizes this information.

The Desktop

The architects of the original Mac OS wanted to create an organizational system that closely mimicked the way people store information in real life. And because they intended the Mac to use a graphical user interface (GUI), the designers had to come up with some way to represent this system with pictures. so they decided to use the desktop/folder analogy that you've grown to love. (You're in good company. Microsoft thought so highly of the idea that it "borrowed" the GUI for Microsoft Windows.) The idea was simple and elegant. The Mac's screen would display a work space much like the top of a desk. (What? You thought calling the Mac's work surface the *Desktop* was just a coincidence?) On this Desktop would be displayed any disks and volumes (a volume can be an entire disk or a portion of a disk called a *partition*); a menu bar containing a string of menus chock-full of commands; and, of course, the Trash, an icon that represents the means of disposing of items you no longer wanted (and, in a fairly nonintuitive analogy, the way to eject or unmount disks).

Within a volume would be a hierarchy of folders, with each folder, when opened, displaying its contents in a window. Within these folders, users could store groups of files. Unlike earlier operating systems, the Mac OS rarely demanded that files grouped together be related in any way.

Careful readers noticed that I fudged a bit when I mentioned grouping related items. In some cases, certain items must be gathered together and placed in a particular spot in the Mac OS's folder hierarchy. The following sections discuss those items.

The System Folder

The *System Folder* is a special folder necessary for the Mac OS to function. This folder must sit at what is termed the *root level* of the volume. When you hear this *root-level* business, it simply means the level you see when you first open your Mac's hard drive. In recent years, Apple has refined the Mac OS by placing some other folders at the root level—specifically, an Applications folder and a Documents folder. These two folders are mostly for your convenience. The Mac OS may store files in these folders (your Outlook Express or Eudora email files, for example), but you don't have to put anything in these folders if you don't care to.

Other folders and files within the System Folder, however, have to remain inside the System Folder for the Mac to function properly. The two most important of these folders are the System and Finder.

The *System* is a collection of other files within a special kind of folder called a *suitcase*. These files—which include sound files, keyboard layouts, and some invisible stuff that you can't (and wouldn't want to) see—are major components of the Mac OS.

The Finder is actually a kinda-sorta application. It's the application that you see when your Mac first boots up. Within the Finder application, you do things such as empty the Trash, duplicate files, create aliases, and eject disks.

The System and Finder must be in the System Folder for the Mac to recognize, or *bless*, that System Folder. Likewise, all the components inside the Extensions folder and most of the items in the Control Panels folders won't work if they are placed outside their host folders or those host folders are moved outside the System Folder. The Mac's typefaces (known as *fonts*), for example, are available to your applications when they're placed inside the System Folder's Fonts folder.

Extensions and Control Panels

What, exactly, are extensions and control panels? The name *extensions* provides a clue to their purpose. *Extensions* are items that *extend* the capabilities of the Mac OS. A particular extension will allow the Mac to work with a certain joystick, whereas another will let your Mac recognize a Palm Pilot plugged into the Mac's USB port. *Control panels* are small applications that allow you to control the enhanced functions provided by extensions. Control panels can work without the benefit of an extension, providing enhancements of their own. Extensions and control panels load at startup and, when loaded, become part of the Mac OS.

Preference Files

Every application I can think of requires some variety of preference file. In the preference file are stored—yup, you guessed it—user-defined settings. When you ask Microsoft Word 2001 to no longer display Max (the animated assistant) or to cease checking your grammar as you type, those settings are stored in the Word Settings preference file. Preference files are stored in the Preferences folder inside the System Folder. If you move a preference file out of the Preferences folder the application will still function. When you launch the application the next time, a new preference file will be created and, as you might have expected, you lose all your carefully customized settings.

> **The Finder Preferences.** *You recall that I said the Finder was a kinda-sorta application? Well, it's enough of an application to have its own preference file, called (aptly enough) Finder Preferences. Like any preference file, Finder Preferences can become corrupted. But unlike other preference files, when the Finder Preferences file becomes corrupted, all kinds of odd (and sometimes terrible) things can happen. Because the Mac OS is so consistent, the cure for a corrupt Finder Preferences file is simply tossing it out. When the Mac next starts up, the Mac OS—knowing that you take this sort of action when a preference file is missing—creates a new, uncorrupted Finder Preferences file.*

Startup Items/Shutdown Items Folders

Somewhere in the second half of the 1990s, Apple came up with yet another cute trick, including two new items in the System Folder: the Startup Items folder and the Shutdown Items folder. Their names explain it all. When you want an application or file to launch when the Mac starts up, you place it in the Startup Items folder. Likewise, when you want an application or file to launch when your Mac begins the shutdown process, place it in the Shutdown Items folder.

I can just imagine Mom asking, "But honey, if you're shutting down your Mac, why would you want it to *launch* something?" Good question. Here's the answer:

At times, you need little programs to kick in before your Mac says bye-bye. If you want to scan your hard drive for viruses or corruption automatically, for example, you'd place a disk-scanning utility in this folder. If it knows its stuff, this utility will do its job and quit; then the Mac will shut down.

You can do far sillier things with this folder. You can record the sound of your little brother burping, save it as a sound file, and place it in the Shutdown Items folder. Now whenever you shut down your Mac, you'll hear your sibling's gaseous bark.

Gee, Mom, aren't you glad you asked?

Let's Get Organized (Mac OS X)

As I commit these words to print, the Mac world is in a period of minor upheaval. No, I don't mean that Apple plans to implement the ill-advised Flower Power design across its product line or, once again, force its users to employ the wretched, pucklike Round Mouse. Bigger events are afoot—the transition from an operating system that's matured over some 17 years to a new operating system built from the ground up. I mean, of course, the move from the original Mac OS (Mac OS 9.2 and earlier) to Mac OS X.

I can't emphasize enough this "built from the ground up" business. Unlike other operating systems that claim to be new (read: Microsoft Windows 95/98/Me/XP and so on), Mac OS X isn't built on the back of the Mac OS we're all familiar with. Instead,

Apple created a new operating system based on something called Mach (an operating system conceived in 1984) and a version of the Unix operating system called FreeBSD 3.2. On top of this, Apple added technologies for displaying text (Quartz), 3-D graphics (OpenGL), and multimedia (QuickTime). Farther up the heap are Mac OS X's programming environments (Classic, Carbon, Cocoa, and AppleScript). At the top of the heap is Aqua, the toolbox that makes up Mac OS X's throbbing, translucent interface.

OK, Mom is understandably bored. This isn't a Mac OS X book, and it's not important that you understand the underpinnings of Mac OS X to use this book. I just want you to grasp a few Mac OS X concepts and understand how it differs from the Mac OS you know. For purposes of this book, though, you should know the following things about Mac OS X.

A Familiar Interface

Apple has made every effort to make Mac OS X familiar to its users. Sure, underneath the Aqua interface is a lot of Unix gobbledygook, but Apple does its very best to hide it from you (though you're welcome to look if you like). Under Mac OS X, you'll find the same Desktop/folder analogy that appears in earlier versions of the Mac OS.

File Placement

Mac OS 9.2 and earlier require certain files and folders to live in a particular place for the Mac to do its job. The same is true of Mac OS X. In fact, Mac OS X may be even more finicky about where items are kept. If you move your Users folder (mine is called chris) out of Mac OS X's Users folder, for example, the Mac won't be able to find your environment. (I'll discuss this concept in Chapter 6.)

The End of Extensions

Mac OS X isn't extensible in the same way as the classic Mac OS. When you boot up Mac OS X, you won't see a parade of extensions and control panels, because no such things exist in this new operating system. Apple has made it very clear that it has no intention of providing the kind of access programmers need to patch Mac OS X. Also, from what I've heard, the company has threatened to break any utilities that attempt to patch the OS in ways frowned upon by Apple. So although we lose some extensibility, we also lose extension conflicts, which were among the most nagging problems of the old Mac OS.

Preference Files

Mac OS X has preferences files, just like Mac OS 9.2 and earlier. You know that tossing a preference file in the earlier Mac OS can cure an ailing Mac. That method works in Mac OS X as well.

No More Big Crashes

Mac OS X has something called *protected memory*, which means that each process running under Mac OS (a process can be an application or a task performed by the OS) has a bit of memory it can call its own. The memory boundaries under the old Mac OS were a bit more fluid. Although Mac OS 9 and earlier tried to keep each application's mitts off another's memory, it wasn't always successful. When an application encroached on another's memory, one application or the other might crash. And when that application crashed, it was likely to bring the whole computer down with it.

Under Mac OS X, applications can still crash, but if they do, they crash by themselves, leaving everything else on the Mac running blithely along.

> **OK, Maybe Just a Very Few Big Crashes.** *Although a crashing application shouldn't bring the computer to its knees, something called a kernel panic can. I'll get into this topic in Chapter 6, so suffice it to say for now that a kernel panic is to Mac OS X what one of those cozy California power blackouts is to your home electrical system. When the kernel panics, everything goes phhht. Fortunately, the cure for a kernel panic is simple: Just restart your Mac.*

The Unfinished OS

Mac OS X is a work in progress. When Apple first released Mac OS X on March 24, 2001, it did so because Apple's Big Kahuna, Steve Jobs, promised that it would—not because Mac OS X was even a quarter of the way baked. The first truly usable release of OS came in September 2001 with Mac OS X 10.1. But even that version is missing lots of the goodies in Mac OS 9.2 and earlier—including drivers for scads of hardware devices you'd like to plug into your Mac.

What the OS Can't Control. Before the operating system kicks in, it makes no difference to the Mac whether you're running Mac OS 9.2 or Mac OS X; your Mac will go through the same hardware startup procedures. If you have bad RAM, a corrupt hard disk, or some kind of cabling problem, your Mac's kaput until you fix it, modern operating system or no.

What It All Means

I understand that some people may wonder about the practical use of the preceding pages. Fair enough. I'll try to help you put this information to work.

As I explained earlier in this chapter, two groups of actions take place when you press the Power button on your Mac:

- The Mac's hardware comes to life, performs some diagnostic checks and does its very best to carry out the electronic and mechanical functions necessary for the Mac to do its job. Those tasks include moving data in and out of RAM and on and off the hard drive; displaying video on your monitor; receiving input from the keyboard and mouse; and establishing links to your printer, other external devices, and the Internet.

- The Mac's ROM and operating system kick in and turn this pile of circuits and wires into a Mac—a machine capable of crunching numbers, processing words, playing games, surfing the Web, and helping you compose and send mushy email messages to your sweetie.

When you understand the sequence of events that take place when power first touches your Mac and it successfully starts up, you can begin to make educated guesses about what might *keep* it from attaining that successful startup.

At the risk of putting you off these pages so early in the proceedings, I'll give you a pop quiz to see whether you've got the idea. (And *yes*, penmanship counts.)

Question 1: You press the Power button on your Mac running Mac OS 9.2 and earlier, and nothing happens. Is this a hardware or software problem?

Answer: Hardware.

Why: Before the Mac's software can do anything—even have the opportunity to make your Mac crash—the Mac has to start running. If you press the Power button and nothing happens at all—no whirring, no display on the monitor, no keyboard lights blinking on—you definitely have a hardware-disconnect problem somewhere.

I address this issue specifically in Chapter 2. But for those of you who just can't wait, my guess is that a problem like this can be attributed to no power getting to the Mac (it's unplugged), a keyboard that's not plugged into the Mac (when you've attempted to power up the Mac from the keyboard's Power button), a dead internal battery, a dead power supply (the circuitry necessary to deliver power to the rest of the Mac), or a broken Mac. On a PowerBook, I'd add the possibility of a drained battery or a power-manager circuit that needs to be reset.

Question 2: You press the Power button on your Mac running Mac OS X, and nothing happens. Is this a hardware or software problem?

Answer: Hardware.

Why: It makes no difference what operating system you're running; hardware is hardware. If you have a bad RAM module, it will be just as naughty under Mac OS X as it is under Mac OS 9.2.

Question 3: Your Mac running Mac OS 9.2 or earlier starts up, displays the Welcome screen, begins loading extensions (those icons that march across the bottom of the screen), and stops halfway through. The mouse moves the pointer on-screen, but the Mac won't continue to boot. Is this a hardware or software problem?

Answer: Software.

Why: The Mac's hardware has finished most of its job. It's started the Mac, performed the diagnostic tests, found a bootable drive, and given the Mac the A-OK to start loading the Mac OS; without that A-OK, you wouldn't see the welcome screen. When you see that welcome screen, the Mac OS is top dog, and any problems that ensue are likely attributable to some software glitch.

I talk about this problem in Chapter 3, but I'll provide a hint on this one here as well. This problem is likely the result of an extension conflict. A couple of those add-on doodads that extend the capabilities of the Mac OS are not seeing eye to eye, or an extension and the Mac OS itself are in conflict. Their struggle has become so heated that the Mac cannot continue to boot. The solution to this problem is to locate and disable the offending extension or extensions.

Question 4: Your Mac running Mac OS X starts up, displays the spinning beach ball, and takes you to the Log In screen, when you expected to be taken directly to the Desktop. Is this a hardware or software problem?

Answer: Software again.

Why: Just as in Mac OS 9.2 and earlier, after hardware has done its job—bringing the Mac to life and bringing RAM, video, and the hard drive into the mix—what follows generally is the responsibility of software. In this case, Mac OS X seems to have lost track of your Users folder. (Remember, I told you that it has to remain within Mac OS X's Users folder.) To put things right, you can dive into the murky depths of Mac OS X's Terminal application or reinstall Mac OS X.

Question 5: Your Mac running Mac OS X doesn't work with your printer, but that printer works fine with Mac OS 9.2 and earlier. Is it a hardware or software problem?

Answer: Software.

Why: The fact that the printer works with Mac OS 9.2 is a dead giveaway. Remember, Mac OS X isn't finished yet. A compatible Mac OS X driver may not be available for your printer. Fortunately, you can always boot into Mac OS 9.2 and use your printer from there.

Question 6: Your Mac running Mac OS 9.2 or earlier starts up, the march of extensions proceeds normally, the Desktop appears, and your Mac freezes. Is this a hardware or software problem?

Answer: Sorry, this is a trick question. It could be either.

Why: Now, calm down a second, Mom. I know your inclination is to inquire, "What good is this chapter if the problem could be related to any of a million things?!" But—and I mean this with the greatest respect—you're wrong. It can't be any of a million things. In fact, it can be only one of two things: hardware or software.

I realize that this answer sounds like the ravings of someone who claims that you have a 50-50 chance of winning the lottery—either you win or you don't—but my intention isn't to rave or be glib. I'm simply suggesting that rather than throw your hands up with the idea that you'll never figure out what's causing this complex piece of machinery to have a bad case of the jim-jams, you take a step back and look at the most obvious possibilities.

In this case, you know that the Mac has frozen. You don't know why, but you do know that the Mac is suffering from either a hardware problem or a software problem. With that in mind, what do you do?

Simple. Eliminate one of the suspects.

Here's a tip you can take to the bank: In nearly every instance, it's easier to eliminate hardware as the problem. Why? Because you can remove a piece of hardware physically. It's more difficult to remove bits of software or determine whether they're broken.

In this example, I'd shut down the Mac and remove every external device attached to the computer save the keyboard, mouse, and monitor. If the problem disappears when I next boot the Mac, I know that some piece of hardware I'd removed was in conflict with the Mac. From there, I'd follow the advice I provide in Chapter 3 for dealing with hardware conflicts—again, starting with the most obvious and working my way through to the point where I either fix the problem or resolve that something is broken.

If ditching the hardware didn't solve the problem, I'd look for software solutions, stripping my Mac's software down to its most basic components by disabling extensions and control panels. (I tell you at length how to do this in Chapter 3 as well.) If that didn't fix the problem, I'd work through a series of solutions until I put things right or decided to simply start over and install a brand new copy of the Mac OS. (Yup, I tell you how to do all this, too. See Chapter 2.) If the Mac refused to respond to such treatment, I'd break out my diagnostic/repair utilities (see Chapter 5).

And so you reach the crux of the chapter and, ultimately, this entire book. As Sherlock Holmes was so fond of saying, "When you have eliminated the impossible, whatever remains, *however improbable,* must be the truth."

I Can't Get Started!

Making Your Mac Get Up and Go

Nothing puts a damper on your day like sitting down at your Mac, pressing the Power button, and—after staring dumbly at your monitor for the better part of 10 minutes—realizing that your computer has no intention of ever starting up. Worse yet, you jam the Power button over and over, pressing the Reset button, and alternating prayers and curses improve matters not one iota. What on earth are you supposed to do?

Before following your first inclination (*my* first inclination, anyway) and taking a sledgehammer to your recalcitrant computer, you might want to spend a few minutes trolling through this chapter for an answer. Startup problems are common, and fortunately, most are treatable.

The Lifeless Mac

It's a rare Mac that, when you push the Power button, does nothing at all. At the very least, your Mac should blink an LED or two, make some kind of whirring noise, cause your monitor to light up (or make that "fizzy" sort of sound when the monitor first blinks on), or emit the kind of tone that makes you think, "Oh, dear, *that* sounds like trouble."

At the risk of offending my readers this early in the book (I generally try to reserve that kind of thing until at least Chapter 8), I'd like to suggest that the most common cause of this behavior is operator error—you've neglected to do something that provides your Mac the life-giving essentials it needs to start up. These essentials include:

There's no power getting to your Mac

Although you may consider your Mac to be an amazing productivity tool, a gateway to a world of knowledge, and your very best friend, it's also an electrical appliance. If you fail to supply your Mac with its recommended daily requirement of watts, you'll quickly learn how convincingly it can imitate a cinder block.

Certainly, no one would willingly deprive his or her Mac of this life-giving force, but it's remarkably easy to pull the plug unwittingly. When you're searching for the weak link in your personal power grid, check the following:

- Is the power cable plugged securely into your Mac as well as the power receptacle?
- Is the power receptacle receiving power? Try plugging a lamp into it to find out.
- Is the power receptacle switched off? Perhaps that light switch over by the door has a purpose.
- If the Mac is plugged into a power strip, is the power strip switched on?
- Have you neglected to pay your power bill?
- If you're using an iBook or PowerBook and attempting to run from a battery, are you sure that the battery is fully charged? Recent Mac portables sport tiny switches on their batteries that, when pressed, indicate how fully juiced the battery is. If you suspect a dead battery, plug your portable pal into a functioning power receptacle.

There's no spark getting to your Mac

I know as much about the way an automobile functions as I do about the mating habits of the Ruby-Snouted Pygmy Toad, but I believe that when you turn the key in your car, an electrical charge is sent from the battery to some thingamajig that ignites the fuel that allows your car to take you to Harry's House of Ham for a passel of pork and pie. Your Mac works in a similar fashion (except for the pork and pie, of course). When you press the Power key on your Mac's keyboard or on the Mac itself, that key sends a signal to the Mac that it's time to rise and shine. If this signal is interrupted, your Mac won't boot. If you've verified that your Mac is getting power, these are the next things to check:

Examine the cable. When you're attempting to start up by pressing the keyboard's Power key, ensure that the keyboard's cable is attached securely to the keyboard and to the Mac itself. If this cable has come loose, the necessary signal sent from the keyboard to the Mac won't be transmitted. A quick way to determine whether the connection between the keyboard and the Mac is the problem is to press the Mac's Power button. If the Mac fires up, give your keyboard and its cable a stern look and begin troubleshooting.

To troubleshoot such a problem, first determine whether you have a solid connections among the cable, Mac, and keyboard. Switch off the Mac if it's on, unseat the cable, and plug it back in. If the cable allows (if you have an ADB keyboard cable, for example), swap one end for the other. Try the keyboard's Power key.

If the Mac still won't start from the keyboard yet perks right up when you push the Power button on the Mac, you likely have one of two problems: The cable between the keyboard and the Mac is no good and needs to be replaced, or your Mac wasn't designed to be powered on from the keyboard.

Huh!? That's correct—iMacs released in the summer of 2000 (and those that followed) cannot be started from a keyboard. If you have one of these iMacs, and you use the Apple Pro Keyboard that shipped with your computer, you'll never run into this difficulty, because the Apple Pro Keyboard doesn't have a Power key. But prepare to be disappointed if you press the Power key on one of the older USB keyboards that Apple shipped with countless iMacs, the Blue and White Power Mac G3, and the early Power Mac G4 (you know, that eensie-teensie keyboard that all right-thinking Mac users loathed from the minute they laid hands on the miserable thing). Apple removed the circuitry necessary for these iMacs to boot from anything other than the Power button on the front of the case.

Check the battery. No, I have no intention of carrying on with my automotive analogy; I promise that I won't ask you to check the oil. The truth is that most Macs—excluding some of the portables—have an internal battery that, in addition to keeping enough juice flowing to your Mac to maintain certain System settings, helps start up your Mac when you press the Power key. If this battery has given up the ghost, your Mac may not start. These batteries are supposed to last about five years, but in some iMac models, they've gone kaput in as little as a year. A clue that the battery has indeed gone to meet its maker is a System clock that reverts to a time when people were still getting around in horse-drawn buggies or when Dwight Eisenhower was entrusted with the keys to the White House (1904 and 1956, respectively).

Some PowerBooks and iBooks lack an internal battery. Rather, the regular-ol' batteries that power the portable when it's not plugged in maintain these settings.

Were this book called *Absolutely Every Cotton-Pickin' Thing There Is to Know About the Mac—No Fooling*, I'd provide complete details on where the battery sits in each Mac model released by Apple and third-party manufacturers. But it isn't and I won't for this simple reason: Only one thing inside your Mac looks like a battery. *The battery!* If you open your Mac's case (don't worry; I mention the means for doing so in many Mac models in Chapter 7) and poke around, you're sure to run into the battery. It's usually colored some combination of pink and purple and is about two-thirds the length of a AA battery and a bit thicker. These batteries are either 3.6- or 4.5-volt lithium or alkaline batteries. If you're dying to know the exact specifications of the battery inside your Mac, Apple provides a helpful document in its Technical Information Library: http://docs.info.apple.com/article.html?artnum=11751.

But frankly, when folks ask me about battery replacement, I invariably issue these instructions:

With the power off, crack open your Mac; search for the thing that resembles a battery (it *is* one); remove the cap that keeps the battery in place if such a cap exists (not all Macs have them); extract the battery; take it to your local Full Service Electronics Boutique; place the battery on the counter; and, with appropriate aplomb, ask, "Could you give me another one of these, please?"

This way, the onus for finding a replacement battery is completely on the poor schmo working behind the counter. You don't have to struggle with embarrassing questions about part numbers or voltage ratings.

Reverse these steps to replace the battery.

Reset the Power Manager. Portable Macs (PowerBooks and iBooks) have an integrated circuit on their motherboards that controls such aspects of the computer as backlighting, sleep, hard-disk spin-down, and trackpad control. This integrated circuit is called the Power Manager. Over time, the Power Manager can become corrupted (you know what they say; "Absolute power corrupts absolutely"). And when the Power Manager is absolutely corrupted, it's possible that your laptop will refuse to start up when you press the Power button.

Regrettably, the procedure for resetting the Power Manager differs from model to model. Fortunately, I believe that I have just enough space to squeeze in the many methods for putting your Power Manager back in the pink (see the sidebar "Resetting the PowerBook and iBook Power Manager" in this section). Note: When you reset the Power Manager, you'll lose some of your System settings, such as the correct time and date.

Resetting the PowerBook and iBook Power Manager

Mac laptop feeling blue? Resetting the Power Manager may be just the thing to return the spring to its step. Here are the methods for resetting the Power Manager on every PowerBook and iBook model made:

PowerBook 100. Disconnect the AC adapter and battery, turn the battery contact switch on the back of the computer to the down position, allow the PowerBook to rest without power for 5 minutes, simultaneously press and hold the Reset and Interrupt buttons on the side of the PowerBook for 15 seconds, reinstall the battery, plug in the AC adapter (if your battery isn't charged), and turn the battery contact switch back to the up position.

PowerBook 140, 145, 145B, 170. Disconnect the AC adapter and battery; allow the PowerBook to rest without power for 5 minutes; using a couple of paper clips simultaneously, press and hold down the Reset and Interrupt buttons on the back of the PowerBook for 10 seconds; reinstall the battery; and plug in the AC adapter (if your battery isn't charged).

PowerBook 150. Disconnect the AC adapter and battery, grab a straightened paper clip and use it to push the Reset button on the back of the PowerBook for 10 seconds, plug the AC adapter into an outlet, plug the adapter into the PowerBook, push the Reset button briefly (you'll hear a tiny popping sound from the speaker; don't worry), and push the Power button on the back.

PowerBook 160, 165, 180. Disconnect the AC adapter and battery, allow the PowerBook to rest without power for 5 minutes, reinstall the battery, and plug in the AC adapter (if your battery isn't charged). If that doesn't do the trick, use two paper clips (or, heck, live it up and use a couple of ballpoint pens) to hold down the Reset and Interrupt buttons simultaneously for 10 seconds.

PowerBook 500 Series. Disconnect the AC adapter and battery, allow the PowerBook to rest without power for 5 minutes, simultaneously press and hold down Command-Option-Control-Power for 10 seconds, reinstall the battery, and plug in the AC adapter (if your battery isn't charged).

PowerBook 200 and 2300 Series. Press and hold down the Power button on the back for 45 seconds.

PowerBook 190, 1400, 2400, 3400, 5300 Series and PowerBook G3 (the original black one bearing the model number M3553). All these PowerBooks require the use of the Reset button. On the 190, you'll find this button below the Video Out port. The 1400's is between the ADB and Serial ports. The 2400's button is above the floppy-drive connector. On the 3400 and G3, the button is left of the Serial port. And the 5300's Reset button has—along with the 5300 itself—been burned to a crisp, so what do you care? (Sorry, but did you know that these PowerBooks are famous for catching on fire?) Seriously, the 5300 Series' Reset button is below the charred Video Out port.

To reset these PowerBooks, start the computer by holding down the Reset button for 20 seconds. If the PowerBook won't come to life, try this Reset-button trick another couple of times.

PowerBook G3 Series (Wall Street, M4753). Simultaneously press Shift-Fn-Control-Power, wait 5 seconds, and press the Power button.

PowerBook G3 Series (Bronze Keyboard, M5343). Press the Reset button on the back, wait 5 seconds, and press the Power button.

iBook and iBook (FireWire). Using a paper clip, press the Reset button (below the Power button at the bottom of the screen); wait 5 seconds; and press the Power button.

iBook (Dual USB). Press the Reset button (above the Audio/Video port on the left side of the iBook), wait 5 seconds, and press the Power button.

PowerBook (FireWire), PowerBook G4 (Titanium). Press the Reset button (between the Video Out and Modem ports), wait 5 seconds, and press the Power button.

Press the Cuda button. Open your Mac (with the power off!), and hunt around for a round button about the size of a saccharin tablet. This button is called the *Cuda button* (see the sidebar "The Cuda Button" in this section). Press and hold down this button for a few seconds; then reassemble your Mac. Pressing this button sometimes brings an otherwise-comatose Mac to life.

> **The Cuda Button**
>
> The Mac contains a microcontroller chip that looks after such functions as turning the System power on and off, managing System resets, maintaining parameter RAM (PRAM), and scrutinizing the Mac's real-time clock. This microcontroller is called the *Cuda chip*—a chip that you can reset by pressing the appropriately named Cuda button.
>
> If your Mac is seriously messed (it won't start up, or you get a Sad Mac, the Chimes of Doom, or both when you press the Power key) and nothing else seems to work, I'm a firm believer in opening the Mac, locating this button, and pressing it for a few seconds. The button usually is black or red, often is located near the Mac's internal battery and, as I mention elsewhere in this section, is darned tiny. Doing so may force your Mac to reconsider its recently reluctant actions and play ball. On the other hand, pressing the Cuda button may do nothing more than provide you the satisfaction of knowing that you've done absolutely everything you can to make your Mac see sense.

Think power supply. I've dealt with the easy "U-Can-Fix-It" stuff: cables and the battery. But there's one more character to consider in this power play: the Mac's power supply. The power supply is responsible for feeding power to your Mac, and if it goes on the fritz, it must be replaced. Occasionally, you'll see warning signs that the power supply is ready to go; the monitor displays distorted patterns or you need to pound your Power key a few times to make your Mac start. Often, though, the single indication you have that your power supply is shot is a Mac that refuses to start up.

It's possible to obtain replacement power supplies from parts dealers who advertise in the back of *Macworld* and other Mac-centric magazines. With many early modular Mac models (the Macintosh II family, for example), it's not difficult to remove and replace these things. But if you have a newer Mac with a less-accessible power supply or are the least bit shy about mucking around with the guts of your computer, save yourself some heartache rather than a few bucks, and take your Mac to the shop. (Call first to see whether the shop can actually obtain a replacement power supply.)

The Mac really is on; it's just that...

Way, way back in the days of the Mac II and other six-slot behemoths, Macs bore the kind of fans you find in small-to-medium-size wind tunnels. Fire up one of these babies, and unless you have the aural acuity of, say, Ludwig Van Beethoven, you know quite well that your Mac is powered on.

As Apple has made Macs cuter and more compact, it's also made them quieter. If you have an iMac, a PowerBook or iBook, or the dearly departed Power Mac G4 Cube, the only indication you may have that the computer is actually switched on is a screen that's lit up or a lightly throbbing LED. I know you're going to feel a bit sheepish if this turns out to be your problem, but just in case:

> **Check the monitor.** Is it switched on?
>
> **Check the monitor cable.** Is it plugged in securely?
>
> **Check the video card?** Is it completely seated?
>
> **Check the brightness control.** For all I know, your 7-year-old son thinks it's a hoot and a half to turn the brightness all the way down on your PowerBook just to see how long it takes you to figure out the problem.
>
> **Is your Mac sleeping?** A sleeping Mac that's diagnosed as dead isn't nearly as improbable as it seems. The fact is, this whole "wake from sleep" business is still a work in progress. I've opened my sleeping PowerBook G4 more times than I care to recount with the expectation that it will pop to life, only to be let down when no action ensued. A sleeping Mac usually gives an indication that it's asleep; an LED might blink or pulse, for example. But if the Mac crashed while it was in suspended animation, you might not see such a signal. For this reason, it's not a bad idea to press your Mac's Restart button or Command-Control-Power to attempt to force-restart your Mac.

The Mac is well and truly hosed

It would be swell if we could fix all our personal, financial, and technological problems single-handedly, but at times, matters have spun so far out of control that only a Trained Professional will do. If your Mac won't respond to any of the treatments I've suggested so far, it's probably time to call in the experts and give Apple a jingle. For information on receiving technical support from Apple, see Appendix A.

If Apple can't solve your problem, you've pretty well exhausted your options. You must bundle up your Mac and seek salvation at *The Shop*.

Taking your Mac to the shop generally means locating an Apple Authorized Dealer, carting in your computer, and shelling out a fair number of shekels to return it to its former state of grace. In some cases, the shop will perform the repairs on-site, but more commonly, Macs are now returned to Apple for service. This arrangement is both comforting and a little irritating. It's comforting because if the only Apple Authorized Dealer in your neck of the woods is a gargantuan appliance outlet where the service technicians know more about washing machines than Macs, you have the assurance that a qualified technician—rather than Bluto over there with the monkey wrench—is going to work on your baby. And it's irritating because once your Mac leaves the dealer's premises, there's nothing on heaven or earth you can do to expedite your repair. Your calls to Apple's technical-support line with offers of chocolate-chip cookies in exchange for the return of your beloved Macintosh will go unheeded. Although Apple has a pretty fair track record in regard to turning around repairs, if the company is having difficulties obtaining a part that your Mac requires, you'll wait until that part arrives and Apple has the time to install it, bub.

The Sad Mac

Far more common than Macs that do nothing when you flick on the power are those that show brief signs of life and then grind to a halt, displaying an unfriendly icon on a black screen or sounding an intimidating tone. This icon (termed a *Sad Mac*) and these error tones (known as *the Chimes of Doom*) are sent out into the world when some portion of the Mac's startup hardware test fails. Although a Sad Mac or the Chimes of Doom strikes fear into the bosoms of every Mac user, they don't always indicate that your Mac is destined for a trip to the shop. Before fainting dead away, take a gander at these possible causes and solutions for your unhappy Mac.

Bad RAM

If you've read the "Holy Cripes" emergency pages of this book, you know that a Mac that displays an unhappy countenance or sings an ominous tune after you've installed additional memory likely suffers from nothing more than an incompatible RAM module or one you've failed to tuck securely into its slot. (To learn how to install RAM in many Mac models, see Chapter 7.) The obvious way to test that RAM module is to shut down your Mac, remove the offending memory, and start your Mac again. If the Mac boots without complaint, bad or unsecured RAM is your problem. Before picking up the phone and raising holy heck with the company that sold you the RAM, try reseating it.

If the Sad Mac or Chimes of Doom returns, and your Mac sports multiple RAM slots, switch off the Mac, open its case, and try swapping RAM modules around. You know, take the RAM in the first slot and fling it into the third slot, and move the recently evicted RAM from slot three into slot two. While you're playing this digital version of three-card monte, be sure to keep careful watch on which of these RAM modules is the one you recently introduced to your Mac. If the module is incompatible or just plain bad, you'll want to be sure to return the right one.

Earlier in this chapter, I mentioned that pressing the Cuda button sometimes works miracles on a seemingly dead Mac. Mashing this button sometimes clears up these kinds of startup crashes as well. Give it a shot.

Card tricks

RAM modules aren't the only components of your Mac that can come loose. If you have some variety of modular Mac that accepts AGP, PCI, PDS, LC, Comm-Slot, or NuBus cards—a Power Macintosh or earlier beige desktop model, for example—one of these cards may not be as snug as it could be and is causing conniptions for your Mac. To be sure that everything's right in this regard, open your Mac (again, with the power *off*), and reseat any internal video and add-on cards.

If you've just introduced a new add-in card to your Mac—such as a SCSI, sound, or video card—your internal alarm should have rung the minute you hit the Power key and your Mac gave you the raspberry. Reseat such a card, and if your Mac continues to reject it like a bad penny, remove any devices you may have attached to the card. If you've added a SCSI card to your Power Mac G4, and you've strung a SCSI cable between that card and an old scanner that you picked up at the local flea market, remove the SCSI cable from the card and restart. If all's right with the world, the attached device may be the problem, rather than the card. If the Mac continues to misbehave with nothing attached to the card, remove it and seek help from the card's manufacturer.

SCSI voodoo

If you're relatively new to computers, you probably have the idea that these thinking machines should work in a logical and predictable fashion. Most of the time, they do. But there's also a certain black magic to these things. Some of the darkest black magic is in the Small Computer System Interface (SCSI). If you have a Mac that was made in the past few years, the acronym SCSI may be unfamiliar to you. Count your blessings that it is.

SCSI was the means by which Macs of the late 1980s and most of the 1990s communicated with such peripherals as hard drives, removable media drives, scanners, and (rarely) printers. Ideally, SCSI works this way: A single SCSI chain supports as many as seven SCSI devices, and each of these devices has a specific SCSI address, or ID. On the Mac, SCSI ID 7 was reserved for the Macintosh itself. ID 0 was almost always assigned to the internal hard drive, and ID 3 traditionally was set aside for the CD-ROM. That means that if you wanted to add an SCSI device, you'd set its ID to 1, 2, 4, 5, or 6. The rule of thumb held that the last device in the SCSI chain had to be *terminated*—meaning that the last device in the SCSI chain was capped off in such a way that signals sent down the SCSI chain weren't echoed back up the chain, thus keeping the signal clean and pure.

Sounds like the kind of science you can take to the bank, right? Wrong. If you bothered to read the fine print, you saw a list of exceptions as long as your arm. If the SCSI chain exceeded 10 feet in length (and this limit includes internal cables, which you can't see), you were probably hosed. If the cables were of poor quality, you were probably hosed. If such-and-such device was at the end of the chain instead of at the beginning, you were probably hosed. If you had a SCSI scanner at the end of the chain on Mondays and in the middle of the chain on every third Wednesday, you were probably hosed. *Sheesh.*

Apple eventually rid Macs of this SCSI pestilence and replaced it with USB and FireWire, but SCSI lives on in older Macs and via add-on SCSI cards. What does this have to do with you and your Mac? Just this: If you have a SCSI port on your Mac or have added a SCSI card, and your Mac flashes a Sad Mac at you on startup, take a moment to consider SCSI as the culprit. The quickest way to clear SCSI's good name is simply to remove the SCSI cable from the Mac's external SCSI port. (Please do this with the Mac shut down. *Hot-swapping*—plugging and unplugging cables with the Mac switched on—is a definite no-nay-and-nary with SCSI.) If the Mac responds to this treatment in a happy fashion, you're in for the thrill of a lifetime: troubleshooting SCSI!

Troubleshooting SCSI

As I mention outside this sidebar, SCSI is anything but scientific. In many cases, getting a SCSI chain that carries two or more devices to work properly is a hit-and-miss matter. But you can take certain measures to give yourself a leg up. They include:

Keep the total cable length less than 10 feet. This cable length includes the cables inside your Mac as well as the SCSI peripheral, so keep that length *well* under 10 feet.

Use quality SCSI cables. Honestly, I've set more than a dozen erring Macs back on the path of righteousness simply by suggesting to their owners that they stop being such miserable cheapskates and invest in high-quality SCSI cables. Good cables really do make a difference.

Use the right kind of cables and adapters. SCSI comes in a variety of flavors—SCSI, SCSI-2, and SCSI-3—and connectors. Macs that originally shipped with SCSI bear a 25-pin connector (except for PowerBooks, which have a square 30-pin connector). Newer SCSI cards have much smaller 50-pin or 64-pin connectors. You can use newer SCSI peripherals with older SCSI connectors as long as you have the proper cable or adapter. (You can, for example, connect a SCSI-2 SCSI hard drive that sports the smaller connector to your old Mac IIci.) Older Macs can't take advantage of these devices' speed, however. SCSI speed is limited by the host SCSI device, so if your IIci runs at SCSI-1 speeds, that's all you'll get from that fast SCSI hard drive.

Terminate the first and last device in the chain. If you're using the internal or external SCSI connector that came with your Mac, the first device in the chain—your Mac—is terminated, so don't sweat it. If you've added a SCSI card, however, check the manual for termination instructions. The card should ship in a terminated state, but it doesn't hurt to check. Very definitely terminate the last device. Most SCSI peripherals include a switch that allows you to turn termination on and off. If yours doesn't have such a switch, jog down to your local electronics emporium and purchase an external SCSI terminator—a gray, blocky kind of thing that clamps onto the SCSI port and provides termination.

Make allowances for scanners. SCSI scanners are like an opera company's coloratura sopranos; you must graciously acquiesce to their every unyielding demand. Such scanners are particularly finicky about their place in the SCSI chain. Some scanners prefer to be at the end of the chain. Others desire to be first in line. Still others aren't quite sure where they're most comfortable and demand that you juggle the position of every SCSI device in the chain a dozen times or more before finally consenting to work in the configuration you tried the first time.

If all else fails, ignore everything in this list. Ultimately, that's what makes SCSI so damnably damnable. Even though the preceding guidelines are *supposed* to provide a trouble-free SCSI chain, they sometimes don't. To troubleshoot a chain that just won't work, start by simplifying. Attach one device and test. Then attach another and test. Keep going until something breaks down; then move a device from one position in the chain to another. At one time, I had a SCSI chain that refused to work unless the third device in a four-peripheral chain was terminated. (Go figure.) At a point like this, the best advice I can offer is to be creative and patient. Good luck.

Confused startup disk

Your Mac requires a startup volume that's capable of booting and one that contains a kosher System Folder. A corrupt, incomplete, or missing System Folder shouldn't cause your Mac to exhibit Sad Mac kinds of behavior, but a startup disk that's damaged in some way (corrupt boot blocks, for example) can lead to a Sad Mac or Chimes error.

To determine quickly whether this situation is the cause of your Mac's woes, just boot your Mac from a different startup disk. In most cases, the easiest way to do so is to insert the startup disk that shipped with your Mac (a Disk Tools floppy disk, if you've got a fairly aged Mac, or a CD-ROM for a more thoroughly modern Mac) and attempt to boot the Mac from that disk. Booting from a floppy isn't a problem; just shove the thing into the Mac's floppy-drive port, press the Power button, and wait and wait and wait and wait while the Mac churns to life. Booting from a CD is the slightest bit trickier. To boot from a CD, hold down the keyboard's C key at startup. You'll know that the Mac has booted from the CD when the Mac takes longer than usual to start up and finally displays a startup screen that appears to have been invaded by flying saucers (actually, pictures of CD-ROMs). You can also boot your Mac from some troubleshooting CDs—such as Alsoft's Disk Warrior, Micromat's TechTool Pro, or Symantec's Norton Utilities—and from System software CDs such as the Mac OS 9 disc. Even better, you can create your own bootable troubleshooting CD. In Chapter 5, I show you how.

If you have a non-Apple Macintosh (yes, youngsters, there really was such a thing once upon a time), such as a Power Computing, Umax, APS, or Motorola clone, the C-key trick may not work. Y'see, the CD-ROM drives in some of these clones are not compatible with Apple's CD-ROM drivers; these machines shipped with third-party CD-ROM drivers such as FWB's CD-ROM Toolkit. Therefore, pressing the C key on startup does you no good whatsoever. When you're dealing with these clones (or with an Apple Mac that doesn't care to boot from the CD, for reasons of its own), try pressing Delete-Option-Command-Shift (DOCS). This key combination instructs the Mac to search somewhere other than the internal hard drive for a bootable volume. In addition to booting from a CD, this method is a perfectly delightful way to boot from another hard drive that carries a legitimate System Folder.

It really is a hardware problem

If every Sad Mac and Chimes of Doom error were caused by something as trivial as an unsecured RAM module or confused startup disk, Apple's engineers could have saved themselves a lot of hard work. Instead of creating dialog box after dialog box of arcane error codes, they could have cobbled together a couple of messages that appeared at startup, such as "Hey, buddy boy, seems we have a RAM problem here. Either insert it properly or get it out of here!" and "Oh, for pity's sake, where's my startup disk!?"

But when you're faced with a Mac that exhibits these kinds of symptoms *and* won't boot from an alternative startup disk, you should consider that when your Mac displays such a sad face, it's doing so because the Mac really is in need of serious repair. What kind of repair are we talking about? Regrettably, the kind of repair that requires you to wish your Mac many happy—and *swift*—returns. Yes, this kind of thing may prompt a call to Apple and a trip to the shop.

The Questioning Mac

No, not the *questionable* Mac—surely you know whether it's a Mac or not. *Questioning*. The Mac that, after you press the Power button, displays a picture of a floppy disk with a question mark or a folder that alternately displays the Mac OS logo and a question mark. The questioning Mac is one that tells you that it has searched far and wide and can not find a startup disk that contains a valid System Folder.

This problem doesn't apply to those of you who, for whatever bizarre reason, intentionally ripped the hard drive from the Mac's interior. But for the rest of us, a Mac whose sole goal in life is to blink a bit of punctuation rhythmically is one whose sights should be set higher.

What would cause your Mac to behave in such a way? Let's take a look.

Peripheral problems

The hardware items dangling from the outside of your Mac—SCSI, USB, and FireWire devices—can keep your Mac from starting up as it should.

SCSI again. Earlier in this chapter, I talked about SCSI voodoo and the effect it can have on your Mac. In addition to keeping your Mac from booting or causing it to boot with a Sad Mac, a screwy SCSI setup can bar your Mac from finding a valid startup disk. For this reason, if your Mac displays this questioning behavior, it's not a bad idea to switch off your computer, disconnect the SCSI chain, and try starting up again. If your Mac starts up and discovers that the internal hard drive really does have a working System Folder, it's time to flip back a page or two to the "Troubleshooting SCSI" sidebar and brush up on your SCSI troubleshooting skills.

If you boot your Mac from an external SCSI drive, of course, this drive must remain. Any other devices attached to the chain should go.

USB. USB—the Universal Serial Bus that makes it easy to plug in such peripherals as printers, input devices, and removable media drives—was supposed to end all this voodoo nonsense by providing a port that would rid our computers of such peripheral conflicts. It hasn't. A pass through any online troubleshooting forum will reveal message after message complaining about Macs that won't start up because a USB printer and USB-based removable media drive just don't see eye to eye.

To determine whether USB is your Mac's problem, disconnect all the USB devices attached to it (except the keyboard and mouse), and see whether that action puts things right. If the Mac boots after such treatment, jump onto the Web and download the most up-to-date drivers you can find for your peripherals. Peripheral vendors hear about it in short order if their thingamabobs don't work with someone else's doohickey, and most vendors are conscientious about issuing updated drivers.

Also, if you're not running the most recent version of the Mac OS (by this, I mean Mac OS 9.2 or earlier, not Mac OS X), and if your Mac will accept a more recent version of the OS, consider upgrading. The drivers released when Apple first embraced USB were—how shall I put this politely?—*less than perfect*. They got significantly better with each revision of the Mac OS. A simple OS upgrade may be all your Mac needs to vanquish USB conflicts.

Take a look at your USB hub as well. Inexpensive hubs may not provide the kind of power necessary to keep your USB peripherals happy. I found that my collection of USB devices worked more harmoniously when I introduced a powered Belkin (www.belkin.com) hub into the equation.

If your USB conflicts don't disappear even after driver, Mac OS, and hub updates, you may have to learn to live with the conflict. No, I'm not suggesting that you should leave all your USB stuff plugged in and allow your Mac to slack off. Rather, you may have to unplug one of the offending USB devices (an Iomega Zip drive, for example), boot the Mac, and then plug the USB device in after the Mac has started up.

This workaround is possible because, unlike SCSI, USB is *hot-pluggable*—meaning that you can plug and unplug USB devices while that Mac is switched on. When you plug a USB device into a running Mac, the Mac OS should see that you've done so and should load the USB driver that allows that device to function. On one of my Macs, I have a USB device that reads my digital camera's CompactFlash media card. If that device is plugged into my USB hub at startup, it's dollars to doughnuts that my Mac either won't boot or will crash as soon as I see the Mac's desktop. Therefore, I wait until my Mac has started and then plug the card reader into a free USB port. When I do, I hear a little hard-drive whirring, indicating that the Mac has laid out the welcome mat for this doodad. Then the device is ready to read.

If you've tried and failed to boot your Mac from a USB drive, Apple suggests that you attempt to boot the Mac some other way—with the System CD that shipped with your Mac, for example—and disable the drivers that came with the drive. (I talk about how to enable and disable drivers in Chapter 3.) The idea here is that the USB drivers may be out of date, and when you disable them, Apple's own USB drivers may allow you to boot from the drive.

FireWire. FireWire (a.k.a. IEEE 1394 or iLink) is an Apple-designed technology for moving data between FireWire-compatible devices quickly. Recent Macs, digital camcorders, hard drives, and a host of other removable media drives are among these compatible devices. As with USB, FireWire devices are hot-pluggable. To mount a FireWire drive, just string a FireWire cable between your Mac and the drive, and you're in business.

Many recent Macs that natively include FireWire ports can be booted from a FireWire drive; the Blue and White Power Mac G3 and Power Mac G4 (PCI Graphics) are the exceptions. You may find, however, that your Mac will display the flashing question mark even though you have a FireWire drive that contains a perfectly delightful System Folder attached to your Mac. Obviously, you should first make sure that the FireWire drive is on and that its cable is connected firmly to both the drive and to the Mac. But you should also consider the order in which you powered on your Mac and the drive.

Like all SCSI drives, some FireWire drives prefer to be switched on before the Mac. Yup, even though FireWire drives are hot-pluggable, many of them won't boot a Mac if the Mac was fired up first.

Corrupt System Folder

Now that you've eliminated peripheral devices from your list of suspects, if your Mac still displays the flashing question mark, it's time to switch to full-on troubleshooting mode. If your Mac worked perfectly well the day before and now displays a questioning countenance, the System Folder on your startup drive may have become corrupted.

To diagnose a corrupt System Folder, boot from the System disk that came with your Mac (in case you've forgotten how, see "Confused startup disk" earlier in this chapter), and take a gander at the System Folder inside your startup disk. This folder should sport the two-faced Mac OS icon, which indicates that the System Folder is "blessed"—meaning that the Mac OS thinks it's perfectly OK for the Mac to boot from this System Folder. If you see a System Folder without this icon, that's your problem, and you must discover its cause. Causes (and their solutions) include:

Blessed Art Thou. The two-faced icon indicates that this System Folder is "blessed."

Corrupt Preferences file. The Finder Preferences file can become corrupted, particularly after your Mac has crashed. If corrupted, this file can keep the System Folder from being blessed and your Mac from starting up. To repair the problem, open the System Folder's Preferences folder, locate the Finder Preferences file, and drag it to the Trash. Then restart.

Failure to recognize the Finder and System files. Why? Beats me. As the bumper sticker says, "Confusion Happens." The quick fix for this one is to drag the System and Finder files out of the startup disk's System Folder, close that System Folder, drag the System and Finder files back onto the closed System Folder, open the System Folder, and close it again. After performing this Finder foxtrot, hope that the OS icon appears on the System Folder. If it does, restart your Mac.

Corrupt Finder file. If the Finder file is corrupt, your Mac won't boot. Reinstalling the System Folder will certainly fix the problem (I tell you how to do this later in this chapter) but jeez, what a hassle. And because it *is* such a hassle, I keep a copy of a working Finder file close by. When I suspect that my Finder is corrupt, I drag the old one into the Trash (you'll find it inside the System Folder) and replace it with a working copy.

Note: When you attempt this trick, make sure that the Finder is the same version as the one you're replacing. If your Mac originally came with Mac OS 9.0, for example, and you're currently running Mac OS 9.1, make sure that the Finder replacement is version Mac OS 9.1, not Mac 9.0. You can tell which version it is by clicking the icon and then pressing Command-I (or choosing Get Info from the Finder's File menu). When you do, you'll see the version number near the top of the window.

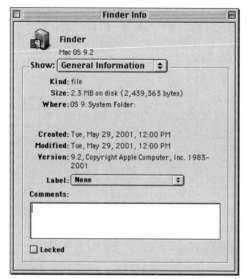

Like a Version. The Get Info window reveals that this is version 9.2 of the Finder.

Another note: If replacing the Finder doesn't work, try the same trick with the System file (also located in the System Folder).

PRAM problem. Parameter RAM (or PRAM) is a bit of RAM set aside on your Mac's motherboard that holds software settings important to your computer. These settings include the time and date, the status of AppleTalk (switched on or off), and information about the current startup disk. PRAM can get corrupted, and to clear its confusion, you must zap it. Zapping hardly sounds like a technical operation, I know, but I assure you that it's a real technique, really called zapping.

To zap your PRAM, hold down Command-Option-P-R right after you hit your Mac's Power button. You'll hear the usual startup tone, followed by another startup tone. After the second tone, let go of these keys and wait while your Mac starts up. If the procedure was successful, your Mac should boot without a hitch. When it does start up, you'll have to change some of the Mac's settings. The time and date will be off by a few decades, for example.

Note: Zapping the PRAM, like rebuilding the Desktop, is one of those "Hey, give it a try, what have you got to lose?" troubleshooting solutions. Any time you encounter a startup problem, it's worth zapping the ol' PRAM if you run out of better ideas.

General corruption. Then there are times when your System Folder is so funked up, you can't tell what exactly is troubling it, and none of the solutions I've offered so far makes a bit of difference. You've done what you can by manipulating files and folders and zapping the PRAM. It's time to turn to your troubleshooting utilities.

The first step is to boot your Mac from a startup CD (or floppy disk, if your Mac is that old) and launch Disk First Aid, located in the Utilities folder. When the Disk First Aid window appears, click the volume that refuses to boot and then click the Verify button. Disk First Aid will examine your drive, looking for any obvious problems. If it finds any, it will tell you what they are in language that you may or may not understand. Should Disk First Aid find a problem, click the Repair button; the utility will attempt to fix the drive.

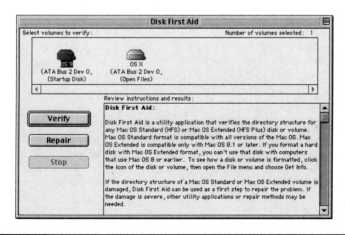

Clicks and Fix.
Pray that clicking Disk First Aid's Verify and Repair buttons will cure your Mac's ills.

Now, here's the real I-wouldn't-lie-to-you scoop: Disk First Aid is a pretty weak diagnostic/repair utility. After pouring molasses into the interior of your hard drive, strapping it to the undercarriage of your car for a week, dousing it with gasoline, and setting it ablaze, odds are that Disk First Aid would report, "Hey, everything looks good to me!" OK, perhaps it's not *that* bad. Disk First Aid can find some of the more obvious problems, but it often fails to sniff out the tougher stuff, and when it does find problems, it can't repair them as well as some third-party utilities.

If Disk First Aid reports no problem—or reports problems but can't seem to fix them—you must turn to a third-party solution, such as Disk Warrior, TechTool Pro, or Norton Utilities. There's no guarantee that one of these tools will bring your Mac back from the dead, but the likelihood of doing so will certainly increase. I discuss each of these utilities in depth in Chapter 5.

Should even these third-party wonders fail to bless your System Folder and allow your Mac to start up as it should, a clean install is in your immediate future.

How to: The Clean Install

Throughout the book, I casually suggest that when you have problems with Mac OS 9.2 or earlier, you perform a clean install of your System software. "OK, swell," you say, "but what is this clean install of which you speak so highly?" Just this: A clean install places a brand-spanking-new System Folder on the hard drive of your choice. While doing so, it renames your old System Folder Previous System Folder.

By the way, it's also possible to perform a "dirty install" (though I'm not sure anyone but me calls it by that name). This variety of System software installation updates your old System Folder, replacing out-of-date items.

There are good reasons for choosing a clean install over a dirty one. With a clean install, you know that you're getting a completely hygienic, uncorrupted System Folder. With a dirty install, a corrupted thingamabob—a thingamabob that caused the problem that compelled you to perform the installation in the first place—might remain. Also, with a clean install, there's no danger that the installation will overwrite any updated files that you may have installed earlier. If just

continues on next page

yesterday, you installed the Apple SuperDuper Modem Thingie version 1.3, and today, you perform a dirty install that overwrites it with Apple SuperDuper Modem Thingie version 1.2, you'd have to reinstall (and perhaps redownload) the more modern version after performing the dirty install. With a clean install, you can simply move version 1.3 from the Previous System Folder to the new, clean System Folder.

Here's how to perform a clean install of recent versions of the Mac OS 9 and earlier:

1. Insert your System software CD.

   This CD can be either the Software Install CD that came with your Mac or a System software CD that you purchased (the Mac OS 9.0 CD, for example). It's often easier (or necessary) to perform a clean install by booting from the CD. To do so, with the install CD in the drive, hold down the C key at startup.

2. Double-click the Mac OS Install icon.

   The Install Macintosh Software dialog box appears.

3. Click the Continue button.

4. Select a destination disk in the next window (your Mac's startup drive, for example).

5. In this same window, click the Options button.

   A dialog box appears, offering you the option to perform a clean installation.

6. Select this option, and click OK.

7. Click Select in the Select Destination window.

8. If you like, read the text in the Before You Install window; then click Continue.

9. Be the very first person on earth to actually do so and read the Software License Agreement in the next window; then click Agree.

10. Click the Start button in the Install Software dialog box to begin the installation.

In the same dialog box, you'll see Customize and Options buttons. Clicking the Customize button allows you to choose exactly which components of the Mac OS you want to install. You can install only the basic OS, or you can go whole-hog and install such things as language kits (which provide support for foreign languages) and the Network Assistant Client. Clicking the Options button grants permission for the installer to update your hard drive's disk drivers and generate an installation report. Leave this option checked unless you've used third-party drive-formatting software.

Hard drive: MIA

Worse than a corrupt System Folder is one belonging to a drive that—as far as your Mac is concerned—doesn't exist. Although you're darned sure that no one entered your home or office and swiped your Mac's hard drive while your back was turned, it's quite possible that your hard drive is so corrupt that the Mac fails to recognize it.

You'll realize quickly that your hard drive is missing in action when you boot from your system CD or floppy disk and find no hard-drive icon on the desktop. And now that it is missing, what can you do about it? Well...

If you have a PowerBook, reset the Power Manager.
After a bad crash, my PowerBook G4 couldn't locate the hard drive. Resetting the Power Manager (see "Resetting the PowerBook and iBook Power Manager" sidebar earlier in the chapter) caused the drive to reappear.

Disconnect peripherals. Yup, it's time to detach cables again. A misbehaving SCSI chain can confound a Mac enough that a volume fails to appear. Also, drives that have the same SCSI ID will exhibit this behavior.

Check cables. If you're attempting to boot from an external drive, be sure that the cable that runs from that drive to your Mac is secure. If the cable appears to be secure and the drive still doesn't appear, swap in a new cable. If you want to be really thorough, you can reseat the data and power cables on an internal drive, although the likelihood that these things will come loose is pretty low.

Run Disk First Aid/third-party troubleshooting tools.
You'll breathe just a bit easier if you learn that your Mac can see your drive in some fashion. If the drive appears in the Disk First Aid window or is recognized by a third-party tool, you can try to repair whatever damage keeps your drive from being recognized.

Run Drive Setup/third-party formatting software.
If Disk First Aid or another troubleshooting tool can't see your drive, you have my permission to panic just a little bit. A drive this far gone is one that's badly befuddled.

Your next step is to run Apple's Drive Setup (in the Utilities folder on your System CD). Drive Setup is the software you use to prepare your Mac's hard drive for reading and writing. Unless your hard drive is completely out to lunch, it should appear among the list of drives in the Drive Setup window, though it may not be mounted.

Found It! Drive Setup may be able to locate a missing drive.

If the hard drive appears in your formatting software's list of available drives, you can attempt to mount that drive. To do so within Drive Setup, click the entry that reads < not mounted >. This entry is your hard drive. Then choose Mount Volumes from the Functions menu. Cross your fingers and hope that your hard drive appears in the list of drives. After the drive is mounted, you can attempt to repair it or perform a clean install of your System software.

Mount It! Better yet, Drive Setup may even be able to mount your shy drive.

If you formatted your drive with a different utility—FWB's Hard Disk Toolkit or Intech's Hard Disk Speed-Tools, for example—Drive Setup may not recognize your drive. Therefore, try to access your drive with the software you used to format the drive originally. Third-party formatting software also provides a way to mount unmounted drives. Check the manual to learn how.

Last-ditch efforts

You've waded through this section patiently in the hope of finding a way to bring your Mac back from the dead. You've tried every suggestion I've offered in the chapter, yet your Mac's hard drive simply cannot be found. Now what?

I can offer you four options:

Restore from your backup. Fortunately, losing a drive this way isn't all that big a deal, because you can always restore your data from the backup that you maintain religiously. All you have to do is... *what's that?* You say you don't have a backup? You mean to tell me that you've entrusted every bit of precious information—your financial records, pictures of your grandchildren, business invoices—to a hard drive that was absolutely destined to die one day, and you haven't bothered to make a backup? *Are you insane!??* It's time for us to have a little chat. See the sidebar "No Backup: Are You Insane!??" in this section.

Call Apple. I mean, heck, why not? You can tell your troubles to someone, and who knows—maybe Apple can offer a solution that helps.

Call DriveSavers. This company (www.drivesavers.com, 800-440-1904) specializes in recovering data from hard drives that have taken a trip to No-Boot Hill. DriveSavers' services are not cheap, but if you really, *really* need the data that was on that drive, and you don't have a backup, DriveSavers is the best resource for getting that data back.

Biff your hard drive. Look, I mention this knowing full well that I'm going to get loads of angry email from readers who think this suggestion is absolutely the worst advice I could give to anyone. But in all fairness, I have to mention it because in rare cases, it works.

Here's the requisite warning: If you wallop your Mac (and, therefore, its hard drive), and your Mac never starts up again, or delivers the kind of shock calculated to kill a dozen elephants, don't blame me. What if you *really* don't care about its data and are willing to end what little life it may cling to in the hopes of maybe, *mayyyyyyybeeeeee* making it work again? In that case, with the power off, give your Mac (or the drive enclosure, if it's an external drive) a tiny shot with the heel of your hand. That jolt may unstick a stuck drive long enough for you to mount the drive and *immediately* back up the data on it. I stress *immediately,* because a drive that chugs back to life after this kind of treatment is one that will repay such ill use by grinding to a halt the next opportunity it gets.

No Backup: Are You Insane!??

I realize that it's a bit cruel of me to chastise you for failing to maintain a comprehensive backup of your data when your hard drive appears to be toast. After all, what could be greater motivation to back up in the future than seeing your data go down the drain? But honestly, troubleshooting a Mac when you know that you can replace its data is totally different from working without a safety net. Nothing is more nerve-wracking than attempting to repair your Mac when you know that if you can't bring it back, you've lost countless hours of work (and perhaps your Great Aunt Sophie's prize-winning pickled-egg recipe).

Really, my heart goes out to you. I've been there, and I know that you won't make the same mistake twice. My hope is that those who've picked up this book for its pure reading pleasure will stumble across this sidebar, place a thoughtful hand to chin, and remark, "Say, this Breen fella's on to something! Maybe I *should* back up."

In Chapter 8, I describe how to create your own network backup server, and I suppose I could simply direct you there for further instructions. But I know full well that at the first mention of the word *networking*, many people's minds glaze over, and any subsequent words that appear on the page are interpreted as "Glubba slubba blubba flubba plooba dooba doo."

To ensure that you don't lose these important backup tips among all the dooba doo, allow me to make a few short points:

- You *must* back up your data.
- You don't have to back up all your data—just the data you can't live without. This category includes not only things like personal correspondence and Quicken files, but also your email client's address book and Web browser's bookmarks.
- Unless you have lots of backup storage, don't bother backing up your applications. You can always reinstall them from the disks on which they shipped.
- Retrospect and Retrospect Express, made by Dantz (www.dantz.com, (925) 253-3000), are the only tools I recommend for a complete backup. Retrospect Express is less expensive and doesn't support network backups or certain backup devices (tape drives, for example). Use Retrospect to create an automated backup schedule. If a backup takes place automatically, you won't have to think about it and, therefore, put it off for another time.
- When you're creating a backup schedule, think about how devastated you'd be if you lost a day's work, or two days' work, or a week's work. Then create a schedule that reflects these levels of devastation.
- Choose a reliable backup medium that balances capacity, cost, and value of your data. Removable media drives such as Zip, Jaz, and Orb are not reliable backup devices in the long term, and the media cost mounts up when you're backing up several gigabytes of data. Digital tape, magneto-optical, and CD-RW are more reliable and, ultimately, cost less to use.
- In a pinch, you can always back up your documents online—to your iTools iDisk, for example.

Finder Mishaps

Crashes, Freezes, and Other Finder Funk

You press your Mac's Power button and dutifully wait to hear the computer's startup sound and view the Happy Mac before tripping upstairs for the morning's first cup of coffee. Having creamed and sugared the breakfast beaker to within an inch of its life, you return to your office, sit down before the Mac, grasp the mouse, and...*nothing*, although everything on the Mac's Desktop appears as it should. Menu bar? *Check.* Hard disk icon? *Check.* Trash icon? *Check.* Desktop picture of former boyfriend being smacked with a banana cream pie? *Check.* Scrubbing the mouse across your mousepad produces not a millimeter of pointer movement. Recalling Chris's admonition to check cable connections, you disconnect and reconnect your keyboard and mouse cables, and...*nothing*.

Welcome, my friend, to the world of Finder funk—a world where extensions come into conflict, hardware peripherals struggle for supremacy, applications refuse to launch, and icons lose their identity; a land that (I assure you) all Mac users must visit from time to time.

But never fear. In this chapter, I tell you how to avoid entering this land on a regular basis and—should your Mac take you there despite your best efforts—show you how to put things right in short order.

Common Causes of Finder Funk

I'd like to stress again that the Mac OS is a logical beast. It behaves, and *misbehaves*, in a mostly predictable fashion. When your Mac locks up halfway through the startup process, the mouse freezes the moment the Desktop appears, applications suddenly quit, or icons turn from descriptive to generic, there's usually a good reason. Fortunately, that good reason can generally be determined by the kind of behavior that problem causes. And once you've witnessed that behavior, it's almost always possible to affect a cure.

So what are the likely causes of such crashes and freezes? In order of likelihood:

- Extension conflicts
- Hardware conflicts
- File or application corruption
- Buggy software

And that's about it. These four variables are the cause of nearly all the problems that plague your Mac as it starts up. *Nearly?* OK, I'll come clean. There's one last variable—a variable that every troubleshooter must face. That variable is:

- Something else

I don't care what kind of fix-it business you're in—auto repair, plumbing, construction, medicine, or marriage counseling—there will come a time when you can't determine the source of a problem. Macintosh troubleshooting is no different. After searching far and wide for the cause of a crash or freeze, I have on occasion had to step away from the keyboard and pour a fizzy libation after reaching the conclusion that this one just beats the heck out of me.

But unlike many of the fix-it jobs I've listed here, it's not always necessary to find the root cause of your problem. Although it may be fun to play detective and sleuth around your Mac in the hope that you'll uncover the flawed font or triple-combo-platter of corrupt extensions that cause your Mac to freeze like a St. Paul puddle in February, knowing exactly what's causing your Mac to misbehave isn't as important as knowing how to cure the aberrant behavior caused by the problem.

If Gigantosoft's Gargantuan GraphicsFest 2.3 crashes every time you launch it, for example, you could dink around with your Mac for days trying to discover why, or you could just reinstall the sucker. Sure, you won't have the satisfaction of learning that the program's corrupt AddMonkeyFur filter was the culprit, but you'll be back to work (or play) a heck of a lot sooner.

So that's pretty much the game plan for this chapter. You'll take a look at the four main causes of Finder funk and deal with ways to prevent or fix these problems. As for *something else,* look for the "When is it time to stop screwing around with this stuff and make the Mac work?" quiz later in the chapter, where I offer general fix-it advice for mysteriously uncooperative Macs.

Extension Conflicts

Extension conflicts are among the most common causes of startup errors under Mac OS 9.2 and earlier. What exactly *are* extensions, and what makes them so discordant? Read on, dear reader, read on.

The Story of the Extensible Mac OS

Once upon a time, a company named Apple created a spiffy computer operating system—an operating system that featured a graphical user interface that included windows, menus, and a cute little trash can stuck down in the lower-right corner of the screen. When the operating system (and the Macintosh computer that housed it) were first released, the many-headed masses cried as one, "Oooh! Ultra-spiffy!" and stayed up all night making little black-and-white pictures with MacPaint.

But as time went on and the many-headed grew bored with MacPaint, polite mutterings were heard from the Mac faithful. "Spiffy though the Mac OS may be," they offered, "it sure would be nice if a verbally abusive, animated moose appeared in the top-left corner of my Mac every so often."

"Fine by us," responded those who created the spiffy operating system. "We've designed this operating system to be *extensible,* meaning that you can create programs that will change the behavior of the OS. As a matter of fact, we have already created some of these programs ourselves. We call these things *extensions*.* We've created other programs called *control panels* that also enhance the operating system. You'll find extensions in the Extensions folder and control panels in the Control Panels folder inside your Mac's System Folder."

"And exactly how do these things work?" the curious users asked.

"Simple. When the Macintosh OS first starts up, it looks in the Extensions and Control Panels folders and fires up the programs it finds. When fired up, these extensions and control panels alter (or *patch*) the OS."

"Very nifty," the multitudes responded. "But this sounds complicated. Is it foolproof?"

"Oh, er..." the creators stammered, "now that you mention it, there is one tiny thing you might want to keep in mind. These programs can come into conflict with one another or with elements of the Mac OS."

"And when they do...?" the suddenly alarmed users asked.

"Your Mac can freeze or crash or otherwise fail to boot properly."

"Wait a minute," a few folks interjected. "That stinks!"

"Perhaps," the creators admitted, "but you can protect yourself from these kinds of conflicts by simply avoiding any software that adds extensions or conflicts to your System Folder."

"Oh. So as long as we don't add the Talking Moose or the program that makes your Mac belch when you eject a floppy disk or that flying-toasters screen-saver thingie, we're OK."

"Not quite," the creators responded as they peered down while tracing random patterns in the dirt with the toes of their Doc Martens. "There are a few other programs you might want to avoid a few years from now."

"Such as?"

"Microsoft Office, FileMaker Pro, Norton Utilities, TechTool Pro, Conflict Catcher, Photoshop, QuarkXPress, PageMaker, Illustrator, Toast, SoundJam, AppleWorks, iTunes, iMovie, QuickTime Player, iDVD, Final Cut Pro...."

---

*OK, OK, I know extensions were first called *inits*, but bringing up that fact plays holy heck with the narrative.

"Holy cats!" the many-headed howled. "You mean to tell us that all those applications install extensions or control panels!?"

"Well, yes," the creators sheepishly admitted. "But just wait until Mac OS X! We're designing that operating system so that it *can't* be patched! Extension conflicts will be a thing of the past!"

"You mean no more Talking Moose?"

"Right. No more Talking Moose."

"Wait a minute," a few other folks interjected. "That stinks!"

The End

Preventing Extension Conflicts

The moral of this story is that extension conflicts are an inherent and common danger in Mac OS 9 and earlier. You can cut way back on extension conflicts by refusing to install any software that relies on extensions and control panels, but let's face it—nearly every Macintosh application in existence requires that you use some kind of add-on doodad. Also, some of the more interesting and entertaining utilities and Finder enhancements you'll stumble across are based almost completely on extensions and control panels.

So what can you do?

> **Be judicious.** A functional Mac that runs Mac OS 9.2 or earlier must necessarily employ programs that rely on extensions and control panels. But that doesn't mean you have to junk up your System Folder with unnecessary numbers of these files. I understand that to run Microsoft Word, for example, the application must add a slew of extensions to your System Folder. The program won't run without them. But do you *really* need your Desktop to reflect the look and feel of a Casio DW-5600 G-Shock watch? If you've slapped such an interface onto your Mac with some customization control panel/extension combo, and your Mac blows up on every third startup, perhaps you should reexamine your priorities. Of course, if an attractive Mac is more important to you than one that's stable, gussy up that Mac till the cows come home with my blessing. Otherwise, ix-nay on the unk-jay.

Pare them down. Just because a piece of software ships with a pantload of extensions and control panels doesn't mean you have to install them all or—if they're installed automatically—leave them all switched on. Heck, the Mac OS Installer bungs several extensions and control panels into your System Folder that are completely unnecessary for many people. I, for example, have given the ax to all the Speech thingamajigs, several printer drivers, DialAssist, Launcher, Multiple Users, and Web Sharing because I don't use the features they provide. I've also switched off all but one of the extensions and control panels installed by Norton Utilities, as well as Apple's own Control Strip control panel and extension and the Apple Menu Items control panel, because I've found that these files cause more problems than they cure.

Extension Management

Throughout this chapter, I breezily discuss switching extensions and control panels on and off. But how do you go about doing such a thing? Unless you have a more capable tool, such as Extension Overload from Teng Chou Ming and Peter Hardman or Conflict Catcher from Casady & Greene, you use Apple's Extensions Manager, that's how.

Extensions Manager, like most Apple software, has an intuitive interface. Just choose Control Panels from the Apple menu and Extensions Manager from the submenu. When the Extensions Manager window appears, you'll notice checkboxes next to the items' names. To disable an item, just uncheck the box next to it. To enable an item, check the box.

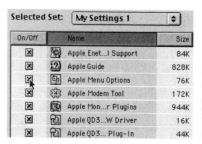

Click; There It Isn't. With a single click, you can enable and disable extensions and control panels.

You can also enable or disable entire folders of extensions and control panels. To do so, choose As Folders from Extensions Manager's View menu, and click the box next to a folder. If a check appears, all the items in that folder are enabled. No check means everything's disabled. Why you'd want to enable and disable your entire Extensions or Control Panels folder is beyond me, but should you care to do so, there you are.

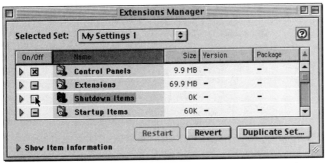

Folder-all. Should you care to disable entire folders of startup items, the View > As Folders command will allow you to do so.

More useful than working with folders this way is the ability to turn packages on and off. *Packages* are groups of extensions and control panels grouped by function. All the AirPort add-ons, for example, are gathered together in a package. Why would you want to do such a thing? Two reasons:

- If you're troubleshooting a fussy Mac, switching off packages is an easy way to pinpoint more quickly where a problem lies. If you switch off the QuickTime package, for example, and your problem disappears, you know that something related to QuickTime was a contributing factor.

- At times, you may want to run a leaner system—one without a lot of extraneous junk that may interfere with such procedures as creating a CD or playing a game. You can trim that system faster by turning off packages rather than individual items.

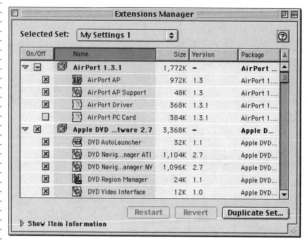

Nice Package. Viewing your startup items as packages allows you to disable related items easily.

To disable extensions and control panels, of course, it helps to know what these things do. Given that extensions bear names such as FBC Index Scheduler, CarbonLib, HID Library, and NBP Plugin, it's often difficult to discern the purpose of some extensions. But the system gives you a couple of ways to learn the purpose of these files.

Way 1 is to choose Extensions Manager from the Control Panels submenu in your Apple menu. In the resulting Extensions Manager window, you'll see a long list of the extensions and control panels installed in your Mac's System Folder. Near the bottom of the window, you'll spy a right-pointing triangle next to the words *Show Item Information*. Click this triangle to reveal the information area below. Now click any item in the list of extensions and control panels and—*huzzah!*—the purpose of that item appears.

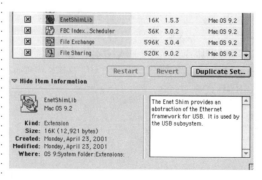

More Info. Extension Manager's Item Information panel hints (sometimes obscurely) about the purpose of an item.

Way 2 relies on Apple's Balloon Help—you know, the help system that no one on earth (including most developers) ever uses. When it works, it works this way:

Open your System Folder and then the Extensions folder within. Choose Show Balloons from the Finder's Help menu, and place your mouse pointer over an item in the Extensions folder. With any luck, helpful text enclosed in a balloon appears. Lacking that luck, a balloon appears with completely unhelpful text—either a generic description that tells you that this file adds functionality to the system (gee, *thanks!*) or a description so full of jargon and acronyms that you're left more confused than you were when you began.

Way 3 won't tell you exactly what an item does, but it can help you learn what other files are associated with that item. You can learn whether an extension is part of QuickTime or Apple's speech-recognition software, for example. To associate files in this way, open Extensions Manager and choose As Packages from the View menu. Doing so groups extensions and control panels into packages, (sets of related programs). When you understand that File X is part of the Mac's networking package, you may be more or less inclined to disable it.

Way 4 is Teng Chou Ming and Peter Hardman's Extension Overload. This $20 application tells you the purpose of every add-on doodad you're likely to find in your Extensions and Control Panels folders. Also, you can use Extension Overload to enable and disable extensions and control panels, fonts, contextual-menu items, and control-strip modules. This is a wonderful utility and one that every troubleshooter should have on hand. You can find a copy at www.extensionoverload.com.

Way 5 is another utility I regard highly: Casady & Greene's Conflict Catcher. Conflict Catcher is Extensions Manager the way it should have been made. Like Extensions Manager, Conflict Catcher allows you to switch extensions and control panels on and off, but it does much more. That "much more" includes the ability to control the loading of fonts; contextual-menu items; control-strip modules; Apple menu items; Internet search sites; Location Manager Modules; and a host of plug-ins for such applications as Illustrator, Photoshop, QuarkXPress, Netscape, and Internet Explorer. I could go on and on about Conflict Catcher (and I will a bit later in this chapter and in Chapter 5), but in the meantime, it's important only to know that Conflict Catcher provides a more extensive database of what various add-ons do.

Even More Info. Extension Overload provides a broader peek than Extensions Manager into the purpose of startup items.

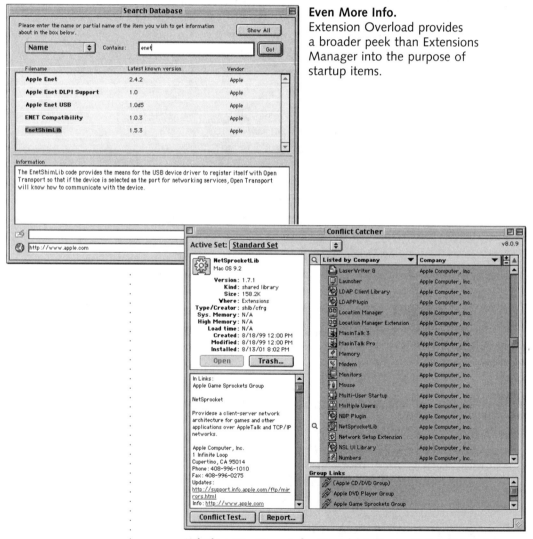

Whole Lotta More Info. Casady & Greene's Conflict Catcher also reveals the intent of extensions and control panels.

Troubleshooting Extension Conflicts

The moment my Mac freezes on startup, I restart it by pressing the Reset button. (Actually, I press the Command-Control-Power keys, because my Mac restarts with this key combo; newer Macs without keyboard Power buttons and iMacs can't be restarted this way.) As soon as I hear the Mac's startup tone, I press the Shift key.

And I push that Shift key for good reason: It keeps extensions, control panels, and items in the Startup Items folder from launching. When my Mac then boots up without a hitch, I've learned something very valuable: My Mac has an extension conflict. With this one simple action, I've pinpointed the problem and am prepared to take Appropriate Action.

In this case, Appropriate Action means sniffing out the errant extension (or extensions) and either making it play nicely with the other extensions or booting it the heck out of town. "Very nice, Chris," you're doubtless thinking, "but how can you tell, among this mishmash of extensions, which one is being naughty?" The answer is: through trial and error.

Wait, wait! Don't rush to the bookstore to demand your money back. I know this sounds like a daunting process, but there ways to make it easier and, if you're an even marginally observant person (and I'm sure you're that and more), you can make a pretty good guess at which extension is the source of your grief. I'll run through a couple of typical scenarios to show you how this process works.

> **The Usual Suspects**
>
> After years of troubleshooting Macs, I've developed a healthy fear of certain control panels and extensions. I don't know what it is about these things, but when I switch them off, my Mac seems happier. My personal hit list includes Apple Menu Options, Control Strip, Microsoft Office Manager, all extensions and control panels that ship with Norton Utilities except the Norton Sharing Lib extensions (an extension necessary for Disk Doctor to work), Kaleidoscope, and Palm Desktop. You may need some of these things, of course, and if you do, switch them on with my approval.

Tommy's Tale: The Intuition Method

Tiny Tommy Tucker had a very happy Mac. Each day, it booted up with nary a complaint and ran and ran and ran and ran without ever crashing. Tommy loved his Mac and gave it a loving pat each night as he shut it down.

One day, Tommy downloaded a Desktop customization utility recommended by some fancy-pantsy Macintosh magazine columnist. Tommy installed the utility and dutifully restarted his computer, as the utility's installer requested. After restarting, Tommy found that his pointer no longer moved, and his Mac failed to recognize anything he typed on the keyboard. Tommy's Mac was frozen.

The Tuckers are nobody's fools, and it took Tommy no more than a couple of seconds to realize that because his Mac had been a very happy Mac before he installed the customization utility, that utility must have done something to make Tommy's Mac unhappy.

After directing an unprintable curse at the fancy-pantsy columnist, Tommy pressed his Mac's Reset button and held down the spacebar as his Mac restarted. He did so because this action causes the Extensions Manager to appear before most extensions and control panels have loaded, thus allowing you to turn off any extensions that may be giving you problems.

Tommy sifted through the list of extensions and control panels, and found one extension and one control panel that bore the name of the recently installed utility. He unchecked the box next to these two items and clicked Continue to resume startup. Tommy held his breath as the icons marched across the bottom of his Mac's screen and crowed in triumph when the Desktop appeared and his pointer and keyboard worked as they should.

Bluto's Tale: The Halving Method

Big Bluto Blowhard had a sometimes-happy Mac. Each day, it booted up with nary a complaint, and every so often it ran for several hours before it finally crashed for no apparent reason. Bluto liked his Mac well enough that he did his best to avoid slopping beer on it. One day, after restarting for the sixth time, Bluto found that his pointer no longer moved, and his Mac failed to recognize anything he typed on the keyboard. Bluto's Mac was frozen.

Bluto also knew the trick about holding down the spacebar at startup to produce the Extensions Manager, and this he did while directing yet another unprintable curse at the Trilateral Commission (which, as everybody knows, runs the world and keeps people like Bluto from ever having a romantic relationship that lasts longer than two days). When the Extensions Manager window appeared, Bluto groaned in despair as he scrolled through a list of hundreds upon hundreds of extensions that one shareware utility after another had casually tossed into his Extensions and Control Panels folders. "How the &%*$# am I going to have time to shield my trailer from spy satellites when I've got this mess to sort through!?" Bluto wondered.

Then Bluto recalled that a character who, conspiratorially enough, bore his name in Chris Breen's *Mac 911* book and had faced a similar problem. Breen's instructions went something like this:

Restart the Mac, and hold down the spacebar to produce the Extensions Manager. When it appears, choose Mac OS *X.x* Base (*X.x* equals the version of the OS your Mac uses) from the Selected Set pop-up menu. Click Continue to resume startup. If the Mac starts up and performs correctly, there's no conflict among the small subset of default extensions and control panels installed by the Mac OS.

Bluto's Base. Choose the Base set of extensions to help determine whether you have an extension conflict.

Choose Extensions Manager from the Control Panels' submenu and, from that same Selected Set pop-up menu, choose Mac OS X.x All. Press the Restart button to restart the Mac. When the Mac once again boots successfully, you know that there's also no problem with the complete set of extensions and control panels installed by the Mac OS.

The trick now is to determine which of the third-party extensions and control panels you've added to your System Folder are the cause of your problem. You can begin by using the Intuition method, but with a plethora of add-ons, it may not prove to be successful.

A more reliable method in situations such as this is called *halving*. Halving is simplicity itself and works this way:

1. Go through your non-Apple extensions and control panels, and turn half of them off.

   You'll find this step more effective if you view your extensions as packages and turn off groups of packages rather than individual files.

2. Restart your Mac.

   If the problem remains, you know that the aberrant extensions or control panel is among those that are switched on.

3. Restart with the spacebar down, and when Extensions Manager appears, disable half of the extensions and control panels that were switched on previously.

4. Click Continue and watch what happens.

   If the Mac has problems, the culprit remains among those extensions and control panels left on. If the problem disappears, it was in the group of items you just disabled.

5. Repeat this halving process until you know for certain that when Extension X is switched on, your Mac takes a dive.

6. Get rid of Extension X.

The Limitations of Halving

As much as I'd enjoy letting Bluto twist in the wind, I'd hardly be serving the rest of you if I claimed that halving was the perfect way to troubleshoot extension conflicts. In the first place, halving can be a tedious process. On one of my completely junked-up Macs, for example, I have 473 extensions and control panels. Halving this many items could take a long, long time. Also, extension conflicts sometimes arise not from a single oddball extension, but a combination of extensions. Your Mac may whistle a happy tune when Extension X runs, but if Extensions Y and Z are also present, *blammo!* Halving might help you narrow your search to Extension X, but it wouldn't tell the whole story. And it might lead you to the wrong extension—one that your Mac absolutely requires to function properly.

Given these limitations, what can you do?

You can take my earlier advice to live a simpler life and use fewer extensions and control panels. Your Mac will certainly be more stable and, because it won't be bogged down with loads of little background chores, will run faster. But I understand that such "Do as I say and not as I do" advice isn't terribly practical. Every Mac needs a few spoonfuls of these things, and even though many add-ons aren't absolutely necessary, they make the Mac a lot more fun to use. So *now* what do you do?

Pick up a copy of Conflict Catcher.

Conflict Catcher

I told you earlier that Conflict Catcher acts much like Extensions Manager in its capability to switch on an off add-on items, but the main reason people purchase the program is for its automated conflict-testing feature. Conflict Catcher takes the halving process and does most of the work for you.

The basic idea is that when you suspect that you have an extension conflict, you run Conflict Catcher and tell it that you have a problem. The utility then asks you to name any add-ons that you particularly suspect and instructs you to designate any extensions and control panels that absolutely must be left on. Then it tests the suspects by switching on the basic Mac OS stuff and those suspects and restarts your Mac. You tell the program whether a problem occurred. If so, you've arrived at a solution and must find a way around those suspects. If the problem doesn't recur, Conflict Catcher begins halving, asking you to restart and, after each restart, to report the results. After a series of restarts, Conflict Catcher tells you which extensions it believes are the problem.

But it doesn't stop there. Conflict Catcher goes on and checks to see whether any other extensions and control panels need to be part of the mix for your problem to start. If so, the utility ferrets them out, and it's up to you to deal with things. If not, the problem is solved.

I'll rave more about Conflict Catcher in Chapter 5. Suffice it to say for now that when it comes to troubleshooting extensions conflicts, I can't think of a more valuable tool.

Dealing with Things

Now that you've located the problem add-on, what do you do?

Check it. Under normal circumstances, that item might comport itself with honor, but currently, it may be ailing. Conflict Catcher and other troubleshooting utilities such as TechTool Pro and Norton Utilities have the capability to check files for corruption. If the item is diagnosed with some kind of illness, put it out of its misery by tossing it in the Trash and replace it with a fresh copy.

Update it. Try locating an updated version of the extension or software that installed the thing. Extensions and control panels that worked beautifully under System 7.5 may break like a Christmas ornament in a hippo's pocket under Mac OS 9.2.

Change its load order. If no update is available or the thing still blows up even after the update, try changing the order in which it loads. To do this, place a space before the first character of the doodad's name to force it to load early in the startup process or a tilde (~) to force it to load late. Odd as it sounds, some extensions and control panels will become model citizens when their load order is shifted.

Research it. The MacFixIt Web site (www.macfixit.com) is one of the best places on the Web to learn about what does and doesn't work on the Mac. If you can't seem to make an extension or control panel work, drop by MacFixIt and search its archives for any mention of that troublesome item. It's possible that other Mac users have had the same kind of problem and can provide assistance.

Kill it. If it's something you can live without—an extension that arrays a chain of blinking squid around the border of your Mac's screen, for example—get rid of it.

Hardware Conflicts

I know, I know—you thought I covered hardware conflicts six ways to Sunday in Chapter 2. I'm afraid that hardware conflicts can not only manifest themselves in ways that keep your Mac from booting but also cause your Mac to crash or freeze after it has booted. Such hardware conflicts are remarkably similar—some might say *identical*—to those that prevent a Mac from starting up. They include:

- SCSI conflicts
- USB conflicts
- Bad RAM

I discussed much of this material in Chapter 2, but for those of you who need a reminder, I'll cover the basics here.

SCSI Conflicts

As I mentioned in Chapter 2, SCSI is an inexact science. A funky SCSI chain can crash your Mac during the startup process or twiddle its thumbs until your Mac is completely booted and then start messing with your Mac's mind.

If you've determined that extension conflicts are not the source of your problem, and your Mac has a couple of SCSI devices, try unplugging everything from the SCSI bus save your internal hard drive. If the problem goes away, SCSI is a likely suspect. You should leap into your troubleshooting overalls and begin mucking with the SCSI chain as I suggest in Chapter 2.

USB Conflicts

Yup, I've told the USB story before as well. Unlike SCSI conflicts, USB conflicts generally don't keep your Mac from running as it should. Rather, conflicting USB devices cause one USB peripheral or another to remain conspicuous by its absence. If you have both a USB Zip drive and USB Epson printer attached to your Mac, for example, one of these devices may not be available when your Mac is up and running.

To fix such a problem, you might do the following:

Upgrade your USB drivers. A new driver might resolve the conflict.

Upgrade the Mac OS. Apple's USB drivers get better with each iteration of the Mac OS.

Unplug one of the peripherals. I know it's a pain, but sometimes, the only way to force USB peripherals to get along is to unplug one of them, start up the Mac, and then plug the misbehaving peripheral into the USB port. USB is slicker than SCSI in that it attempts to mount a USB peripheral when the Mac OS "sees" a USB device appear on the USB chain.

Get a hub. Recent desktop Macs provide three USB ports—two on the Mac and one on the Mac's keyboard. The two ports on the Mac are supplied with plenty of power. You can plug any Mac-compatible USB device into the Mac's USB ports and have a reasonable expectation that if it doesn't work properly, it's not because it's not getting enough juice. The same cannot be said for the keyboard's USB port. I've plugged more than a couple of peripherals into the keyboard only to be greeted with a warning that the device isn't receiving enough power.

To address such a problem, you should look to a *powered* USB hub. Such a hub should put an end to such warnings.

By the way, I emphasize *powered* because it's quite possible to purchase an unpowered hub—one that pulls its power from the Macintosh. Frankly, I've never seen the sense of using unpowered hubs; they can't deliver the kind of power necessary for many peripherals to function. Ultimately, how useful are they? Do you *really* plan to plug more than two USB peripherals into your iBook on that trans-Atlantic flight? If so, maybe you should consider packing a good book and giving this whole technology thing a rest for a few hours.

Getting the Right Hub, Bub

Just because you've chosen a powered hub over one that sucks power from the Macintosh doesn't necessarily mean that you have the right hub. Unfortunately, not all powered hubs are created equal. To illustrate the point, here's a true-life tale:

Grant, a visitor to *Macworld*'s Troubleshooting forum, was having a heck of a time with his Power Mac G4 Cube (a Mac that has since been discontinued). Grant had a pair of the Apple-branded Harmon-Kardon USB-based speakers and the USB Apple Pro Keyboard included with the Cube. Apple recommends that with such a configuration, the keyboard must be plugged into one of the Cube's USB ports, and the speakers must be plugged into the other. Well, swell, but what happens if you also have a USB printer, camera, PDA, removable drive, and toaster? If the Cube's USB ports are full, and the port on the keyboard can't handle such devices, what on earth are you supposed to do?

Rightly ignoring Apple's admonition, Grant purchased a powered USB hub and then plugged the hub into one of the Cube's USB ports, the speakers into the hub, and the keyboard into the Cube's other USB port. After powering up his Cube, Grant received the message that the speakers would not function because they weren't receiving enough power. He tried plugging the keyboard into the hub and the speakers into the Cube. No go.

I turned to the fine folks at *Macworld* Labs for an answer and in short order received this one: get a better hub. The Lab Rats plugged a Belkin (www.belkin.com) four-port USB hub into the Cube, the keyboard into the hub, and the speakers into the Cube—and everything worked beautifully. I relayed this information to Grant, who dutifully purchased a Belkin-powered hub and discovered that it indeed solved his problem. I've read several other reports of people who have had great success with Belkin hubs.

There certainly are other hubs that work as well in such situations. I have a no-name powered hub that ticks along quite nicely when it's attached to a printer, CompactFlash media reader, and Palm dock. This hub was significantly less expensive than the Belkin hub.

I was fortunate to get a hub that worked; you may not be so fortunate. But because I like a bargain as much as the next guy, you have my permission to pick up a cheap hub. Just be sure to keep the receipt.

Bad RAM

A RAM module that's completely shot will almost assuredly cause your Mac to issue an ominous tone, perhaps display some kind of error, and undoubtedly sit there like a big lump of cheese. But you can purchase RAM that, while not completely bad, may not be up to snuff. It may be close enough to spec to allow the Mac to boot but still cause problems later. Such problems may include error messages that accompany an application that suddenly quits (including the Finder) and a Mac that unceremoniously crashes.

Determining that RAM is the cause of your problem rests primarily in your powers of observation. If you recently installed additional RAM in a mannerly Mac that now behaves like the spawn of Satan, a bad RAM module is the first thing you should investigate. By *investigate,* I mean you should remove that RAM module (or, if you purchased several modules at one go, swap each in and out to see how it performs) and see what happens.

> **Avoiding Bad RAM**
>
> Although it's perfectly possible to purchase poor RAM from any RAM vendor, you'll have better luck if you work with a reputable merchant. I've been buying RAM from an Austin, Texas, company called TechWorks (www.techworks.com) for years and years, and in that time, I've received only one bad module. The company offers good tech support, allows you to shop by both phone and the Web, happily accepts returns and exchanges, and delivers RAM that meets or exceeds Apple's specs. If Apple's stamp of approval means anything to you, I might also mention that Apple occasionally uses TechWorks' RAM in its products.
>
> But TechWorks is hardly the only reputable RAM merchant on the planet. Its RAM prices are a bit higher than those of some other outfits, so if price is of paramount importance to you, you might want to shop elsewhere. To find the best prices on RAM, visit RAMSeeker (www.ramseeker.com). RAMSeeker tracks current prices on RAM from several vendors.

File or Application Corruption

If your extensions and hardware check out satisfactorily, you should next turn your attention to file corruption. It's an unfortunate fact of computing life that bad things occasionally happen to good files. After a crash, freeze, or some other unexpected interruption, open files or your Mac's hidden directory and database files may be munged to the point where they turn from the path of Goodness and Light to unspeakable evil.

If you've run a troubleshooting utility on your Mac, you're probably aware that files routinely get corrupted—their modification dates are incorrectly set, icons don't display properly, or they contains data that they shouldn't. Most of the time, your Mac never gives an indication that some of its files are corrupt. As long as those files necessary to the Mac's health remain in a reasonably uncorrupted state, your Mac trots right along.

If an important file gets corrupted, however, watch out. A confused Desktop database file can cause applications to lose their icons and the Mac to act up in a host of odd ways. A corrupted Finder can cause your Mac to crash the moment the Desktop appears. A corrupted application can keep that application from launching. And something as seemingly innocuous as a corrupt font or preferences file can cause the equivalent of a meteor to strike your Mac.

The Confused Desktop

The Mac keeps track of the location of files on your hard drive with the help of the invisible Desktop DF file. Information about icons are kept in the just-as-invisible Desktop DB file. If these files are corrupted, your Mac may slow, icons will turn from descriptive to generic, the drag-and-drop function no longer seems to work, and you may receive an "Application not found" error when you double-click a file that you know darned well should open.

When you notice this kind of corruption (generic icons are a dead giveaway), you should perform the Mac's most popular troubleshooting operation: rebuild the Desktop. Rebuilding the Desktop is a cure akin to popping your finger into your mouth the moment after you cut it. Whether it's likely to help or not, it's the first remedy people try.

When you R the D, the Mac scans your hard drive for all the files therein and makes note of the location of these files in an invisible directory (the Desktop DF file). That invisible file already exists, so when you rebuild it, the Mac basically says "OK, I don't give a hoot what's listed in the Desktop DF file now; we're going to take another look and update that information."

There are a couple of ways to rebuild the Desktop. The Apple-recommended way is to hold down the Command and Option keys as your Mac starts up. Keep these keys pressed until you see a message that asks whether you really want to rebuild the Desktop. Because you've gone to all the effort to hold down these two keys, you might as well click OK.

(This, like much of the information in this chapter, applies only to Mac OS 9.2 and earlier. Mac OS X doesn't understand this whole "Rebuild the Desktop" business.)

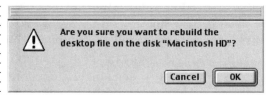

Two-finger Salute. To rebuild the Desktop, hold down the Command and Option keys at startup.

The Apple method is OK, but it's not as thorough as it could be. Y'see, the Apple method keeps the original invisible database files. If these files are essentially corrupted, the corruption remains after the rebuild. For this reason, you'll get a cleaner rebuild if you toss out the old Desktop DF and Desktop DB files.

You can perform this task manually, but to do so, you have to muck with invisible files. Although there's a certain dangerous thrill that comes with doing such a thing, in this case, it's unnecessary. To toss the old Desktop DF and Desktop DB files, simply download a copy of Micromat's (www.micromat.com) free TechTool Lite. Among a couple of other tricks—including the capability to zap the Mac's PRAM—TechTool Lite will diagnose your Desktop files and, if you like, toss them out. When the Finder next loads, it creates brand-new ones.

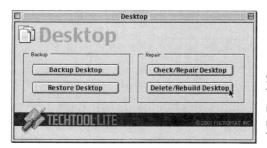

Starting Fresh. To create brand-new Desktop files, use Micromat's TechTool Lite.

The Usual Suspects

Although any file can become corrupted, particular files seem to have a penchant for it. When corrupted, some files almost certainly cause problems. They include:

Finder Preferences file. No. 1 in this particular Hit Parade is the Finder Preferences file, located inside the Preference folder inside your System Folder. When scrambled, this little sucker can seriously mess with your Mac. When I troubleshoot a Mac, I usually toss this file out whether it needs it or not. Don't worry—when you do toss it, the Mac makes a new one. Sure, you'll lose a few System settings, but the effort is worthwhile in case this file was causing your Mac's grief.

Other preferences files. If a particular application crashes every time you launch it, try pitching its preferences file. As is the case with the Finder preferences file, the application should create a new preferences file (but don't toss the file and empty the Trash until you're sure that you don't want the old preferences file back). In a recent search for corrupt preferences files, I discovered that my TCP/IP and Apple Menu Items preferences files were hosed. Replacing them made my Mac work more reliably.

Before you toss a preferences file, think about what that file might do. Preferences files often contain settings that you'd prefer not to lose. When I tossed my TCP/IP preferences file, for example, all the settings—IP address, DNS server, subnet mask, everything—disappeared from the TCP/IP window. If I hadn't written those settings down, I would have had to call my ISP and ask for that information. To prevent these kinds of problems, jot down any settings that might be lost when you toss a preferences file.

The Finder. I mentioned this trick in Chapter 2, but it's worth repeating. The Finder file contains a load of resources for managing tasks on your Mac, and if this file is corrupted, just about anything can happen (well, except for anything *good*). For this reason, I keep a clean copy of the Finder on a removable disk (I have one on both Zip and CD-R), and when my Mac appears to have lost its wits and I've slapped it about with the usual fixes, I boot from my emergency disc and replace the Finder.

Font files. Corrupt fonts can cause applications to crash and freeze when you launch them. You might suspect that a font has gone funky if a particular system font no longer displays correctly (the words in the Mac's menu bar or file and folder names are jagged, for example). Tracking down corrupt fonts can be a tricky affair without some variety of third-party utility, but you can try a few home remedies.

One method is to double-click the fonts in your System Folder's Font folder. When you open an uncorrupted font file, a sample window appears that shows you what the font looks like. A corrupted font won't open; instead, you should receive an error message indicating that the font is damaged.

Another method is to pull your fonts out of the Fonts folder and into a folder on your Desktop. Then drag the lot of them onto the closed System Folder. Before filing your fonts away, the Mac OS gives your fonts a once-over to make sure that their IDs don't conflict. This once-over may reveal a corrupt font as well.

If these home-grown cures don't work, you can use a third-party utility to track down a corrupt font. Our old friend Conflict Catcher has the capability to scan for damaged files, including fonts. Adobe's (www.adobe.com) $65 ATM Deluxe can also scan for damaged fonts, as can Morrison FontDesign's (www. morrisonsoftdesign.com) $70 Font Doctor, DiamondSoft's (www.fontreserve.com) $90 Font Reserve, and Extensis's (www.extensis.com) $100 Suitcase.

Diagnostic and Repair Utilities

When your Mac is ailing, it may need more medicine than you can deliver with the previous troubleshooting techniques. The following diagnostic and repair utilities may provide the magic your Mac needs.

Disk First Aid

If you suspect that your Mac suffers from corruption, the first thing to do is to scrutinize it with a diagnostic and repair utility. Apple includes such a troubleshooting utility, called Disk First Aid, on the System software disk that was shipped with your Mac as well as on Mac OS discs.

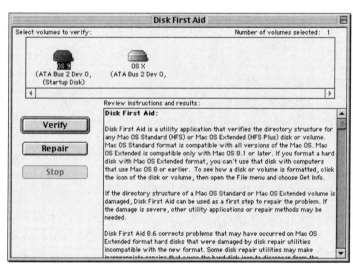

Free and Easy. Though it's not a comprehensive utility, Disk First Aid is the first troubleshooting tool to turn to.

As I've mentioned elsewhere, Disk First Aid is hardly the most comprehensive diagnostic/troubleshooting utility on the market, but it's a utility that everyone owns and is a safe and sane product—meaning that when Disk First Aid detects a problem, its treatment rarely causes additional trouble. Unlike third-party troubleshooting utilities, Disk First Aid does not check for wrongdoing in every file on your hard drive. Rather, it largely confines itself to the structure and integrity of the Mac's directory and database files.

To diagnose your Mac with Disk First Aid, follow these steps:

1. Start up your Mac from a system CD (use the most recent CD you own) or floppy disk.

2. Open the Utilities folder on the CD, and launch Disk First Aid.

3. In the Disk First Aid window, select the volume that's giving you trouble (this is likely to be your startup volume), and click the Verify button.

   Disk First Aid will diagnose the volume, and if it discovers a problem, it will tell you so. If it can actually do something about the problem (an all-too-rare occurrence, I'm afraid), it will tell you that as well.

4. If repair is possible, click the Repair button and wait while Disk First Aid does its stuff.

Other repair utilities

Although I devote another portion of the book to utilities that I've found helpful in my long troubleshooting career, I hate to keep you on pins and needles in regard to diagnostic/repair utilities, particularly when you may be reading this section because you have an immediate problem. So now I'll discuss what to do should Disk First Aid fail to do the job.

As this book goes to press, three major diagnostic/repair utilities are available to you: Alsoft's (www.alsoft.com) Disk Warrior, Micromat's (www.micromat.com) TechTool Pro, and Symantec's (www.symantec.com/nu/nu_mac) Norton Utilities for Macintosh. Call it kismet, these files are listed in alphabetical order not only by vendor name but also in order of my personal preference. Here's the dope.

> **Disk Warrior.** Disk Warrior is a one-trick pony, but the trick it performs is so worthwhile that there's no need for additional features. It works this way: The Mac has an invisible directory file that keeps track of where all the files on your Mac reside. When this file is corrupted, your Mac can crash, freeze, or comport itself in an otherwise unseemly fashion. Disk Warrior builds a new directory file from information that it recovers from the old directory file.

This service may not sound like a big deal, but it is, considering that the kind of directory errors that Disk Warrior addresses can disable your Mac in a hurry. No other utility fixes this kind of corruption nearly so well. Disk Warrior has saved my patoot on more than one occasion and is on my list of Absolutely Must Have utilities.

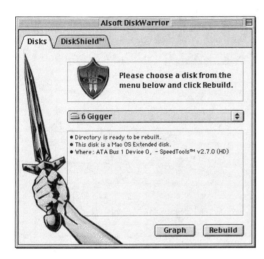

Simple Is as Simple Does. Disk Warrior may do just one thing—repair deep-seated directory damage—but does it very, very well.

TechTool Pro. TechTool Pro is a utility that tries to be all things to all people. It diagnoses hardware (things such as RAM, video memory, serial-port connections, keyboard, and mouse), deals with software corruption, includes an extensions-conflict component, and scans for viruses. Like Norton Utilities, TechTool Pro includes a component that keeps track of changes you've made to your Mac and can help recover files that you've accidentally (or purposely, I suppose) trashed.

I've had mixed results with TechTool Pro over the years. For the most part, I haven't found its hardware-testing component to be terribly helpful, but perhaps that's only because my hardware always toes the line. Likewise, its software diagnostic and repair utility often failed to fix nagging problems.

Recently, I've taken more of a shine to TechTool Pro. Micromat religiously updates the thing, and with each update, the program improves. TechTool Pro recently diagnosed and repaired a couple of nagging problems on my Mac, and for this reason, I now include it in my troubleshooter's toolbox.

Everything but the Kitchen Sink. TechTool Pro seemingly scrutinizes every part of your Mac save the smudges on its screen.

Norton Utilities. Norton Utilities is the grandpappy of all troubleshooting utilities. Its main components are Disk Doctor, a software diagnostic and repair utility; and SpeedDisk, a program that optimizes the way files are placed on your hard drive. (I'll talk about file optimization in Chapter 5.) Norton includes a passel of other applications: a program to erase your hard drive more thoroughly than Apple's Drive Setup can, a couple of file-recovery utilities, and a control panel called Disk Light that places a little blinking icon in the Mac's menu bar to display hard-disk activity.

Although I think that SpeedDisk is a worthwhile utility, my faith in many of Norton's other components has been shaken. Half of them are pretty useless (such as Disk Light and LiveUpdate, a program that searches automatically for updates to this utility, which seems to be updated only once every couple of years), and the rest sometimes cause more problems than they cure. On a couple of occasions, I've run Disk Doctor and asked it to repair one thing or another, and my Mac emerged from the process in worse shape than when it began. For this reason, Norton Utilities runs a distant third in my preferred list of troubleshooting utilities. If I can't seem to solve a problem with Disk First Aid, Disk Warrior, or TechTool Pro, and I know that I have a complete backup of my hard drive, I'll let Norton take a crack at it.

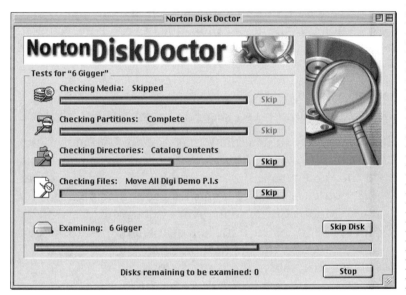

What's Up, Doc? Norton Disk Doctor's performance is, unfortunately, a hit-and-miss affair.

Buggy Software

I'm perfect—as I know you are—but we share this planet with people who make mistakes. These people include tinkers, tailors, candlestick makers, and computer programmers. When programmers make mistakes, they introduce bad bits of code into a program. These bad bits are known as *bugs*. Some bugs can remain in a piece of software for years and years and cause no harm; others can crash an application or your Mac in less time than it takes to say, "Bring me the head of Bill Gates!"

Bugs should be detected in the early days of testing, of course, but some applications contain a bajillion lines of code, and there's no way to anticipate the kind of software and hardware each user will tack onto his or her Mac. Also, heaven forbid, a company or two may rush a product to market in a half-baked state because of some selfish need to rake in enough cash to keep its creditors at bay for another week. For those reasons, bugs slip through, and you pay the price.

Unless you're a *really* good programmer, there's very little you can do directly about buggy software. If you must continue using the program, you can pay attention to what actions cause the application or your Mac to blow up and attempt to avoid those actions. If the application quits every time you issue the Save command or type the letter *e,* however, avoidance is no solution.

Dealing with bugs

So what do you do if you suspect that you have a bug?

> **Confirm.** Try to determine that it really is a bug. You can do this by repeating a series of actions and arriving at the same result. If, when using UltraWebPaintDeluxe 7.2, you discover that it crashes every time you select the Whipped Cream tool, great—boot your Mac with a limited set of extensions, and see whether that tool continues to crash the application. If so, there's a good chance that you've discovered a bug.
>
> **Research.** If you've discovered a bug, it's likely that other users have, too, and you might be able to learn from their experiences. The folks at MacFixIt (www.macfixit.com) routinely report on bugs discovered in major (and sometimes not-so-major) Mac applications and offer workarounds when available. Mac-centric newsgroups are another place to ask about buggy software.
>
> Apple is not terribly forthcoming when it comes to bugs in its products. At times, the entire Mac community buzzes about a bug or shortcoming in an Apple product, and Apple remains officially mum on the subject. And because Apple is a bit shy about revealing its mistakes, when it does document bugs, it hides that documentation in the AppleCare Knowledge Base.

As part of your research, look for application updates online. Such an update may fix the bug that's been haunting you. VersionTracker (www.versiontracker.com) provides links to product updates in one convenient location.

Report. If you can't find a solution online, call the application vendor's technical-support number. If you're lucky, the vendor has found a workaround or has issued an update that fixes the bug. If you're not so lucky, the vendor will deny that the bug exists.

Be prepared to walk through the steps necessary to trigger the bug. Keep in mind that whenever you talk with tech support, you should be sitting in front of your Mac. Tech-support reps often want to walk through the process with you.

Something Else

Look, if Mac troubleshooting were a science, there'd be no need for me to write this book. Apple could slip a three-fold plastic card into the documentation packet that accompanies each new Mac. That list would include every Mac problem you'll face, along with its solution. With this handy piece of plastic, we could all troubleshoot our Macs in a matter of seconds and use the time we saved to take up spelunking.

The truth is that this troubleshooting business is sometimes as much voodoo as it is science. You can run through every troubleshooting technique I've listed throughout this book, and nothing will work. *Nothing.*

I completely understand the thrill of the chase, but try to keep this in mind: For most of us, the Mac is supposed to be the means to an end. It's a tool, not the means itself. At some point, it makes sense to stop trying to find the cause of your Mac's problem and just make the darned thing act like the digital helper it's supposed to be.

How will you know when you've reached that point?

Only you can say for sure, but perhaps this little quiz will help.

When is it time to stop screwing around with this stuff and make the Mac work?

1. Have you tried every troubleshooting technique suggested in this book?

   If Yes, proceed to 2. If No, try them.

2. Have you scoured the Web for answers to your problem?

   If Yes, proceed to 3. If No, check with MacFixIt (www.macfixit.com) and the *Macworld* Troubleshooting forum (www.macworld.com/cgi-bin/ubb/Ultimate.cgi). If you said No because your Mac is in such sad shape that it can't get to the Web, proceed to 3.

3. Have you contacted Apple or a software vendor for information on this problem?

   If Yes, proceed to 4. If No, what's the delay? Get with it!

4. Have you slipped into a nearby bookstore and surreptitiously scanned the pages of Ted Landau's *Sad Macs, Bombs, and Other Disasters* in the hope of finding a solution to your problem?

   If Yes, you should be ashamed of yourself. Buy a copy; it's a terrific investment. If No, buy a copy; it's a terrific investment.

5. Do you have endless time and patience to throw at this problem?

   If Yes, have a ball (but may I suggest that many worthwhile charitable organizations would happily make use of any time you can spare?). If No, what say we just put the Mac to rights and get on with our lives, shall we?

Fixing the Darned Mac

Unless your computer or hard drive suffers from some terrible physical malady, you can make your Mac a happy creature once more. To make it so, I suggest the following.

Reinstall Troublesome Applications

Has a particular application got you down? Are you tired of adjusting that application's memory allocation in the vain hope that goosing that allotment will result in a stable working environment? Have you already tried tossing preferences files and associated extensions and control panels? Give up and reinstall the bugger.

Perform a Clean Install of Your System Software

If you suspect hat the source of your Mac's anguish is a flawed item in the System Folder, and you can't track down that flaw, install a new System Folder. I reveal how to do this in Chapter 2. What I don't reveal is how to move your third-party extensions and control panels from your old System Folder to the one you just installed. Although you can perform this task manually, *criminy,* what a tedious chore! For this kind of job, I turn once again to Conflict Catcher.

If you peek in Conflict Catcher's Special menu, you'll spy the Clean-Install System Merge command. When you invoke this command, Conflict Catcher asks you to select the System Folder you'd like to boot your Mac with (presumably the one that you just clean-installed) and your Previous System Folder. After you make this decision, Conflict Catcher suggests that you restart your Mac and hold down the spacebar to bring Conflict Catcher forward before the rest of the Mac's startup items load. This suggestion is a fine one, given that CC sloshes about with your startup items, and it's best not to have many of those startup items running when CC begins that sloshing.

When invoked, the Clean-Install System Merge process rummages around in your Previous System Folder and presents you a lengthy list of startup items, fonts, and other System Folder effluvia that you might care to add to your current System Folder. It's up to you to choose what to bring over. After you make your choices and give CC the go-ahead,

CC brings the items over, along with any files necessary for these items to function properly (preferences files that may contain that item's serial number, for example).

Although I'm enamored of this feature, it does have a drawback. If something in your old System Folder was putting your Mac through such hell that you were motivated to perform a clean install, copying that something to your new System Folder could land your Mac right back in the soup. For this reason, I suggest that you be very selective about what you move over.

Reformat the Drive and Begin Again

This procedure is pretty much the Court of Last Resort. If you've tried everything—and I mean *everything*—it may be time to start anew. With a comprehensive backup of your data, you can have your Mac up and running in a few hours. Balance this time against the days you could spend beating your head against the wall, searching in vain for a solution.

The key to the viability of this solution versus a desperate one is the aforementioned comprehensive backup of your data. With backup in hand, you can unleash just about any heinous action, short of more extreme forms of physical abuse, on your Mac.

Have you backed up lately?

And Other Stuff

Common Conundrums of a Well-Meaning Mac

I wish I could say that after your Mac has successfully booted and displayed the squeaky-clean visage of the Desktop and its assorted icons, every operation on your computer will tick along without incident. Regrettably, I can't. Although many a Mac problem is hinted at during the startup process, some problems won't reveal themselves until after you've launched an application, tried to log onto the Internet, or attempted to print an invitation to the annual backyard egg-and-spoon race.

In this chapter, I examine some of the most common problems you're likely to encounter with everyday applications and chores.

Applications Gone Bad

If you've launched your copy of SuperWhizzoPaint 6.2.7 only to be confronted with a cryptic error dialog box, had your Web browser vanish in the middle of downloading the SuperWhizzoPaint 6.3.2 update, or locked up your Mac while attempting to send a terse email message to support@superwhizzopaint.com, you have some idea of where I'm going: applications that misbehave on an otherwise well-mannered Mac. I'll begin by examining why applications act up.

Bugs

Last time I counted, my copy of SuperWhizzoPaint had exactly 3,872,164 lines of computer code. Given this many lines of code, it's possible that somewhere along the line, a programmer typed O when he meant 0. I mean, heavens, there are days when I'm lucky to punch in my four-digit ATM PIN number correctly.

When such mistakes are introduced, they can cause unexpected things to happen—a program freeze or unexpected quit, for example. If you're lucky, the application will throw up an error message before it goes down for the count, and if you're *really* lucky, you'll be able to make some sense of that message.

As a user, there's not much you can do to deal with software bugs directly. After all, your software license agreement probably forbids you from going in and fixing the bug yourself (yeah, right...). But you can do your part by making sure that you really *have* discovered a bug. To verify that a bug exists, you should consistently be able to reproduce the behavior that causes the problem. If the application crashes every time you type the letter *t*, for example, there's a good chance you've come face to face with a bug.

When you're sure that you're dealing with a bug, tramp around on the Web to see whether other people are having the same problem. MacFixIt (www.macfixit.com) and the *Macworld* forums are good places to look. Also log onto the application vendor's Web site and check its support area to see whether the bug is mentioned there. While you're there, check for any application updates that might eradicate the bug.

If the bug appears to be unknown, give the folks in tech support a jingle and tell them what's happening. The tech may be able to help you deal with the problem.

The other option when dealing with buggy software is simply to avoid using it. I understand that certain applications would be inconvenient and expensive to replace—SuperWhizzoPaint, for example—and therefore, you have to put up with problems until a fix arrives. But if that $5 shareware copy of Joe's Handy Dandy Text Munger isn't doing the trick, and a dozen other shareware apps can do the same job, dump Joe's shoddy work and try a different tool.

Conflicts

What, we're still dealing with conflicts!? Yes, like you, I'm heartily sick of these discussions of software conflicts, but I'm afraid that's the nature of the Mac OS 9.2 and earlier troubleshooting beast. You see, software conflicts can raise a ruckus beyond the startup process. A conflict may not rear its bitter little binary head until you've launched an application or asked that application to perform a particular chore.

You should be well aware of how to deal with Mac OS 9 and earlier software conflicts by now:

1. Use Extensions Manager to create a lean and mean set of extensions and control panels.

   Start with the Mac OS 9.x Base set, and add any extensions and control panels you need to run the application.

2. If the problem remains with a base set of extensions, try booting the Mac with the Shift key held down to disable extensions and control panels.

   (Note: Some applications, such as Norton Utilities, won't run without their extensions switched on.)
   If things are hunky-dory with all extensions off, it's time to look for the bad apple.

3. If problems remain, see the "Bugs" section earlier in this chapter.

Memory Allocation

If you've used a Mac running Mac OS 9.2 and earlier for more than a few weeks, you've undoubtedly encountered mostly benign-but-annoying Type 1 errors. Despite what an error dialog box or Apple's technical documentation might tell you about such errors, they often crop up when insufficient memory has been assigned to an application. Fortunately, this problem is easy to fix:

1. With the application closed, click its icon.

2. Press Command-I, or choose Get Info from the File menu.

3. In the resulting info window, choose Memory from the Show pop-up menu.

4. Increase the number entered in the Preferred Size text box.

   Note that memory in this field is allotted by kilobytes. So if you want to allot an extra megabyte of memory to the application, add an extra 1,000 KB.

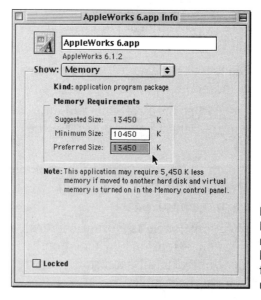

Now I Remember. Boosting application memory may keep your programs from quitting unceremoniously.

The idea here is that you're instructing the application to set aside the amount of memory you've entered in this Preferred Size box, whether the application needs it or not. This procedure may prompt the question "How much additional memory should I give my application?" The answer: as much as you need to keep the application from crashing.

You can do this by adding 500 KB, launching the application, and seeing how things go, allotting more RAM each time the application quits. Or you can do it the Breen Way.

As I write this chapter, memory costs just a bit more than a bucket of gravel. You can add 256 MB of RAM to your Mac for around $50. If, by the time you read this book, RAM is still inexpensive, I suggest that you drop as much RAM into your Mac as you can (some models hold as much as 1.5 GB!). That way, if an application rudely quits with a Type 1 error, you can avoid this 500 KB pussyfooting and throw dozens of extra megabytes of RAM at the application. If it continues to malfunction, you've learned that lack of memory isn't the problem.

While we're on the subject of memory allocation, let's talk about virtual memory. What makes virtual memory so, well, *virtual* is that it's not the kind of computer memory you may be accustomed to thinking of: small chips that hold a computer's Random Access Memory (RAM). Instead, it's memory that's placed on the hard drive and accessed like RAM.

Because virtual memory is contained on the hard drive rather than on computer chips—and because your computer can access RAM much faster than it can a hard drive—using virtual memory can slow your computer. If it slows your computer, what good is it?

Back in the days when 8 MB of RAM cost about the same as a new Dodge Dart, virtual memory was a very cool way to open applications that required more RAM than your Mac had on-board. Sure, your Mac was slower when you used it, but at least you could run that copy of Microsoft Word 6 or open more than one application at a time.

Given that RAM is so inexpensive, is virtual memory still worthwhile? For the most part under Mac OS 9.2 and earlier, no. *However* (and this is why I'm introducing the subject here), some applications running under Mac OS 9.2 and earlier will crash if they're unhappy with the state of virtual memory. With virtual memory switched off, SuperWhizzoPaint may crash. Switch it on, and the application is happy as a pig in slop. The opposite can be true as well; with virtual memory on, an application may act up.

Applications *shouldn't* misbehave in this manner, of course, but when all else fails, it's not a bad idea to toggle the state of virtual memory. To do so:

1. Choose Control Panels from the Apple menu and then choose Memory from the Control Panels submenu.

2. Locate the Virtual Memory portion of the Memory control panel, and choose On or Off.

3. If you're switching VM on, allocate 1 MB more of virtual memory than the amount of real memory you have in your Mac.

Much Like Memory. Although it's not as fast as real RAM, virtual memory can allow your Mac to run more applications than RAM allows.

If you have 128 MB of RAM, for example, allocate 129 MB of virtual memory. This setting allows VM to do its job without gobbling up massive amounts of hard-drive space. If you're using VM for its original intended purpose—fooling your Mac into believing that it has a ton of RAM—set this number high enough to accommodate your needs.

A few notes in passing:

Note 1. Virtual memory is a nonissue under Mac OS X, which allocates memory in a different way from Mac OS 9.2 and earlier; it has its own virtual memory scheme. So don't bother scouring Mac OS X's System Preferences window for a way to adjust memory: In Mac OS X, virtual memory is on all the time. Although you can still adjust the memory allocation of applications running in Mac OS X's Classic environment (that Get Info trick I detailed earlier in the chapter), the Memory control panel doesn't work in Classic. If you try to use the Memory control panel in the Classic environment to switch virtual memory on or off, you'll see an error message indicating that this feature is not supported in Mac OS X.

Note 2. If your Mac has a huge scoop of RAM in residence —say, a gigabyte—the Memory control panel, overwhelmed by your greed, will tell you that you have too much RAM on-board to allow virtual memory to be switched on.

Note 3. Although Type 1 errors are notorious pump-up-the-memory indicators, other error types can also crop up as the result of too little memory. On occasion, you can put Type 2 and 3 errors to rest by throwing more memory at the problem. Conversely, increasing memory may have no effect on these Type errors whatsoever. I mean, if the Mac were *really* smart enough to know exactly what the problem was, it probably would be smart enough to fix it without your intervention.

Note 4. Low memory can also cause an application to quit without sending up any kind of error at all. If an application routinely quits for no apparent reason, try a memory boost.

Browsers

Every so often, someone sends me a question that begins "I'm using [insert Web browser name here], and it [insert unexpected behavior here]!" I stop reading and paste this bit of canned text into the reply:

Dear Reader,

You're having problems with your browser because it's a browser! Please don't take this behavior personally. In all likelihood, you've done everything you can to make your browser behave—allotted it a load more RAM (even tripled the amount of RAM it requires), cut way back on your extensions, tried opening fewer pages, turned graphics off, turned Java off, used it only on every third Wednesday of the month—and yet it repays you in this horrid fashion.

It's not your fault. Browsers, by their very nature, are funky. If you've tried all the remedies I suggested above, try reinstalling your browser or—if that fails to do the trick—switch to a different browser.

Your friend,

Chris

Preferences Files

After I've confirmed that an application isn't buggy, doesn't appear to conflict with something else on the Mac, and has enough memory, I direct my steely gaze at its preferences files. As the name implies, preferences files can hold all kinds of user-configuration settings: preferred fonts, window arrangements, and word processing styles, for example. When an application's preferences file is corrupted, all sorts of wacky things can happen.

Fortunately, dealing with funky preferences files is a simple matter. With the application closed, locate the preferences file—usually housed in the System Folder's Preferences folder—and drag it onto the Desktop. (Drag it to the Desktop rather than the Trash, in case the preferences file wasn't the problem, and you want to restore your old preferences quickly by moving the original preferences file back into place.) When you launch the application the next time, that preferences file will be replaced with a new one, and ideally, your problems will be at an end.

When you create a new preferences file, you lose your old preferences. This situation can mean that you'll have to spend some time once again telling the Microsoft Assistant to get lost or configuring AppleWorks so that the default font is Palatino instead of Times, but making these adjustments should be no more than a minor inconvenience.

I'll add a couple of notes here as well:

- Under Mac OS 9.2.x and earlier, not all applications place their preferences files in the System Folder's Preferences folder. You'll find, for example, that the email clients Eudora, Outlook Express, and Entourage put their support and preferences files in the Documents folder at the root level of your startup drive. And some applications place their preferences files somewhere inside the application's folder—the Adobe Photoshop 5 Prefs file is inside the Adobe Photoshop Settings folder inside the Adobe Photoshop 5 folder, for example.

- Native Mac OS X applications have preferences files as well, and giving these files the big toss can be just as helpful when an application misbehaves under Apple's latest operating system. You'll find these preferences files by following this path: ~/Library/Preferences (where "~" is your users folder).

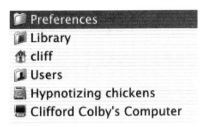

Preferred Path.
To find your application preferences under Mac OS X, just follow the path.

Microsoft Word Preferences

While we're on the subject of preference files, let's talk about Microsoft Word for a moment. Like many people, I believe that beneath Microsoft's chinos-and-khaki edifice beats a cheating black heart, but its Macintosh division has churned out some very impressive products in the past few years—including Microsoft Office 98, Office 2001, and Office X.

That said, I think that Microsoft Word 98, 2001, and X are annoyingly presumptuous—automatically creating hyperlinks, capitalizing words at the beginning of sentences, selecting entire words when you click them instead of the space between two letters...and don't even get me started on Max, the goofy animated "assistant" who hops around like grease on a griddle. If, like me, you want to tame Word's most "helpful" features, try this:

1. In Word 2001, choose Preferences from the Edit menu to open the Preferences window, click the Edit tab, and uncheck the When Selecting, Automatically Select Entire Word checkbox.

   In Word 98, you'll find the Preferences command in the Tools menu. To reach it in Word X, choose Preferences from the Word application menu and click Edit in the left pane of the Preferences window.

2. In this same Preferences window, click the Spelling & Grammar tab, (in Word X, click Spelling and Grammar in the left pane), and uncheck any option in the Grammar section.

   (Ain't no gol-durned grammar checker gonna tell me how to write good.)

3. Choose AutoCorrect from the Tools menu, click the AutoCorrect tab, and uncheck the Capitalize First Letter of Sentence checkbox.

   Switching this option off allows you to begin a sentence with the word *iMac*.

continues on next page

> **Microsoft Word Preferences** *continued*
>
> 4. In this same window, click the AutoFormat tab, and uncheck the Ordinals (1st) With Superscript, Symbol Characters (--) With Symbols (—), and Internet Paths With Hyperlinks checkboxes.
>
> 5. Repeat step 4 in the AutoFormat As You Type tab.
>
>   Doing so allows you to type 2nd without fear that the trailing *nd* will turn into a couple of tiny letters that can completely mess up your *Mac 911* book template, lets you type a couple of hyphens in a row without Word turning them into a single em dash, and keeps all your text black and un-underlined when you type http://www.buttoutandletmecreatemyownformattingdammit.com.
>
> 6. In Word 2001, choose Turn Assistant Off from the Help menu to keep Word's virtual assistant, Max, from bouncing off the walls. In Word X's Help menu, deselect Use Office Assistant to accomplish the same task.
>
>   Killing Max in Word 98 is a little more difficult. Max lives inside the Assistants folder, which is inside the Office folder inside the Microsoft Office 98 folder. To give Max the ax, drag the Max file out of the Assistants folder. Now when you click the Office Help button, the traditional Microsoft electronic help system will appear (provided that you haven't installed any other Assistants in this folder; if you have, drag them out as well). If you'd simply prefer that Max dispense with the noisemaking and jumping about, open the Preferences window (choose Preferences from the Tools menu), click the General tab, and turn off the Provide Feedback with Sound and Provide Feedback with Animation options.

Corruption

An application that quits or freezes may do so because it's ailing. Applications and their support files can, unfortunately, get munged up after a crash and become unstable. It's very difficult to tell whether an application is corrupt. Diagnostic/repair utilities occasionally can pick out a funky application, but for the most part, you won't really know that an application was corrupt until you replace it with a clean copy.

To do so, I insert the application's installation disc, run the installer, and pray that the installer has an Uninstall option. If an installer complies with the Apple way of doing things, you should be able to uninstall an application by following these steps:

1. Run the installer.
2. Click Continue through any introduction windows and license agreements until you get to the Install window.
3. Choose Uninstall from the Install pop-up menu, and click OK.

    The installer should now sift through your hard drive and wipe out not only the application but also any of its support files.

The advantage of using this method is that the uninstaller has a far better idea than you do where all its little support files are squirreled away.

Regrettably, far too few applications offer such compliant installers (and I've yet to see an uninstaller in any Mac OS X application installer), and you must dump the application by hand. To begin, toss the application and its surrounding folder into the Trash. Then dig through the Extensions and Control Panels folders for any obviously related support files. If you're cleaning out SuperWhizzoPaint by hand, and you find the SuperWhizzoPaint Extension in your Extensions folder, give it a toss.

It's possible that you won't know which files to hurl. (Who knows whether the dxir4498Lib file is necessary for Super-WhizzoPaint to function?) In such cases, don't sweat it. If the installer knows its business, it will shove a new copy of the application *and* all its support files onto your hard drive.

Now install a clean copy of the application from the original installation disc, apply any updates, restart your Mac, and see what happens. With any luck, this remedy will end your troubles.

Uninstaller Utilities: Don't Bother

If you've come from the Windows world, you've surely seen Windows' Add/Remove application, along with a plethora of third-party utilities for uninstalling software. You may wonder why the Mac OS doesn't include such a utility or why more savvy Mac vendors don't market an uninstaller utility.

The answer is simple: Windows stinks, and the Mac doesn't.

Given that you've purchased this book, I'm likely preaching to the choir. But honestly, when it comes to troubleshooting and adding or removing software and hardware, Windows can be a nightmare. The reason why you find such a crowd of uninstaller utilities for the Windows platform is because they're absolutely necessary.

Most of the time, when you install a piece of software on the Mac, little more than an application and a few support files make their way onto your hard drive. You can remove these files by using the methods I mention outside this sidebar. When you install a Windows application, not only does the application grace your drive but several .DLL (driver) files also may be added to some obscure corner of your Windows folder, along with a host of other support files that are tucked away God knows where. *And* Windows may alter something called the Registry (a database file conceived in Hades) to make the whole mess work. If you carelessly toss a Windows application into the Trash—oops; I mean *Recycle Bin*—and neglect to get rid of those .DLL files (which may now have become attached to some other application) and expunge certain Registry entries, horrible things can happen. To prevent these horrible things, you must run an uninstaller application.

As I write this chapter, two uninstaller utilities are available for the Macintosh: Casady & Greene's $40 Chaos Master and Aladdin Systems' $50 Spring Cleaning. I can't recommend either one, because neither is smart enough to know which files are necessary and which are disposable. Instead, they present you a list of files that may or may not be unnecessary and offer you the option to toss any or all of those files. Should you accidentally trash a file that the Mac needs, your Mac could be in for a world of hurt.

Printing Problems

Several years ago, some yahoo predicted that thanks to computers, we'd soon be working in paperless offices. That's right—instead of slapping a Post-it on the curdled half-and-half in the office fridge, jotting the names of the 15,000 employees we intended to lay off into our Franklin Organizer's To Do list, and tossing a wadded-up sheet of legal paper at the office phone-monkey for the cruel pleasure of it, we'd accomplish all these tasks electronically. I don't know about you, but since I started using computers, the piles of paper around my office have increased twelvefold.

Only a portion of this paper can be explained away by my love of origami. The rest, I'm afraid, has been run through one printer or another.

Because printing is so important, there's no frustration quite like pressing Command-P only to be presented with an error dialog box that claims no printer can be found. (*"What do you mean, 'No printer can be found!?' I can see it right there!"*)

If your printer appears to have pooped out, try these techniques.

Check Connections

Yup, your printer is just as susceptible to loose connections as your Mac is. Be sure that all cables—power, USB, serial, and Ethernet—are plugged in and firmly seated. Also check to be sure that the printer is switched on.

Check the Chooser

If you're using Mac OS 9.2 or earlier, choose the Chooser command from the Apple menu, and click the driver for your printer in the resulting window. If you don't see your printer driver in the Chooser window, make sure that a printer driver is installed in the proper location. Under Mac OS 9.2.x and earlier, printer drivers are stored in the Extensions folder. People using a laser printer probably will use the LaserWriter 8 printer driver in this folder. Specific laser-printer drivers (sort of a subset of LaserWriter 8) are located in the Printer Descriptions folder inside the Extensions folder.

Under Mac OS X, printer drivers are located in the Printers folder inside the Library folder at the root level of the Mac OS X drive (grouped by manufacturer). To look for your printer in Mac OS X, open Print Center (found in the Utilities folder of Mac OS X's Applications folder). If you've added your printer, it should appear in this list. If it doesn't, click the Add Printer button in the Printer List window and select the method by which your printer is connected to your Mac in the pop-up window that appears in the resulting sheet (your choices are AppleTalk, LPR Printers using IP, and USB). If your printer doesn't appear in this list, check for updated drivers on your printer manufacturer's Web site.

Printer Troubleshooting

Try these tips for bringing your printer to the fore:

Are you using the latest version of the printer driver? When Apple updates the Mac OS, printers that used to be recognized by the Mac no longer are. If you recently changed versions of the Mac OS or added new utilities, and your printer stops working, look for updated printer drivers.

If you're running Mac OS 9.2 and earlier, have you tried cutting back on your extensions and control panels? Yes, some extension-based utilities can keep a printer from printing.

Does your printer require AppleTalk? Some older printers that use an older Mac's Printer port require that AppleTalk be turned on. If your running Mac OS 9.2 and earlier, open the Chooser and make sure that the AppleTalk option is indeed switched on. To switch on AppleTalk under Mac OS X, launch the Network system preference, select the configuration from the Show pop-up menu that you use to connect to the printer (Ethernet or AirPort, for example), click the AppleTalk tab, and select the Make AppleTalk Active checkbox.

Is the print queue switched on? If, under Mac OS 9.2 and earlier, you have a desktop printer, click its icon and then open the Printing menu that appears in the Finder. Is the Start Print Queue command checked? If not, choose that command. On occasions, I've switched off the print queue and left my Mac, only to have my wife unsuccessfully attempt to print something from this same Mac.

If you're using a USB printer, have you tried unplugging other USB devices? USB printers are notorious for conflicting with other USB doodads. Unplug other devices and see how you fare.

Are you using an Epson printer? I don't know exactly what it is about these things, but when I hear about a printer that's acting up, my first question is "Is it made by Epson?" More often than not, the answer is "Yeah. How'd you know?"

Please don't misunderstand; I think Epson printers produce beautiful results—photographs on the photo-grade printers in particular. But Epson could stand to work a little harder on its Mac drivers. In the case of an Epson printer doing something odd, run, don't walk, to the Epson Web site and download the latest driver for your printer.

Have you looked for warning lights? The Mac OS should toss up an alert if a printer has a paper jam or is out of paper, but in other cases, the Mac OS may not know to display an alert. It's always a good idea to see whether the printer's LEDs are blinking in some unusual fashion. If so, break out the manual, decipher the error, and try to put things right.

Check any adapters connected to the printer. To network my beloved HP LaserJet 5MP to my officeful of Macs, I use Asante's (www.asante.com) EtherTalk adapter. This doohickey (approximately $100) sports a 10Base-T Ethernet port on one end and a serial port on the other and allows you to include an AppleTalk-compatible printer in an Ethernet network. Every so often, my printer becomes inaccessible to the network because this adapter has become confused. To fix the problem, I simply pull the power from the adapter for a couple of seconds and then plug it back in. When I next attempt to print, the printer's rarin' to go.

Modem Problems

Although the number of people using fast DSL, cable, and satellite broadband connections continues to increase, many Mac users get onto the Web the old-fashioned way: by modem. Here are some common modem problems and their solutions.

No Connection

I'm afraid that I have to ask again: Is it plugged in? Be sure that the plug on both ends of the phone cord is seated properly. Also make sure that your Mac is plugged into a functioning phone jack. To test it, just plug a phone into the jack and listen for a dial tone.

If everything appears to be connected properly, open the Modem control panel and see to it that your modem is selected in the Connect Via pop-up menu and that the kind of modem you use appears in the Modem pop-up menu. Now open the Remote Access control panel, and check it for correct settings (that a phone number is entered, for example). Finally, open the TCP/IP control panel, and double-check that PPP (or some AOL connection protocol, if you use AOL) is selected in the Connect Via pop-up menu.

Also, it's slightly possible that someone switched off your modem's sound in the Modem control panel. The modem may be working perfectly, but you're missing its usual squawk.

In Mac OS X, launch the Network system preference and select Internal Modem from the Show pop-up menu. Double-check your connection settings in the TCP/IP, PPP, and Modem windows—information such as your ISP's domain name server addresses are found in the TCP/IP area, your ISP's phone number is entered in the PPP area, and you select modem scripts from the Modem pop-up menu in the Modem area of the Network window.

Slow and Dropped Connections

Modems try their very best to move data to and from your Mac as cleanly as possible. If the connection over the phone line is noisy, the modem may have to resend or re-retrieve data for it to go through in an uncorrupted state. This operation certainly can slow your modem. Worst case, the phone line may be so noisy that the modem can't maintain the connection at all.

As much as I'd like to blame the phone company for such noisy connections, you may be doing things to increase line noise. If you have your modem plugged into a fax or answering machine, for example, you're likely to have a noisier connection. Likewise, if you have a very long phone cord running from your Mac to the wall jack or a phone cord draped over some electrical cords or appliances, your line may be increasing line noise. The best way to protect yourself from such internal line noise is to use as short a phone cord as possible and run it directly into the phone jack.

OK, *now* I'll talk about the phone company. The phone company is responsible only for delivering connections clear enough for conversation. In other words, that slight crackling you hear that plays merry heck with your modem calls is perfectly okey-dokey with the phone company because it doesn't interfere with your voice calls.

If you call the phone company and complain that your modem is slow or your data calls end abruptly, the person you speak with will sympathize politely and just as politely tell you to go soak your head. For this reason, if you suspect that external line noise is the problem, call the phone company and tell them you're having a problem with your *voice* calls. *That's* something they'll deal with.

But even a thorough inspection of your phone lines may do no good. Some phone lines just can't support data calls faster than about 24 Kbps. When I moved to the country recently, I was dismayed to discover that I rarely connected at over 19 Kbps. I asked around the neighborhood, and sure enough, everyone in the area had the same problem. As Bruce Hornsby taught us lo those many years ago, "That's just the way it is."

> **There Are No Modem Miracles**
>
> A couple of products on the market claim to increase modem speed through the use of "optimized" modem scripts. Don't be fooled by such spurious claims.
>
> Oh, these products appear to work because through some clever programming, these modem scripts can force Remote Access to report serial-port speed (a much higher number) rather than the connect speed you're accustomed to seeing displayed. But it's a placebo. You see this higher number and naturally assume that the modem connection is faster.
>
> *Macworld* tested a collection of these scripts in a controlled environment and found such claims of increased speed to be pure hokum. The scripts were no faster than the scripts that ship with the Mac OS and in some cases were actually slower.
>
> Buyer beware!

Performance Issues

Over time, computers, like their human keepers, tend to slow down. Unlike the case with humans, this less-than-zippy performance isn't due to parts wearing out but to a computer that is overburdened in one way or another. If you've noticed that your Mac isn't the sprightly beast it once was, try these performance-enhancement tips.

Trim Extensions and Control Panels

In Mac OS 9 and earlier, try this experiment: Restart your Mac with nothing but the Mac OS Base set switched on in Extensions Manager. Does your Mac seem to be markedly faster? If so, the extensions and control panels that you regularly run are slowing you.

When you're seeking add-ons that are likely to affect performance, first look to those utilities that churn away in the background: antivirus applications, disk optimizers, and diagnostic tools. That background work can hobble your Mac's capability to get things done quickly. If such a utility offers you the option to switch off background processing, and you're concerned about performance, exercise that option.

Even if something isn't laboring in the background, a plethora of add-ons can grab vital processing cycles and affect performance. Again, if you don't really need something, switch it off.

> **Slow Email Applications**
>
> Does your Mac seem to be as fleet of foot as ever, yet your email client slogs along like it's treading through a glorpy mix of snow, tar, and molasses? There's a good reason: Its message database probably is bloated.
>
> If you're like most Mac users, you swap a fair bit of email over the weeks: daily missives from Mom, tasteless jokes from Margo, mailing-list crud, and the usual tittle-tattle from your lodge brothers. In the process of creating, replying to, and deleting email, the databases in which these messages are kept tend to get flabby. A sure sign of overt flabbiness is an email application that opens slowly and slothlike responsiveness when it finally deigns to open.
>
> *continues on next page*

Fortunately, you can put your email application on a swift diet by compressing its databases. Here's how.

In Microsoft's Outlook Express:

1. Hold down the Option key while launching the program.

   You'll be asked whether you'd like to compact the database.

2. Click Yes (if indeed you want to).

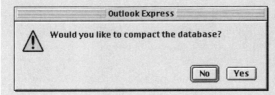

A Fresh Outlook. Outlook Express's Compact Database window.

3. Wait a while until the program is done.
4. Get on with your life.

In Microsoft's Entourage:

1. Hold down the Option key just as you would in Outlook Express.
2. When you see the window that offers you the option to perform a Typical or Advanced rebuild, choose the Typical option.

   A Typical rebuild simply smushes the database. An Advanced rebuild creates a new database—a process necessary only if Entourage's database file is corrupt.

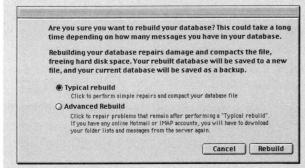

Join My Entourage. Typically, you'll want to choose Entourage's Typical rebuild option.

In Qualcomm's Eudora:

1. In the bottom-left corner of each mailbox window (the In Box, for example), you'll see a small box that includes an entry like 256/3598K/219K; click this box to compact that mailbox.

   The numbers in this box indicate the number of messages in the mailbox, the amount of space those messages take up, and the amount of wasted space in the mailbox, respectively.

continues on next page

> **Slow Email Applications** *continued*
>
> 2. To compact all of Eudora's mailboxes, Option-click this box.
>
>
>
> **A Waste of Space.** Slim your Eudora mailboxes by Option-clicking this box.
>
> Note: Before compacting an email client's databases, be sure to back up these database files. Rarely, these files will be corrupted during the compacting process, and if they are, you could lose not only your saved email but your address book as well.
>
> You'll find Outlook Express and Eudora's database files in the Microsoft User Data folder inside the Documents folder at the root level of your startup drive. Recent versions of Eudora place the Eudora folder (the one you want to back up) in this same Documents folder. Older versions of Eudora place the Eudora folder in the System Folder.
>
> This trick works in both Mac OS 9.2 and earlier and Mac OS X.

Use Real RAM Rather Than Virtual Memory

You may recall that earlier in the chapter, I mentioned that virtual memory is slower than RAM. I wasn't lying; it really is (except in Mac OS X where it's implemented more elegantly). If you can afford it, add more memory to your Mac and switch off virtual memory.

Disable the Mac's Startup Memory Test

When your Mac starts up, it checks the computer's RAM to make sure that all is well. The more RAM you have, the longer this check takes. Considering that RAM rarely fails, I switch this test off. You can, too. In Mac OS 9 and earlier, here's how:

1. Hold down the Command and Option keys while opening the Memory control panel.

    A new option appears in the Memory window: Startup Memory Tests.

2. Choose the Off option.

    When you next start up your Mac, it will do as you requested and skip the memory tests.

Pass This Test. Honestly, your Mac's RAM probably is fine. Kill the memory tests with confidence.

Increase the Disk Cache

The Mac can cache certain functions in RAM. When it does, these functions speed up. If the disk-cache setting in the Memory control panel is too low, your Mac may be slower than it could be. To adjust the disk cache:

1. Open the Memory control panel.
2. Check the disk-cache setting.

    Normally, the Default option will be selected. In most circumstances, this setting is perfectly fine. If you want to try to tweak the setting for greater performance, click the Custom setting option and adjust the cache setting higher.

Earn More Cache! An enlarged disk cache can make for a faster Mac.

Note that you gain only so much benefit from increasing the amount of disk cache. After 8 MB or so of cache, you won't see any performance gains.

Decrease Color Depth

If you have an older Mac—and by this statement, I mean something made before the iMac—your Mac might be a bit perkier if you change the color depth from Millions to Thousands or 256 Colors. You can change color depth in the Monitors control panel or from the Control Strip.

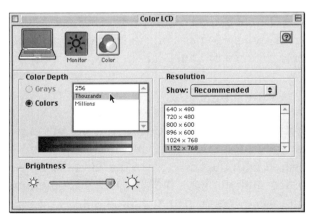

Less Colorful. Older Macs may benefit from a decrease in color depth.

Newer Macs benefit very little from this trick, because these Macs have ultraspeedy graphics cards that can handle any color depth you throw at them with aplomb.

Choose a Startup Disk

If you haven't selected a startup disk in the Startup Disk control panel, the Mac has to waste time rummaging around at startup to locate a bootable volume.

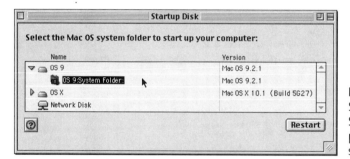

Disk Determination. Selecting a disk in the Startup Disk control panel can goose the startup process.

Rebuild the Desktop

A confused Desktop database file can also slow a Mac running Mac OS 9.2 or earlier (this Desktop database stuff doesn't apply under Mac OS X). Hold down Command and Option at startup to put this file back in order.

Optimize Your Hard Drive

I realize that elsewhere in this book, I said that optimizing your hard drive is likely to assist your Mac's performance only when the hard drive is colossally fragmented. Well, maybe yours is.

Upgrade Your Mac

Adding a faster hard drive, graphics card, and processor certainly will goose the performance of your Mac. In Chapter 7, I show you how.

Buy a New Mac

Finally, some problems will go away only if you throw money at them. If the speed of the Power Macintosh 6100 at home is intolerable compared with the zestiness of the 733 MHz Power Mac G4 at the office, and you have the dough to do something about it, trade up. *Mmmmmm, new-computer smell....*

Tools and Techniques: Classic Mac OS

The Ways and Means to Keep Your Mac OS 9 (and Earlier) Mac on the Straight and Narrow

Picture this: Your kitchen sink is backed up on the night before your shockingly wealthy Great Aunt Elsie is due to pay a visit. Your plan includes concocting the kinds of meals that ensure your name floats to the top of the old biddy's will. Realizing that without the attendant sink, you're sunk, you call the finest plumber in town. Said plumber arrives by limousine in an hour's time, cocks a knowing eye at the swampy sink, and proclaims: "Your drain is clogged with six ounces of animal fat, seven asparagus stalks, and half a pound of coffee grounds (Guatemalan decaffeinated)."

Momentarily struck dumb by the plumber's perspicacity, you finally ask, "How long will it take you to fix it?"

"Fix it? Oh, I won't fix it. I'm simply here to diagnose your problem. I've clearly done so, and now, if you'll just hand over your firstborn child, I'll be on my way."

I paint this picture not only because I understand how vitally important the plumbers' demographic is to the success of any book but also to drive home the point that a competent Mac troubleshooter has knowledge *and* a well-stocked toolkit (plus the wherewithal to put both to good use).

In this chapter, we look at the tools of the trade—the good *and* the bad—and learn how to make those tools work for you.

Diagnostic Tools

If you've read Chapter 3, you know that I've already weighed in on the Mac's best-known diagnostic and repair utilities: Apple's Disk First Aid, Alsoft's Disk Warrior, Micromat's Tech-Tool Pro, and Symantec's Norton Utilities for Macintosh. My opinion of these utilities has not changed one ounce in the intervening pages: Disk First Aid is harmless but only occasionally useful, Disk Warrior is superb, TechTool Pro is worth having, and Norton Utilities is only occasionally useful (and sometimes harmful).

This situation is the status quo as of late-autumn 2001. If you're reading these words after unearthing this tome in some 27th-century archeological dig, you may find that things have changed. For this reason, it's a good idea to glean updated information on these products (as well as new troubleshooting utilities) by devouring the reviews pages of *Macworld* magazine and other Mac resources you trust.

Disk First Aid

Every Macintosh ships with a copy of Apple's Disk First Aid. You'll find it in the Utilities folder on your Mac's hard drive. If you have a recent version of the classic Mac OS (9.2 or 9.1, for example), you'll find the Utilities folder inside the Applications folder at the root level of your Mac's hard drive. A copy of Disk First Aid is also included with the System software CD that came with your Mac.

Disk First Aid doesn't attempt to check or repair applications and documents. Rather, its job is to examine your Mac's hard drive for directory damage—to make sure that the directory is uncorrupted.

Open Disk First Aid, and you'll discover that the program offers you only two options: Verify and Repair. When you select a volume and click Verify, Disk First Aid eyeballs the directory structure of that volume; reports any errors it encounters; and, if it does discover errors, indicates whether it can repair them. The Repair button should more aptly be named the "If It's One of the Very Few Problems I Can Fix, I'll Do What I Can" button. In other words, don't expect miracles when you click Repair.

A few Disk First Aid tips:

- As I mentioned earlier in this chapter, just because Disk First Aid can find a problem doesn't mean that it can do anything about it. Far too often, Disk First reports a problem and then indicates that it can offer no help. In such situations, turn to a more robust diagnostic/repair utility.

- Just because Disk First Aid reports no problems doesn't mean that your Mac isn't completely befuddled. Disk First Aid has a very dim understanding of when a Mac is messed and when it isn't. If your Mac continues to have problems, use a more robust diagnostic/repair utility.

- Should you be diagnosing your startup drive, and Disk First Aid reports that it can repair that drive, you can try clicking the Repair button, and the repair may be successful. But be prepared to boot from your System software CD or emergency disk and run Disk First Aid from there. It won't always be possible for Disk First Aid to repair the drive used to boot the Mac. It's a little like trying to remove your own appendix; it can be done, but the chances of a successful outcome are greater if a third party provides the service.

    If your Mac originally shipped with a now-ancient version of the Mac OS (System 7.1, for example), and you're now running a much later version of the OS (9.1, for example), the older version of Disk First Aid on your emergency disk may be of little use. That copy of Disk First Aid may be unaware of certain changes made in the Mac OS since its creation. Also, more recent versions of Disk First Aid are more capable than previous versions. For these reasons, create an emergency disk that includes a recent version of Disk First Aid. (I show you how to create an emergency disk later in this chapter.)

- This tip has very little to do with Disk First Aid, but I couldn't figure out where else to put it. You know that warning dialog box that appears on startup after your Mac has quit unexpectedly? That's right—the one that claims your startup drive is being diagnosed and repaired by Disk First Aid after an improper shutdown. I can't swear to it, but my guess is that during the hundreds of times that dialog box has appeared, Disk First Aid has never once performed a valuable service.

Because I am so doubtful about this dialog box, I've taken its advice and turned off the Check Disk If Computer Was Shut Down Improperly option in the General Controls control panel. If you'd rather be safe than sorry, leave this option on.

Check Disk
☑ Check disk if computer was shut down improperly.

Don't Show and Tell. Switch off this option in the General Controls control panel to keep Disk First Aid from checking your drive at startup after a crash.

The verdict

It's free, it's on your Mac, it's worth a shot.

> **Creating an Emergency Startup CD**
>
> We hold these truths to be self-evident:
>
> - Your Mac will one day crash badly enough that you will be unable to boot it.
> - You appreciate your Mac (and the stuff on it) well enough that you'll want it to work again as soon as possible.
> - You want to treat your Mac with the most capable tools possible.
>
> Assuming that all these things are true for you, it's likely that you'll want as capable an emergency startup CD as you can create. Oh, sure, you can boot your Mac from the Software Install CD that came with your computer. But honestly, do you want to rely solely on Disk First Aid or Mac OS X's Disk Utility to repair your Mac? And even if have several troubleshooting utilities that can be booted from CD, which one do you choose?
>
> *continues on next page*

With a custom-built emergency CD, you needn't make any of these hard choices. Instead, you can build a CD that contains the tools *you* think are important.

First, you'll require a CD-R or CD-RW drive. Nearly all Macs released since late 2000 carry these drives. If your Mac doesn't have one, plenty of CD-RW burners are available for around $200. You'll also need software to create a bootable CD. I regret to say that Apple's Disc Burner doesn't fill the bill; it can't create bootable discs.

Fortunately, unless you own a Mac that shipped with a CD-RW drive, you have the best tool for the job: Roxio's (www.roxio.com) Toast. Although the OEM version of Toast that ships with most third-party CD-RW drives isn't as full-featured as Toast Titanium, it can create bootable CDs. Here's how I'd go about the job:

1. Running Mac OS 9.2 or earlier, launch Apple's Disk Copy (located in the Utilities folder inside the Applications folder in Mac OS 9.1 and 9.2), and choose Create New Image from the Image menu.

2. In the resulting window, give the image a descriptive name such as Emergency, choose 663,000K (CD-ROM 12cm, Full) from the Size pop-up menu, make sure that the Mount Image checkbox is checked, and click Save.

3. Insert your System Software Install CD, locate the Mac OS Install application, and launch it.

4. Select the Emergency disk image you just created as the destination for the installation.

5. Begin the installation process.

    If you like, you can install a full System or be more selective by clicking the installer's Customize button and installing a slimmed-down System Folder—just the Mac OS 9.2 option, for example.

6. When the installation is complete, open Startup Items inside the System Folder on your Emergency disc, and remove the Mac OS Setup Assistant alias (to keep the Mac from asking you to configure the System each time you boot from this disc).

7. Proceed to install your diagnostic and repair utilities.

    If you're installing Alsoft's Disk Warrior, launch the program's installer and select the Emergency disc as your destination; then launch the copy of Disk Warrior on your Emergency disc and enter your name and serial number. If you don't provide that information, Disk Warrior won't run from your CD.

    Follow much the same procedure for Norton Utilities. After installation, however, I've found it helpful to remove a couple of unnecessary items from the Emergency disc. I've never found Disk Light to be useful, for example, so I drag it out of the Control Panels folder. Likewise, because you can't update the version of Norton Utilities on the CD (it's read-only, after all), I also toss out Live Update.

continues on next page

> **Creating an Emergency Startup CD** *continued*
>
> Installing TechTool Pro 3 is a little trickier. You must first install it on your Mac's hard drive and install any available updates. Then run the copy on your hard drive and choose Preferences from the Edit menu. In the window that appears, uncheck the Auto-Update Protection Files checkbox. Again, because your Emergency CD is read-only, TechTool won't be able to update its protection files, so there's no need for it to try. Quit TechTool. Now install a copy of TechTool Pro 3 and its updates on your Emergency disc. Open the Preferences folder on your Mac, and copy the TechTool Pro Prefs file to the Preference folder of the System Folder on your Emergency disc. This procedure allows the copy of TechTool on the Emergency disc to launch properly without trying to update your protection files.

8. If you're using Toast 4.x launch Toast, choose the Files & Folders option from the Format menu, click the Data button, and then click the New CD button that appears in the same window.

9. Select all the files in your Emergency disc, and drag them into Toast's Files & Folders window.

10. Now burn, baby, burn.

If you're using Toast Titanium (Toast 5, in other words), select Data in the Roxio Toast Titanium window, choose Mac OS CD or Mac OS and PC (Hybrid CD) in the pop-up menu (Mac OS CD is selected by default). Drag the System Folder you created into the data window. Change the name of the CD to something more descriptive ("Emergency," for example). Drag the rest of material you want on the disc into the data window. Insert a blank disc into your CD burner.

Now burn, baby, burn.

Disk Warrior

Let me again state that Alsoft's Disk Warrior is the finest utility currently available for repairing really nasty directly damage—the kind of damage that can keep your Mac from booting up or, if it boots, causes your Mac to behave in untoward ways.

Disk Warrior may be even easier to use than Disk First Aid. If you suspect that you have a problem with a particular disk, boot your Mac from a disk other than the troublesome one (Disk Warrior can't repair the startup drive or the drive on which it resides), select the volume you want to diagnose and repair, and click the Rebuild button. When you do, Disk Warrior looks through your Mac's directory for any corruption and builds a new directory based on information it found in the old directory. When it builds that new directory, it does so without the errors in the old one. After the new directory is built, Disk Warrior reports any errors that it's found and fixed and offers you the opportunity to preview the drive as it will look with a new directory. (After trying the Preview option once, I've never found a reason to do so again. You may feel differently.)

Repair Report. Disk Warrior indicates the repairs it's made before creating a new directory.

When you're sure that replacing the old directory with the new is a good idea, just click the Replace button, and—*presto change-o*—the directory is replaced.

Disk Warrior offers a couple of other options. If you'd like to see how fragmented a volume's directory is, you can click the Graph button, which produces a window that shows you how many directory items are out of order. If you don't like the look of things, you may be more motivated to build a new directory.

This graph is a nice little feature but not a vital one. Directories get fragmented, just as people occasionally stub their toes and sprout pimples. A fragmented directory won't lead to a Mac that dissolves into a molten puddle of goo. If a directory becomes badly fragmented, your Mac could slow a bit when seeking files or starting up; other than that, no worries.

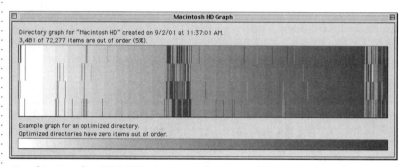

Graphic Gander. Disk Warrior provides a graphic view of just how out of whack your directory is.

Disk Warrior also includes something called Disk Shield. This extension acts as a watchdog over information written to a volume's directory. If Disk Shield detects directory damage or an operation that's likely to damage the directory, it sends up an alert. Then your job is to launch Disk Warrior to view the error. After that, you're free to run Disk Warrior and attempt a repair. Unlike some other utilities that check on the state of your disk from time to time, Disk Shield is not intrusive; you won't even know it's there until you need it. I like this feature and leave it switched on.

Shield's Up! Disk Warrior's Disk Shield keeps tabs on your directory's health.

Mac OS X compatibility

If you boot from the CD or an Mac OS 9.2 or earlier partition, you can repair an Mac OS X volume with the latest version of Disk Warrior.

The verdict

Disk Warrior is an indispensable tool. Buy it.

TechTool Pro

By now, you're probably aware that your Mac can suffer from far more problems than directory damage. Files become corrupted, fonts go bad, a RAM module comes loose, your keyboard develops a stuck key, your Mac becomes infected with a computer virus, extensions come into conflict, your 8-year-old takes it into his pointy little head to trash all your Quicken files to watch the Trash go from skinny to fat to skinny again....

Tools such as Disk First Aid and Disk Warrior can't handle these problems. Their job is to make sure that your hard drive's data structure is sound. When you need a tool to deal with these other issues, Micromat's TechTool Pro is the place to turn.

TechTool Pro tries to be the Swiss Army knife of Mac troubleshooting utilities. The program originally was designed to diagnose hardware problems: RAM, ADB and serial ports, video RAM, modem connections, and SCSI, among many other things. Over the years, Micromat piled on the features, adding data recovery and data protection, extension-conflict diagnosis, virus protection, and hard-disk optimization features. Frankly, when some of these features were introduced, they were half-baked. With version 3, TechTool Pro has become far more robust.

Although TechTool Pro packs all these features into a single interface (one in which you can test components one at a time or run a series of tests in one go), the program contains two major elements: (a) The Hardware Tests and (b) Everything Else.

The hardware tests run through everything from RAM to sound output to the Mac's processor. Just select the elements you want to check, and TechTool blasts through a series of tests.

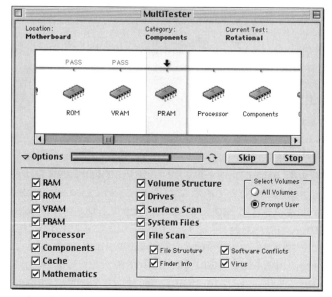

Helping Hardware. TechTool Pro can check many of the hardware components and ports on your Macintosh.

Allow me to be frank just one more time: In all my years of troubleshooting, I have never run into anyone who claims that these hardware tests have pulled their Mac's fat from the fire. I've run TechTool's hardware tests numerous times and have yet to turn up a single problem. Although it's perfectly possible that my Mac's guardian angel puts in a load of overtime, I think it's more likely that these kinds of problems are pretty rare.

That leaves Everything Else. The following sections describe TechTool Pro's main features.

Data recovery

TechTool Pro's data-recovery feature is similar to the file-recovery component of Norton Utilities. This feature allows you to recover files you've accidentally (or purposely, I suppose) tossed out. This is possible because files tossed into the Trash and then emptied from it have not been erased; rather, the directory information for that stuff is removed. The files remain. With that information removed, the Mac is free to write new data over the locations of those files on your hard drive.

TechTool installs an extension and control panel that help keep a record of trashed files. When asked to do so, TechTool will try to bring these trashed items back from the dead. If you've added new files to your Mac, of course, there's an increased likelihood that your trashed files have been overwritten and therefore are unrecoverable. For this reason, when you want to recover files, you should stop whatever you're doing, boot your Mac from your emergency disk (this can be the TechTool Pro disc), and begin recovery.

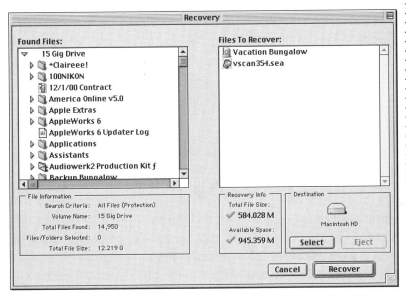

In Recovery. With TechTool Pro (and a little luck), you may be able to recover files that you thought had long ago disappeared from your hard drive.

I run hot and cold on such data-recovery protection schemes. I've found that the extensions necessary to make data recovery work cause more conflicts than they're worth, and I grow tired of such utilities updating their databases while I'm working or when the Mac starts up or shuts down. But then, I never throw anything out, and I maintain an up-to-date backup of my data, so losing files is not a huge issue for me. If you're more cavalier about tossing files, and you have yet to heed my warning to *backup your data right this instant*, such automatic protection may be worth your while.

TechTool Pro also claims that it can recover trashed files without this kind of protection. I recently had the opportunity to test this claim and found it wanting. I purposely trashed all the files on a 500 MB hard drive—one that was not protected by TechTool Pro—and then attempted to resurrect the files.

No dice. TechTool found only a handful of files. The lesson learned is that if you hope to recovered files from your drive with TechTool, you must have its protection components installed and switched on.

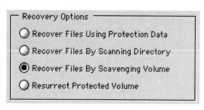

Scavenger Hunt. Even if TechTool Pro has no record of your deleted files, it may be able to recover them by scavenging the hard drive.

Directory maintenance

TechTool Pro offers a directory-rebuilding feature similar to Disk Warrior. Regrettably, I haven't found it to be nearly as effective as Disk Warrior. Enough said.

Optimization

If you're a typical Mac user, you move a lot of files on and off your hard drive. After all these files are moved hither and yon, your hard drive's free space tends to become fragmented. To compensate for the dribs and drabs of free space scattered across your hard drive, the Mac must segment files to make them fit—500 KB here, 1.2 MB there, another 280 KB over there. After a while, your hard drive is littered with these segments. To bring the segments together—making your files all line up again in a contiguous way—you *optimize* your hard drive with a program such as Norton Utilities Speed Disk, Alsoft's Plus Optimizer, or TechTool Pro's optimization feature.

Optimizing your drive is a little like taking a deck of shuffled cards and arranging it by suit and number. The theory is that optimization makes it easier for the hard drive's read head to move data off the hard drive and into memory—meaning that documents should open more quickly.

In the old days of slow hard drives and pokey processors, optimization made some difference. For the most part, it no longer does. Put two dual-processor, 800 MHz Power Mac G4s side by side—one with a badly fragmented hard drive and the other with an optimized drive—and I doubt that you'd feel a difference in performance. If you're using a video or audio application that requires you to move data on and off your hard drive as efficiently as possible, however, optimization may still be worthwhile.

TechTool Pro includes an optimization component. If you're running Mac OS 9 or later, you must boot from a drive other than the one you want to optimize. (You can boot from the TechTool Pro CD, for example.) Also, for TechTool to optimize your drive, it needs about 15 percent free space on that drive to do its job.

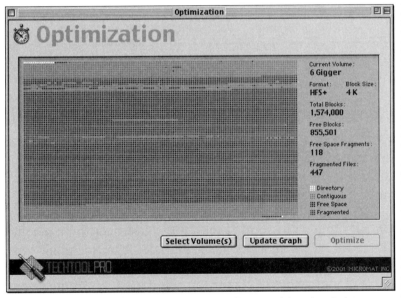

Line Up! You can bring your fragmented files (and free hard-drive space) together with TechTool Pro.

> **Optimization Tips**
>
> I have two optimization tips tucked away that have squatted in my brain for far too long. Here they are:
>
> - If you have copy-protected software on your hard drive (older music software, for example), remove any key-disk installs you have on a drive that you intend to optimize. (If you don't know what a key-disk install is, this tip likely doesn't apply to you. Don't lose any sleep over it.) Key-disk installs work only when the key disk resides in a place where the host application expects to find it. When you optimize your drive, the optimization program may move the key disk. When key disks are moved, their host applications won't recognize them and won't run. Worse, you lose that key-disk install.
>
>   TechTool Pro isn't quite clever enough to anchor such files in place, but it does know that such files exist and will warn you that you must remove them before it can do its job. Nice feature!
>
> - I recently had a good reason to optimize one of my hard drives. StuffIt, Aladdin Systems' famous compression/expansion utility, requires that an unstuffed file be written to contiguous free space. In other words, when a file expands, it can't be fragmented to several locations on your hard drive. I had a hard drive that was so badly fragmented that every time I tried to unstuff a file, StuffIt Expander threw up an error and refused to expand the file. After I optimized the drive, files unstuffed as they should.

Conflict testing

TechTool Pro doesn't offer the kind of extension-conflict testing offered in Casady & Greene's Conflict Catcher. The program can't "halve" groups of extensions and see how they get along, for example. Instead, TechTool Pro includes a database that lists files known to conflict with one another or to be incompatible for recent versions of the Mac OS. After scanning your drive, the program lists those files that it feels are troublemakers and explains why they appear on the Most Wanted list. Although this feature is not as useful as Conflict Catcher's capability to test the files, it's an easy way to seek out likely suspects when your Mac appears to be suffering an extension conflict.

> **Conflict Number: 1001**
> Adaptec Toast 3.5.7 is not fully compatible with System 9 or above. To correct this problem, visit the manufacturer's web site at <http://www.adaptec.com/> and download or purchase the latest version of the program.
>
> The problem file is located here:
> Macintosh HD:Toast Folder:Adaptec Toast 3.5.7
>
> *Major*
>
> **Conflict Number: 1800**
> Hard Disk SpeedTools(tm) 3.0 is not compatible with Mac OS 9.1 or above and you will be be unable to boot from your ATA or SCSI drive afterwards.. To correct this problem, visit the manufacturer's web site at <http://www.IntechUSA.com/> and download or purchase the latest version of the program.
>
> The problem file is located here:
> Macintosh HD:Desktop Folder:From Mac HD:Stuff:HDST™3.0 Update:HD SpeedTools™ 3.0 Update:Hard Disk SpeedTools™ 3.0
>
> *Serious*

Conflict Comments. TechTool Pro can't do anything about application and extension conflicts other than let you know that they exist.

Virus testing

TechTool Pro's virus-testing component is likewise limited. Unlike bona-fide virus-protection utilities such as Symantec's Norton AntiVirus, Network Associates' Virex, and Intego's VirusBarrier, TechTool can't download a list of virus definitions automatically; new virus definitions are included only in new versions of TechTool Pro. Although Micromat seems to offer new revisions of TechTool Pro fairly often, the revisions don't come out as regularly as every month. Should a new virus emerge before Micromat is ready to issue an update, your Mac could be susceptible to the latest cootie. Also, TechTool can't scan for Microsoft macro viruses—a variety of virus that Mac users are most likely to contract.

File tests

I lump together a few TechTool tests in this section: System Files, File Structure, Finder Info, and Volume Structure. These tests are the most useful of TechTool Pro's tests. Each looks for some variety of corruption. Such corruption can be as inconsequential as files with incorrect dates or as dire as a Finder file ready to bring your Mac to its knees. This group of tests—along with Surface Scan, which checks the integrity of your hard drive's media—pretty well duplicates the functions of Norton Utilities' Disk Doctor application. In my opinion, TechTool handles these tasks better than Norton does.

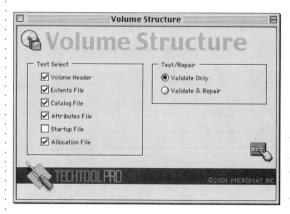

Fixer-Upper. TechTool Pro does a competent job of diagnosing and repairing corrupt files and volumes.

The other blades in the knife

But wait—that's not all. I told you that TechTool Pro is the Swiss Army knife of diagnostic/repair utilities, and I wasn't kidding. The application also includes a component called Wipe Data, which overwrites areas of your hard drive so that files can be nigh on impossible to recover (a handy feature when you have something to hide). Additionally, you'll stumble across components that test your modem, scanner, floppy drive (if you still have such a relic), and the integrity of your Internet connection. Then there are the fish scaler, mini saw, toothpick, tweezers, and pneumatic drill. Wait—I'm kidding. There's no toothpick.

Mac OS X compatibility

If you boot from the CD or an Mac OS 9.2 or earlier partition, you can repair an Mac OS X volume with the latest version of TechTool Pro.

The verdict

OK, so not every part of TechTool Pro is necessary or even the very best tool for the job. This tool kit contains enough worthwhile things—the file-testing utilities in particular—to justify its price.

TechTool Pro gets the *Mac 911* nod.

Norton Utilities for Macintosh

If you've read this book from page 1, you know that I'm less than enthusiastic about Symantec's Norton Utilities for Macintosh. At one time, Norton was a respectable diagnostic/repair utility. Perhaps not coincidentally, Norton was at its very best when compelling and competing tools were on the market—Central Point Software's MacTools Deluxe and Fifth Generation Systems' Public Utilities in particular. Symantec swallowed up the competition, and shortly thereafter, Norton began to languish. Symantec seemed to be less and less interested in supporting the Mac, and updates of Norton were few and far between—even updates necessary to make Norton compatible with the current version of the Mac OS.

To keep those upgrade dollars coming (and honestly, I'm sure with the best intentions of making the program better), Symantec threw a few more features at Norton. Regrettably, some of these additions were either marginally helpful or downright dangerous.

Among the marginally helpful was LiveUpdate, a program that logs onto the Internet automatically to seek out and download Norton Utilities updates. Considering that Norton is updated once in a very blue moon, it's hard to find this feature truly useful.

Undoubtedly the most dangerous Norton feature was a little something called Crash Guard. The idea was that when your Mac crashed, the computer wouldn't freeze; instead, Crash Guard would pop up, allowing you to quit all open applications gracefully and then restart your Mac safely. Although this goal was laudable, Crash Guard caused far more crashes than it cured.

LiveUpdate remains in the latest version of Norton; Crash Guard was shown the door with Norton Utilities 5.

The current version as I write is Norton Utilities 6.0.2. It includes the following features.

Disk Doctor

This feature is, and always has been, the Big Kahuna of Norton Utilities. Disk Doctor is charged with diagnosing your hard drive and files, and issuing repairs when necessary. During the diagnosis process, Disk Doctor performs a surface scan of your hard drive, seeking out areas on the drive that may not record data reliably; it ensures that any disk partitions are set up properly, checks the volume structure of the drive (the directory), and looks at the integrity of the files on your drive.

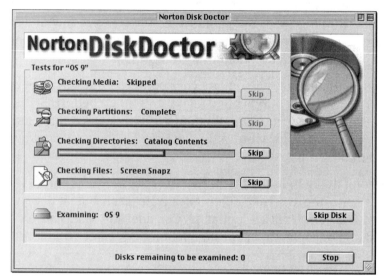

The Doctor Is In. Norton Disk Doctor checks the integrity of your hard drive and the data on it.

When Disk Doctor finds a problem, it lets you know whether the problem is repairable or not. If the problem can be repaired, the good doctor offers you the option to put things right. As an added measure of safety, Disk Doctor includes an option to undo its repairs.

Unfortunately, this whole undo thing is another feature that is more attractive in theory than in practice. Just for laughs, I've had DD repair problems on my hard drive and then asked the program to undo those repairs. Far more times than I care to recount, DD shrugged its virtual shoulders and proclaimed that it couldn't undo that which it had done.

This situation wouldn't unsettle me particularly if all of Disk Doctor's repairs were of premium quality. Regrettably, many are not. After repairing a disk with Norton Disk Doctor, I have often had more trouble with the hard disk than when I began—more crashes and even some cases in which the Mac wouldn't boot at all. Were this incident an isolated one, I might chalk it up to my being born under a bad sign (I've been down since I began to crawl...). But I spend a fair amount of time wandering the Web to see how others fare with their Macs, and reports of Disk Doctor mangling a disk are far from uncommon. Although I'll trust Disk Doctor to repair such minor problems as incorrect dates and bundle bits, I'm extremely wary about allowing DD to touch my Mac after it reports some kind of directory error. At this point, I politely ask Norton to quit and then dash to Disk Warrior.

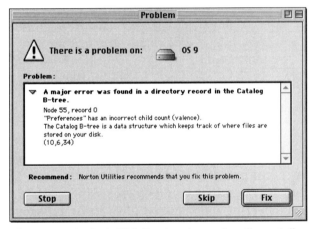

The Doctor Is Out. Disk Doctor does a less-than-stellar job of clearing out tough problems such as B-Tree errors. In such cases, you're in better hands with Alsoft's Disk Warrior.

Speed Disk

On the other hand, I'm pleased with Norton's disk-optimization utility, Speed Disk. Unlike TechTool Pro, Speed Disk offers you the option to anchor files that you don't want moved—those music-software key-disk files I mentioned earlier, for example. Speed Disk also allows you to optimize your drive in a few ways by choosing among several optimization profiles.

When you select the Multimedia profile, for example, Speed Disk maximizes adjacent free space without optimizing the drive completely. This arrangement gives you a lot of contiguous free space quickly and makes room for a large file that you want to keep in an unfragmented condition. When I optimize my Mac's hard drive, this is the tool I use.

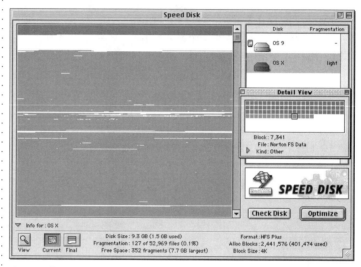

Optimal Optimizer. Speed Disk is one of Norton Utilities' most useful components.

FileSaver, UnErase, and Volume Recover

File Saver is an extension that watches over your Mac and makes note of which files you've tossed. UnErase is the application for recovering those tossed files. Volume Recover is for more heavy-duty jobs—ones in which a drive is fairly well scrambled or you accidentally initialized a drive.

FileSaver is a wonderful idea that occasionally causes problems for me. When my Mac appears to be suffering from extension conflicts, FileSaver is one of the first extensions I turn off. Also, even with FileSaver turned on, I haven't had a lot of success in attempts to bring trashed files back from the dead—perhaps because I tend to write a lot of data to my drive over the course of a day, and those trashed files quickly become unrecoverable. I haven't had much greater success with Volume Recover. Rather than depend on any of these utilities, I make sure that I have a comprehensive backup of my data.

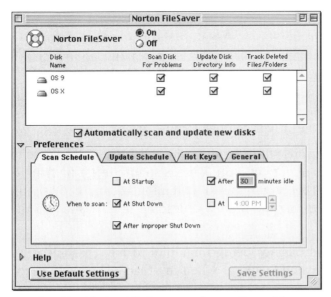

Just Say No. Norton FileSaver can be configured to update its database on a regular basis. If constant updating gets on your nerves, switch off some of these updates in FileSaver's Scan Schedule window.

I heartily recommend UnErase, however, for those situations when you've trashed files and you don't have the protection of FileSaver or TechTool Pro's similar tool. You recall the "toss 500 MB of files" test I performed with TechTool Pro? I repeated the test with Norton UnErase, and UnErase brought back *far* more files than TechTool—around 1,600 files in all. Granted, they bore generic names such as "MS Word 5.x #1503," but at least I had some of my precious data back.

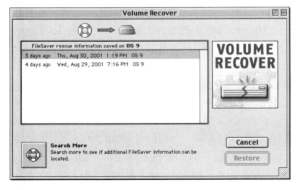

In Recovery. If you don't keep your FileSaver information up to date, Volume Recover may have a tougher time bringing your hard drive back from the dead.

Disk Light

If you're the type of person who really, *really* wants to know how your hard drive spends its waking hours, Disk Light is for you. It puts a little hard-drive icon in the top-left corner of your Mac's screen that blinks when your drives read or write data. (Look for the flashing *R* and *W* to learn exactly which action the drives are performing at any moment.)

Please excuse the rampant editorializing here, but who the heck cares!? If your computing life is so uninteresting that you need to pay attention to this kind of minutia, you really should think about taking up some wholesome hobby, such as dust-mite taming or thimble carving.

Oh, and besides being unhelpful to me, Disk Light is on my list of Prime Suspects when my Mac begins acting up.

Wipe Info

Wipe Info gets the *Mac 911* Thumbs Up. As I've told you, when you trash a file, that file remains on your hard drive until it's overwritten. Even if a portion of a file is overwritten, nefarious folk may still be able to recover bits of embarrassing data from it. That's where Wipe Info comes in. If you'd like a file to be completely unrecoverable, Wipe Info is your tool. Wipe Info uses Department of Defense-approved methods to overwrite your data with enough nonsense to make that data completely unrecoverable.

Fast Find

Some people might suggest that Fast Find—a file-finding utility—is unnecessary, given that the Mac OS ships with a perfectly wonderful finding application called Sherlock. Those who make this suggestion obviously haven't explored some of Fast Find's more subtle features. Having found a file, for example, you can take a peek at some of the information that it contains—a nice idea when you have 892 Read Me files on your hard drive. You can also change the type and creator codes of a file from within Fast Find, as well as make file visible or invisible. Finally, you can edit a file's icon within FF. To be honest with you, I haven't used Fast Find since Sherlock came on the scene, but now that I've taken a second look, I think I'll use it more often.

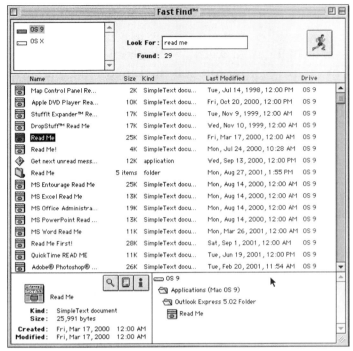

Fast Find Found. Sherlock is good, but Fast Find is a more comprehensive tool for finding (and manipulating) files on your hard drive.

Mac OS X compatibility

If you boot from the CD or an Mac OS 9.2 or earlier partition, you can repair an Mac OS X volume with the latest version of Norton Utilities.

The verdict

Disk Warrior and TechTool Pro demonstrate that you can build a useful diagnostic and repair utility for the Macintosh. Symantec had such a useful utility somewhere around version 3 of Norton Utilities, but the company has allowed Norton to rest on its laurels—laurels that have, I fear, become wilted with each unimpressive iteration of the program.

Extension Management

When I covered extension conflicts in Chapter 3, I pretty well covered techniques for weeding out troublesome startup items. And in doing so, I put forward the proposition that although Apple includes Extensions Manager with each copy of the Mac OS, no better tool for the job exists than Casady & Greene's Conflict Catcher. Because I've already discussed Extensions Manager and Conflict Catcher's capabilities in regard to troubleshooting extension conflicts, perhaps this is a good time to give you a peek at the other wonders they can perform.

Extensions Manager

Apple's Extensions Manager doesn't have a whole lot of other tricks up its sleeve. As I explained earlier in the book, you can use it to view items by packages—thus making it easier to switch on and off groups of related items—and use it to "halve" your extensions manually in an attempt to find the rotten apple among them. OK, you know all that. What else can you do with Extensions Manager? Well, how about the following?

Create custom startup sets

For reasons unknown to me, most users fail to use Extensions Manager's best feature: the capability to create custom extension sets for particular tasks. As you can probably tell by the subject of this book, I spend a fair amount of time troubleshooting Macs and use many troubleshooting utilities (and their extensions) to get the job done. Because such software can be a bit particular about extraneous extensions, I have created a specific set of extensions that contain only those items necessary for the Mac to operate and my utilities to perform. Here's how you can make your own extension set:

1. Begin by opening Extensions Manager, choosing Mac OS 9.x All (or whatever version of the Mac OS you're using) from the Selected Set pop-up menu, and then clicking the Duplicate Set button that appears in the bottom right of the Extensions Manager window.

2. In the Duplicate Set dialog box, give your new set of extensions a descriptive name (My Troubleshooting Stuff, for example).

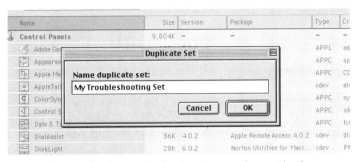

Set to Go. Duplicate a set of extensions and provide them a descriptive name.

3. Now run through the list of extensions, and switch on only those extensions that you really need.

   If you're preparing a troubleshooting set based on Norton Utilities, for example, configure Extensions Manager to display items by package and turn on just the Norton Utilities extensions you need.

   While you're in there flicking extensions and control panels on, be sure to flick *off* any extensions that you know you're not going to need. You likely won't be using Web Sharing or ColorSync, for example, so give them the gate.

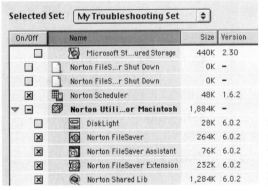

Get Picky. Choose only those extensions you need to get the job done.

4. Close Extensions Manager, and restart your Mac to start using your new set of extensions.

Wait, wait, wait, wait, *WAIT!* OK, OK, I hear you. A chorus of you just chimed, "But, Chris, for pity's sake, I don't know what *any* of these items do! How am I supposed to make an intelligent choice about which items to turn off and which to leave on?"

Excellent question, chorus. Here's my suggestion: If, for some strange reason, you haven't memorized the purpose of each of the 15,000 some-odd items that may grace your Mac's System Folder, and you're concerned about enabling or disabling the wrong things, duplicate that Mac OS 9.x All set of extensions, restart your Mac, and *then* install the software and hardware for which you want to create that extension.

When you do so, all the extensions and control panels necessary to make your software function properly will be installed in your customized set. With everything in place, you don't have to go in and tweak the on/off status of your startup items.

Locate startup items quickly

When you're working in Extensions Manager, you occasionally may need to open the Extensions or Control Panels folder to move or copy an item somewhere else—when you want to make a backup copy of an extension that might be replaced in a software update, for example. Yes, you can slog through the many layers of your hard drive to find the item, or you can use this trick:

1. In Extensions Manager, select the item to which you want to gain access, and choose Find Item (Command-F) from the Edit menu.

   In an instant, that item—along with its enclosing folder—appears before your eyes.

2. Should you care to learn more about an item, select it in Extensions Manager again, and choose Get Info (Command-I) from the Edit menu.

   As you might expect, the item's Get Info window appears.

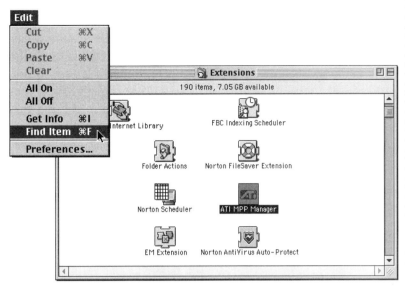

The Hidden Revealed. Extensions Manager's Find command is an easy way to reveal buried files quickly.

By the way, the Edit menu also contains an All On and All Off command, should you want to enable or disable everything at one go. This capability isn't quite as ineffectual as it sounds. I often have a couple of hundred startup items running at a time. (And no, you should not follow my example. I'm a trained professional.) When I want to create a stripped-down set of extensions and don't care to start with the Mac OS 9.x Base set, I simply switch everything off and then pick and choose the few extensions and control panels I want to switch on.

Mac OS X compatibility
You can use Extensions Manager to manage extensions in the Classic Environment.

The verdict
You own it already, and it's a perfectly useful, if somewhat limited, application. Enjoy!

Conflict Catcher

I admit that I'm goofy about Conflict Catcher. It's a utility that I believe every Mac troubleshooter running Mac OS 9.2 or earlier (and even those with only a passing interest in troubleshooting) should have on hand. But I've met knowledgeable folks who disagree with my assessment. Some people contend that it can cause its own extension conflicts and that its services can be replicated, in most part, by Extensions Manager. Willing as I am to accept counsel from other quarters, I generally respond to such judgments this way:

Phooey.

Now that that's settled, take a look at what else Conflict Catcher can do.

Clean-install system merge

When you perform a clean install of your System software, you have this delightfully tidy System Folder. But what about all those cool third-party add-on doodads that you had in your old System Folder? In all likelihood, you'd appreciate having many of those things in your new System Folder. Sure, you could rummage around in the old System Folder and drag those items over. But won't it be a kick in the pants when you try to launch one of these things and find that it won't because it's missing its preferences file or a related extension?

System Merge. Efficiently move items from your previous System Folder to a new one.

That's where the Clean-Install System Merge feature comes in. When you launch this thing, Conflict Catcher goes through your old System Folder and makes a long list of all the add-on items in it. You select the items you'd like to bring to your new System Folder and then tell Conflict Catcher to do its stuff. The program brings over not only those items but also any files necessary to make them work.

I'd almost buy Conflict Catcher for this feature alone.

Scan for Damage

Conflict Catcher is not intended to be a diagnostic/repair utility, but it will do you the courtesy of scanning files for damage if you ask politely. By default, you use this feature to check the items in your Extensions and Control Panels folder for damage, but you can scan other files and folders—particularly handy when you have a corrupt font lurking in your Fonts folder. Scan for Damage is another cool feature.

Secret game

Conflict Catcher allows you to turn on and off plug-ins, contextual-menu items, and control-strip items. Although this feature is admirable, what really rocks my boat is Conflict Catcher's hidden video game.

To reveal the game, open Conflict Catcher, and choose About Conflict Catcher from the Apple menu. When the About box appears, type play; then sit back and watch the fun begin.

Hint: Use the arrow keys to turn, the Option key for thrust, and the Control key to fire.

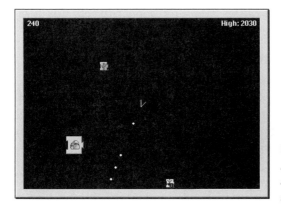

Unexpected Asteroids. And it plays games, too!

Couple of notes

Although I wouldn't like to cheat Casady & Greene out of sales, I feel that it's my duty to inform you that you can download a full-featured demo of Conflict Catcher that works for a few days. If you're really up against it or you'd just like to see how well Conflict Catcher performs, download the demo and give it a spin. If you're as impressed with the program as I am—and you intend to stick with Mac OS 9.2 or earlier for a while—you'll want to buy a copy of your own.

Also, I hate to bring my personal life into these matters, but given a situation a few years ago that wounded me deeply, I feel the need to share. Please bear with me.

Once upon a time, I awarded Conflict Catcher the highest rating *Macworld* magazine has to offer—5 mice—and talked up the program in a big way throughout my review. A couple of months later, I received an email message from a reader who was absolutely furious with me. This reader felt that the program was completely useless because it didn't keep his Mac from crashing after it was up and running. I politely responded that—as I had spelled out in the review—Conflict Catcher's job is to diagnose problems that occur *during* startup, not *after*. His response was far less polite. He claimed that my review had misled him, and he demanded that I personally refund the cost of the program. I demurred. Then, taking advantage of a very obscure portion of the criminal code, I had him incarcerated for a period of no less than 40 years.

Don't let this happen to you. To help you avoid such personal conflicts in the future, I must stress that Conflict Catcher does its job very well—helping you weed out errant extensions and control panels—but it's not a miracle worker. It won't keep your Mac from crashing after it's been running for a while, it won't recover lost files, and it won't wash your car.

Mac OS X compatibility

Conflict Catcher works within the Classic environment. As with Extensions Manager, if you hold down the space bar when the Classic environment first launches, Conflict Catcher appears, allowing you to manage your Classic extensions and control panels.

The verdict

I wouldn't have given Conflict Catcher those 5 mice if I didn't believe in it.

Backup Utilities

Considering that Dantz's Retrospect and Retrospect Express own this market lock, stock, and barrel, I admit that it does seem silly of me to create a category for backup utilities. Although Retrospect really is the only full-featured backup utility on the Mac market, I must mention one other utility that's a perfectly fine application for quick-and-dirty backups. That utility is Connectix's (www.Connectix.com) $39 CopyAgent.

CopyAgent

CopyAgent serves two main purposes: to speed local and network copies and perform automatic file backups. The copy function is a nice bonus, but the most compelling reason to buy the program is for easy file backups. It works this way:

1. Open CopyAgent, and choose Preferences from the Edit menu to open the Preferences dialog box.
2. Click the Copy Scheduler tab.
3. Click the Add button to create a new schedule.
4. Within this schedule, pick what you want to copy (a Daily Work folder that you create, for example), decide where you want to copy that folder to (a Zip drive, for example), and the time when you'd like that copy operation to take place.

    Easy as can be.

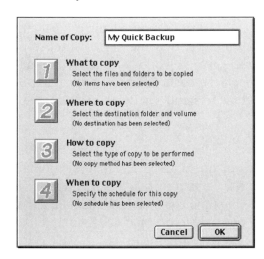

Four-Step Program. Creating quick-and-dirty automated backups is as simple as 1, 2, 3, 4.

CopyAgent is a good method for backing up individual files and folders automatically, but don't kid yourself that it's full-featured enough to serve all your backup needs. For real backups, you need a real backup utility, and that utility is Retrospect or Retrospect Express.

Mac OS X compatibility

The scheduled copy portion of Copy Agent works in the Classic environment. Other parts of the program—the feature for more-quickly emptying the Trash, for example—don't.

The verdict

CopyAgent is a nice little tool for people with modest backup needs.

Retrospect Desktop and Retrospect Express

Hang on a sec while I page back to Chapter 3. Let's see. I've already suggested that those who don't have a backup strategy are insane, that Retrospect Desktop and Retrospect Express are the only tools I recommend for a complete backup, that you set up an automated schedule so that you won't have to remember to remember to backup, and that you use a reliable backup medium.

That, as far as I'm concerned, covers the subject quite nicely. I might, however, remind you that the $50 Retrospect Express does not support network backup and isn't capable of backing up to certain storage devices (such as tape drives). The full-bodied, $175 Retrospect Desktop supports network backup for both Macs and PCs running one of the many varieties of Windows. A five-client pack, which works with any combination of networked Macs or PCs, costs $120. And speaking of networking, I discuss just how to setup a network backup server in Chapter 8.

Mac OS X compatibility

As I write this, there is not an Mac OS X-native version of Retrospect. Dantz tells me a version of Mac OS X is due soon (if not already available by the time you read this) that will allow Retrospect to do its job properly—the Mac OS X-compatible Retrospect 5 will follow shortly on its heels.

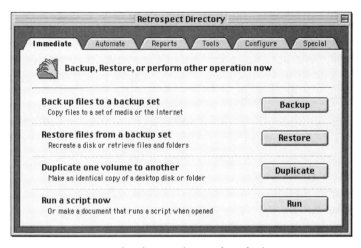

In Retrospect. Don't let the simple interface fool you. Retrospect is a powerful backup utility.

The verdict

Let's slip into this cozy syllogism, shall we?

- You must own a full-featured backup application.
- Retrospect is the only full-featured backup application available for the Mac.
- Therefore, you must own Retrospect.

Antivirus Utilities

I'm sorry to report that some people in this world are not as nice as you and me. Some of these people express their not-niceness by making outrageous demands of waiters; others talk through movies; still others create computer programs designed to cause mischief. This mischief can come in the form of such harmless pranks as messages that unexpectedly pop up on your screen or in more malignant forms that destroy data on your hard drive. These programs are generically termed *viruses*. The people who create them are specifically termed *jerks*.

If you pay the slightest bit of attention to the media, you've heard of computer viruses. These digital cooties bear such colorful names as Code Red, Sircam, and Michelangelo, and they garner a load of press when they're unleashed on the Web. And if you follow the press, you're likely concerned that one of these things is going to make its way to your Mac and commit unspeakable acts on your previously inviolate hard drive.

To those who stay up late at night worrying about such things, allow me to allay your fears: Your chances of contracting a computer virus are slim.

You see, because the jerks who give birth to these things crave the kind of attention their mommies weren't able to provide in those crucial developmental years, they write viruses that are likely to affect the greatest number of people. Fortunately—at least in this case—Macs are relatively uncommon compared with Windows PCs. For this reason, most computer viruses are developed for the enjoyment of Windows users. (Microsoft doesn't help matters by creating operating systems and browsers that are shot full of security holes, but I'll save that discussion for another time.)

The Mac's free ride in regard to viruses is likely to end once Mac OS X is widely adopted. UNIX—the operating system on which Mac OS X is based—has been around for a long time and those miscreants who've concocted UNIX viruses over the years may find Mac OS X a tempting target.

So before I discuss the various antivirus utilities, perhaps I should answer this important question: Do you really need a virus utility?

Perhaps not. This is one of those Chris-is-gonna-tell-you-how-it-really-is-but-don't-blame-him-if-you-don't-take-precautions-and-something-goes-dreadfully-wrong moments. As I write this chapter, few viruses floating around affect Mac OS 9.2 and earlier. If you download software from a reliable source—one of the big sites such as www.versiontracker.com, or an outfit such as Apple or Microsoft—your chances of getting a virus via download is nearly nonexistent. All these places scan files for viruses before they make them available to the public. Your chances of having a virus emailed to you at random is just as slim. Unlike Windows worms such as Sircam, there just aren't a ton of Macintosh viruses that dig into your email program and start sending out files willy-nilly to everyone in your address book. A friend could send you a virus unwillingly, however, so it's not a bad idea to know who your real friends are.

Occasionally, a computer virus sneaks through quality control and appears on a company's CD-ROM. In such cases, the word gets out quickly, and if you surf the Mac news sites, you'll know soon enough which discs to avoid.

That said, why get a virus utility at all? Well, there is the slight chance that a virus will make its way to you—particularly a cross-platform cootie such as a Microsoft Office macro virus (a virus that's triggered when you open a Word or Excel document that contains a malignant macro). Also, things are cool now, but as I mentioned earlier, Mac OS X is a different kettle of fish. I'm not a psychic and obviously can't predict what will happen next year. (Heck, I'm not always sure what's happening right now.) If someone were to come to me today and say, "Chris, I'm down to my last few dollars. Should I buy antivirus software for my Mac running Mac OS 9.2 or earlier or make that long-overdue car payment?" I'd unhesitatingly recommend taking the measures necessary to ward off the repo man. If that same person was running Mac OS X a year from now and we Mac users were experiencing half the quality and quantity of viruses flung at today's Windows users, I might gently prod the questioner's belly and suggest that a brisk stroll to and from work each day would do him no great harm.

What to Look For

I also can't predict what new varieties of antivirus utilities will appear in the next couple of years. But I can tell you what to look for in any such utilities that might appear. Keep a keen eye out for the following:

> **Automatic updates.** A fat lot of good your virus utility does you if it hasn't heard of a cootie that was introduced a few weeks ago. Neither is it any help if you forget to venture out onto the Web to download the latest virus-definition file. A good antivirus utility will download (or at least check for) new virus-definition files automatically once a month.
>
> **Suspicious-behavior scanning.** Suppose that your antivirus program downloaded the latest virus definition file on June 1, and a new virus crops up on June 4. Another update to the definition file isn't due for almost

a month, yet your Mac remains susceptible to this new disease. This can be a very bad thing if your virus utility isn't crafty enough to keep an eye on your computer and throw up an alert when viruslike activity takes place. Although there's no guarantee that such a feature will keep your Mac from becoming infected by a particularly virulent virus, this feature may provide a measure of protection.

Media, Web, and network scanning. Viruses are brought to your Mac in three ways: removable media (such as a CD-ROM disk), the Internet, and a network. When you propel a piece of media into your Mac or receive a file from the Web or a network, your antivirus utility should have the capability to scan that media or file for destructive data. And because most Web downloads come in compressed or archive form—.sit, .bin, .sea, .hqx, or .zip files—the utility must also be able to open and scan these compressed files before they have the chance to infect your computer.

Repair and quarantine. Certain viruses can attach themselves to otherwise perfectly kosher files—files that you might like to use. For this reason, your antivirus utility should be able to remove the infected portion of the file. If the file is incurably tainted or the entire file is a virus, the utility must be able to quarantine or delete the file so that it can't do any further harm.

Antivirus applications can also do undesirable things. These things include:

Lack of stability/extension conflicts. Under Mac OS 9.2 and earlier, antivirus utilities do their scanning magic with the help of extensions and control panels. I've found that these add-ons can make my Mac less stable, and more often than not, I risk the slight danger to which I might be exposing my Mac by removing the antivirus software in exchange for the stability I gain.

Overzealousness. Another sure way to get me to switch off my antivirus software is to have alerts pop up every time I look cross-eyed at my Mac. Fortunately, good antivirus applications allow you to customize the behavior of the utility. You can tell Joe Blow Inc.'s Cootie Killer to butt the heck out when you start up or shut down your Mac, for example. Likewise, when an alert appears, you can tell the program to remember the kind of action that prompted the alert and to never, ever produce an alert when this activity reoccurs.

The Players

Here in late 2001, three main antivirus utilities are on the market: Intego's (www.intego.com) $50 VirusBarrier, Network Associates' (www.nai.com) $50 Virex, and Symantec's (www.symantec.com) $70 Norton AntiVirus. All three utilities offer the options I suggest you look for: automatic updates, suspicious-behavior scanning, scanning of compressed files, and file repair and quarantine.

VirusBarrier is not as configurable as the other two utilities, which is both good and not so good. It stays out of the way (good) but doesn't give you a whole lot of control over the way the program goes about its business (not so good). Norton AntiVirus is *extremely* configurable—to the point, perhaps, that some users might be overwhelmed.

Norton AntiVirus can also be booted from the CD on which it ships—a great feature if your hard drive is infected and your drive is no longer bootable or you need to boot from a disc that can't be contaminated. (A read-only CD-ROM disc is just such a disc.) The utility can scan Mac OS X volumes for viruses as well.

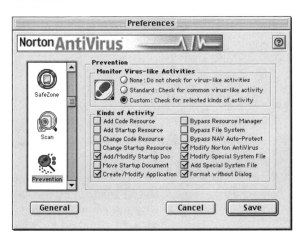

Exercising Your Options. Norton AntiVirus offers you many ways to configure the application. Perhaps too many.

But I have to admit that when I mentioned the two undesirable characteristics—lack of stability and overzealousness—I had Norton in mind. This is another one of those "feeling" things. It just seems that when my Mac has Norton AntiVirus installed, it's less stable. When I switch it off, my Mac seems happier. What definitely is *not* a feeling is that I'm far more harassed when Norton AntiVirus is installed. Although I admire the program's tenacity in protecting me from viruses, I often wish that it would just leave me alone and take care of more of its business in the background. Because the utility is so configurable, you can turn off a lot of the scans and warnings.

And Virex? I saved the best for last. Virex provides me the level of care I desire without making a big show of it. It's a powerful program, but it doesn't demonstrate that power by popping up virus or suspicious-activity warnings throughout the day. Also, my Mac seems to run perfectly well with the Virex extension and control panel installed.

Mac OS X compatibility

In late 2001, Norton AntiVirus is able to scan Mac OS X volumes for viruses when run from the Norton CD or from a Mac OS 9.2 or earlier volume. Mac OS X-native versions of Virus Barrier and Virex are slated for release in early 2002.

The verdict

I prefer Virex. Norton AntiVirus gets nod No. 2 for being so comprehensive, and VirusBarrier comes in third.

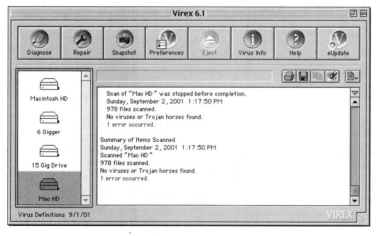

Cootie Killer. Although Norton AntiVirus, Virus Barrier, and Virex will clear out cooties, I prefer Virex for its ease of use and stability.

Firewall Utilities

Because I'm talking about bad things done by bad people, I'll talk firewalls. If you're unfamiliar with the term, a *firewall* is a hardware or software barrier that you place between your computer and others on a network or the Internet.

Why would you need such a thing? When you open a connection to a network or the Internet, it's a *two-way* connection. Information can go out as well as come in. This problem wasn't a big one when everyone used modems to get onto the Internet. Modem users open a connection to the Web to do email or Web surfing, and when they're done, they break that connection. By contrast, DSL, cable, and satellite broadband connections are always on; users don't have to open and shut their passages to the Web. Although the convenience is terrific, it also makes it far easier for other people on the Web to gain access to your computer and, if they so desire, to do some damage.

Now before you get all het up and rip the DSL wire from the wall, consider the subject reasonably. Yes, there are people in this great, wide electronic world who find it amusing to break into other folks' computers. More often than not, these people—who are almost always kids who haven't yet developed more wholesome habits—just want to see whether they *can* access your computer. Rarely do they return to make off with your carefully prepared dung-beetle database. But on occasion, these kids have more wicked motives and attempt to do your computer wrong or use your computer in ways you might not care for.

Much like viruses, this risk is of greater concern to Windows users, because Windows is inherently less secure than Mac OS 9 is. I'm not just bragging; it's the truth.

Of course I must insert the Mac OS X caveat here. No one is quite sure how secure Mac OS X is or how wily UNIX geeks are likely to be about Apple's new operating system. If you're a Mac OS X user with an always-on connection to the Web, I'd recommend a firewall. I'll talk more about such a firewall in Chapter 6.

> ### Slam the Door
>
> If you're running Mac OS 9.2 or earlier, you can make your Mac more secure from hackers immediately. Open the File Sharing control panel, and uncheck the Enable File Sharing Clients to Connect Over TCP/IP checkbox. Doing so makes it very difficult for someone to access your Mac remotely.
>
>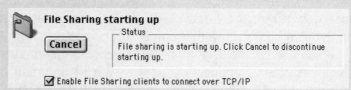
>
> **A More Secure Mac.** Flipping off sharing over TCP/IP makes your Mac less susceptible to outside invasion.
>
> And as for you, Mr. Mac OS X Smarty Pants, who claims that you have to have this option enabled to share files between a Mac running Mac OS X and another running Mac OS 9.2 and earlier, not with Mac OS 10.1 and later—you don't. If you've enabled AppleTalk in the Network system preference for the protocol you use to connect the two computers (Ethernet or AirPort, for example), you can make the connection via AppleTalk.
>
> For those of you who were completely mystified by the preceding paragraph, don't worry; I talk about networking in Chapter 8.

If the Mac OS is so secure, do you really need a firewall? The answer depends on how great a worrier you are. If you'll rest better knowing that your Mac is protected from intruders, go forth and firewall. I'd be the last person to chastise you, because, although I believe that the risk of being hacked is very small, I do run a software firewall on all my Macs. Better safe than sorry, I say.

Now take a look at your options.

Hardware Firewalls

If you want to be ultra-doubly-mega-safe, you'll opt for a box called a *router* that includes a hardware firewall. A router does exactly what its name implies—takes the single signal from the Internet and routes it to one or more computers. During this routing, the firewall component can block access to various parts of your computer selectively. You can set up the firewall so that only the Web-serving functions of your Mac are accessible, for example. These devices include four or more Ethernet jacks and are placed between your Internet connection (your cable modem, for example) and your computer.

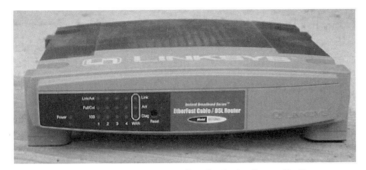

Route About Now. A router with a built-in firewall allows you to share a single IP address among a group of computers as well as protect those computers from Internet and network assault.

A router is largely intended for the computer geeks among us. (I have one, so if you count yourself among that number, there's no shame in it.) A router is ultra-doubly-mega-safe for a couple of reasons. Reason one is because it's a separate hardware device with a separate Internet address. A hacker may be able to get to the router but shouldn't be able to get beyond it to the computers connected to it. Reason two is that routers are highly configurable. You can set up all kinds of convoluted access privileges with these things.

But because they're so highly configurable, routers are not the easiest devices for novice and intermediate computer users to set up. Routers rarely come with Mac-compatible software and usually have to be configured with a browser. If you're not up to this kind of thing—and I don't expect a lot of you to be—skip the hardware firewall and look instead at a software firewall.

If you are interested in a router/firewall combination, I've had very good luck with Linksys products (www.linksys.com). These devices run around $150 or less.

Software Firewalls

A software firewall does the same kind of thing as a hardware router. The difference is that the firewall resides on the host computer, rather than in an external hardware device.

As of middling-late 2001, a couple of software firewalls are available for the Mac. One is Intego's $50 NetBarrier, and the other is Symantec's $49 Norton Personal Firewall for Macintosh. I hate to sound like a broken record, but this area is another one in which a product bearing the Norton name fails to take the prize. I tested both products with a port-probing service on the Internet—a service that looks for breaches in a computer's security—and NetBarrier hid my Mac from these probes more completely than Norton Personal Firewall did. Norton Firewall has a fine interface and a cool self-test feature but it fails to provide the one thing I really want from a firewall: a sense of security.

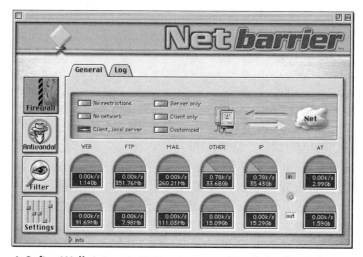

A Softer Wall. Intego's NetBarrier provides all the firewall capabilities that most people need.

Mac OS X compatibility

Not. You need an OS-native firewall utility.

The verdict

Intego's NetBarrier by a nose.

Mac OS X

Troubleshooting the "Trouble-Free" Mac OS

My guess is that the last remaining dodo wished that its great-great-great-great-great-great-great-great-grandfather and Charles Darwin had had the opportunity to meet over lunch and toss around this whole "evolve or die" business. Fortunately, the unfortunate legacy of this large, flightless bird was not lost on Apple Computer. The company well understood that an operating system devised in the early 1980s had a limited shelf life. At some point, Apple must leave the past behind and step boldly into the 21st century.

That step is a little something called Mac OS X (pronounced *ten* not *ex*). Mac OS X is unlike any previous iteration of the Mac OS. More than an upgrade of the Mac OS we know and love, Mac OS X is a new operating system based on NeXT Computer's NeXTStep operating system, which in turn is built on Unix.

Although Mac OS X was designed to reflect the feel of the earlier Mac OS—complete with menus, icons, and windows—it's *not* the earlier Mac OS. That look and feel are in a familiar environment (called Aqua) built on top of an operating system completely foreign to any previous version of the Mac OS.

The X Advantage

From a troubleshooter's perspective, what's so nifty about Mac OS X?

Preemptive multitasking. If you've followed the Windows world in any way, you've probably heard this term. Microsoft has been trumpeting this feature for several years, yet when you ask your average Windows user what it means, they haven't a clue. It means that the operating system can stop and start a job that the computer is performing efficiently to devote the processor's attention to another task. If your Mac is exporting an iMovie to QuickTime, for example, and you launch a spreadsheet and ask the Mac to create a chart, the operating system, through preemptive multitasking, acts as a traffic cop, deciding when the processor should work on the movie and when it should deal with the chart.

The old Mac OS was able to share processes as well by using something called *cooperative multitasking.* In cooperative multitasking, it was the job of applications to manage a processor's time (rather than the job of the OS). If an application failed to manage that time properly, it could crash and bring the whole shootin' match down with it. Because the operating system is the sole arbiter of a processor's time in preemptive multitasking, this tug of war between applications is a thing of the past.

Protected memory. I mentioned this topic in Chapter 1. For those who've forgotten, protected memory is a scheme whereby applications are allowed to glom onto their own portions of RAM. Because applications don't share memory under Mac OS X, you don't face situations in which a memory error causes the entire Mac to collapse. Instead, memory errors are confined to a single application. Should that applications crash, other applications—and the Mac OS itself—are unaffected.

Dynamic memory allocation. Under Mac OS X, applications can grab as much or as little RAM as they need. If you've spent any significant amount of time with Mac

OS 9.2 and earlier, you've undoubtedly seen an error message indicating that such-and-such a program doesn't have enough memory to carry out a particular chore. To skirt this error, you had to quit the application, open its Get Info window, and adjust the amount of RAM assigned to it manually.

This procedure is unnecessary now, thanks to dynamic memory allocation. If an application needs more memory, Mac OS X finds it—either giving up any spare RAM it can find or using virtual memory. (Virtual memory is on all the time in Mac OS X and is much more efficiently implemented than in Mac OS 9.2 and earlier.)

No extensions and control panels. Apple doesn't want anyone dinking around with its pristine operating system, and to protect the OS from such dinking, Apple has made it very difficult for outsiders to patch the OS. Whereas the Mac OS of old could be enhanced by extensions and control panels, Apple has pretty much locked the door with Mac OS X. Users who want to patch Mac OS X must do so in new ways—ways that Apple may very well break with updates to the OS.

From the point of view of users who are looking for an extensible OS and developers who'd like to provide those extensions to their customers, this arrangement isn't so hot. You'll find that many of the utilities you relied on in Mac OS 9.2 and earlier—utilities such as QuicKeys, StuffIt Deluxe, Now Up-to-Date, and Norton Utilities—have *fewer* features in Mac OS X than they did in the old Mac OS. This situation isn't the fault of the folks who produce these tools; they'd love to give you more capabilities with the Mac OS X version. But to ensure the most stable operating system it can create, Apple has barred their way.

This is good news for troubleshooters, however. No extensions and control panels means no extension conflicts—one of the greatest sources of problems in Mac OS 9.2 and earlier.

Where X Has No Influence

Given the preceding section, those of you running Mac OS X exclusively may wonder whether the first half of this book wasn't a waste of your time. You've leaped aboard the Mac OS X bandwagon, so why should you be concerned about the material in the first few chapters?

You should be concerned because a Mac is still a Mac. By this, I mean that it makes no difference whether you're running Mac OS 8.5, 9.2, X, or (heaven forbid) Linux on your Macintosh. If your Mac has a hardware problem—bad RAM, a funky cable, or a corrupt hard drive—it will suffer regardless of which operating system you've installed.

Therefore, it's important to understand when a problem is Mac-related (specifically due to a misbehaving component or connection) and when that problem can be blamed on the OS. Generally speaking, if your Mac fails to boot properly—it appears DOA when you push the Power button, it won't reach the startup screen, you hear error tones, or perhaps you see a blinking folder icon—you should run through the hardware-troubleshooting procedures I outlined in Chapter 2. If your Mac boots successfully and then exhibits some sort of wonky behavior, it's time to scrutinize the OS.

Not Quite Bulletproof

Considering that preemptive multitasking, protected memory, and dynamic memory allocation purportedly end application crashes that bring down the entire Mac OS, and considering that the lack of extensions and control panels eliminates one of the major causes of startup problems, Mac OS X should be trouble-free, right?

Well, no.

Your Mac can still refuse to boot under Mac OS X, applications can still freeze, files can still become corrupted, and your Mac can still crash. You may have these problems less often than in Mac OS 9.2 and earlier, and some of them may be easier to work around in Mac OS X, but Apple's next-generation operating system is hardly invincible.

Given that Mac OS X can't stop a speeding bullet or leap tall buildings at a single bound, the rest of this chapter talks about how you can protect yourself from Mac OS X problems.

Be Prepared

I'm sorry to keep introducing the phrase "as I write this" in this narrative, but the simple fact is that *as I write this chapter,* Mac OS X is not yet completely baked. It was only in September 2001 that Apple released a version that was really worth a darn: Mac OS X 10.1. Previous versions designed for early adopters were, frankly, fairly marginal—slow and incapable of performing such routine chores as burning a CD, playing a DVD, and configuring an AirPort network. Given that Mac OS X will remain a work in progress for many months (and, possibly, years) to come, you'll be doing yourself a favor by protecting your data and making a few provisions before installing Mac OS X.

These provisions include:

Get Religion; Back up Your Data!

I've railed about having a comprehensive backup before, but this time, I really mean it. At times, the only way to get a working copy of Mac OS X back onto your hard drive is to start over and reformat the drive (thus erasing all the data on it).

Here's a for-instance: Shortly before this book went to press, Apple released a couple of updates for Mac OS X that improve security. These updates appeared when you ran Mac OS X's Software Update application and, if you chose to download them, were installed automatically. Unfortunately, most Mac users didn't realize that after these updates are in place, the only way to restore Mac OS X is to reformat the Mac OS X volume (there goes your data!), reinstall Mac OS X 10.1, and then reinstall these security updates.

If you cavalierly reinstalled Mac OS X with the idea that you could perform the same kind of clean-install procedure that you can use in Mac OS 9.2 and earlier (replacing only the System Folder and holding onto your other data), you'd be in for a rude awakening when you realize that everything on your Mac OS X volume has just flown the coop. With a backup in hand, you're inconvenienced rather than devastated.

Also, do you really want to trust your valuable data to an evolving operating system? Big changes are in store, and nobody knows what havoc those changes might wreak. With Mac OS X, you really, really need the safety net that a reliable and comprehensive backup provides.

If you're reading this book in the early months of 2002, a complete backup solution is not available to you. The portions of OS X necessary for a backup utility such as Dantz's Retrospect to backup and restore a bootable volume are not yet in place. Dantz claims those resources will appear in an upcoming version of Mac OS X. When that Mac OS X update ships, a fully Mac OS X-compatible version of Retrospect will ship shortly thereafter.

In the meantime, your best backup bet is to save copies of your documents and third-party applications on another volume. This way, should you have to initialize your Mac OS X volume, your data and non-Apple applications are safe.

Quarantine Mac OS X

I don't mean to imply that Mac OS X is in any way contaminated. I'm just suggesting that you create a place that Mac OS X can call its own—specifically, a partition on your hard drive or a separate hard drive. That way, should you need to erase the volume on which Mac OS X resides, you're killing only your Mac OS X stuff. All your Mac OS 9.2 and earlier data remains intact.

Create a Mac OS 9.2 Volume

Even if you plan to work with Mac OS X exclusively, it's a good idea to maintain a partition with the old Mac OS on it. Why?

To begin with, when you boot into Mac OS X, you don't have access to all the files and folders on your Mac OS X drive unless you log in as a sort of Supreme Being (the root user, in Unix lingo). Mac OS X is designed as a multiple-user environment, meaning that lots of people can use the same computer, yet each person has his or her own environment (an environment that most other users can't muck with). When you boot into Mac OS 9.2 and earlier, you can slog through any Mac OS X folders and files you like.

Second, there's currently no way to boot from an Mac OS X CD-ROM disc into Mac OS X's Desktop environment, where you see your Mac's hard drives, Dock, and so on. Instead, when you insert an Mac OS X CD into your Mac and hold down the C key at startup, your Mac boots into the Mac OS X Installer. The Installer has its uses, but unfortunately, it doesn't allow you to browse your hard drive.

Third, although the Big Boys of Mac troubleshooting and repair utilities—Disk Warrior, Norton Utilities, and TechTool Pro—can help you fix an Mac OS X volume, these utilities (*as I write this*) work only when you run them from an Mac OS 9.2 or earlier environment. Yes, you can boot from the utility's CD, but *sheesh*, what a bother, particularly when you want to run more than one troubleshooting utility.

And finally, Macs manufactured in the past few years have a wonderful feature that allows you to choose which operating system your Mac boots into. Just hold down the Option key during startup, and a screen pops up that displays the bootable volumes on your Mac. Click the volume you want to start from and then click the Arrow button, and your Mac *boots* from that volume. If your Mac OS X volume won't boot for whatever reason, having a Mac OS 9.2 volume at the ready makes it easy to get your Mac up and running.

Mac OS X Problems

You'll find the difficulties you suffer in Mac OS X to be somewhat similar to those you face in Mac OS 9.2 and earlier. The following sections look at these problems and their workarounds.

Your Mac Won't Boot

Rather than copy and paste a huge chunk of an earlier chapter into this space, I'm going to assume that you've determined that your problem is not hardware-related; you've checked all your connections and unplugged any hardware that may be causing conflicts. Your Mac appears to start up properly, making all the right noises and blinking the proper lights. Then, *kablooey*, something untoward happens. That something might include:

Blinking folder icon. The blinking folder icon means the same thing in Mac OS X that it does in earlier versions of the Mac OS: The Mac is unable to locate a bootable system.

Indecipherable text on a dark screen. Instead of being taken to the Mac's Login window or to the Mac OS X Desktop, you're greeted with a few lines of code that mean absolutely nothing to you. This code is a sign that the Mac is trying to boot into Mac OS X but some problem has stopped it along the way.

Solution 1: Try to boot any way you can

Before trying anything tricky, be doubly sure that the problem isn't hardware-related by first attempting to boot from your Mac OS 9.2 volume or from some variety of Mac OS 9.x CD. After booting from Mac OS 9, make sure that your Mac OS X volume exists and that the volume contains the folders (called directories in Mac OS X) that Mac OS X expects to find: the System, Library, Applications, and Users directories. If everything appears to be present and accounted for...

Solution 2: Select your Mac OS X volume in the Startup Disk control panel

Yeah, I know, you thought you were booting into Mac OS X before. I've faced situations in which I wound up in the Open Firmware screen (a gray window with *Open Firmware* at the top that contains more arcane code) after I thought my Mac was supposed to be booting into Mac OS X. By rebooting into Mac OS 9.2 and selecting my Mac OS X volume in the Startup Disk control panel, I was able to boot successfully into Mac OS X.

Solution 3: Boot from your Mac OS X Installation CD and run Disk Utility

Disk Utility is a single Mac OS X application that contains the Mac OS X versions of Apple's basic troubleshooting and formatting tools, Disk First Aid and Drive Setup. To use Disk Utility:

1. Insert your Mac OS X Installation CD, and restart the Mac while holding down the C key.

2. On late-model Macs, you can also restart while holding down the Option key and then select the CD as your startup disc on any Mac OS X-compatible Mac, or insert the disc in Mac OS 9.2 and earlier and double-click the Install Mac OS X application, at which point the Mac restarts with the Mac OS X installer.
3. Click the First Aid tab.
4. On the left side of the Disk Utility window, click the drive that contains your Mac OS X volume.
5. Click the Verify button to check your drive for problems.
6. If First Aid reports problems, click the Repair button.
7. Quit Disk Utility by choosing Quit from the Disk Utility menu (or pressing Command-Q).
8. Quit the Installer application.
9. When the Quit sheet appears (*sheet* is Mac OS X's term for *dialog box*), click the Restart button.

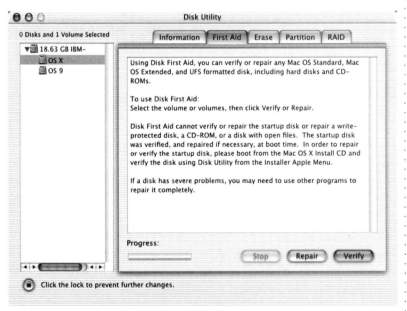

First Line of Defense. Disk First Aid—part of Mac OS X's Disk Utility—may bring your Mac back from the dead.

No Mac OS X Install Disc?

Apple now ships Mac OS X with every Mac it sells. Regrettably, it doesn't include a separate Mac OS X Install disc with some of those Macs. Instead, Mac OS X is included on a set of Software Restore discs and is reinstalled with everything else on your hard drive (after that hard drive has been erased). I pray that this short-sighted policy will no longer be in effect when you read this book, but if it is, there's another way to get to Disk First Aid without the Install CD. Here's how:

1. In Mac OS 9.2 or earlier, open the Startup Disk control panel, and select the Mac OS X volume as your startup disk.
2. Restart your Mac, and hold down Command-S.

   You've just booted into Mac OS X's Single User mode. You'll see a black screen that contains line after line of obscure code. Avert your eyes unless you're interesting in this kind of arcane information. The text will eventually stop flashing down the screen, and you'll see an entry that reads `localhost#`.

3. Type `/sbin/fsck -y` and press Return.

   You've just entered your first Unix command (and aren't you *proud!*) and told Mac OS X to run a Unix repair function called fsck (which stands for File System Check). Apple has glommed Disk First Aid functionality onto fsck, so essentially, you're running Disk First Aid without having to go the Installer.

4. If fsck finds problems and then repairs them, you'll see a message that reads `FILE SYSTEM WAS MODIFIED`, followed by your old friend `localhost#`, so run fsck again until you see the message The volume [volumename] appears to be OK.

   [volumename] is the name of your Mac OS X volume.

5. Type `exit` to continue startup or, if you want to give your Mac a clean start, type `reboot`.

Solution 4: Run a third-party diagnostic/repair utility

In Chapter 5 I mentioned that tools such as Disk Warrior, Norton Utilities, and TechTool Pro can repair corruption on Mac OS X discs. For them to do so, you must have a recent version of these utilities And please—unless you're dead certain that the version you have is compatible with Mac OS X, check with the software publisher's Web site to confirm that your software is compatible. Using older versions of these utilities could make your problems far worse.

Solution 5: Reinstall Mac OS X

If all else fails, there's one sure cure: Reinstall the sucker.

"What!? There's nothing more I can do?"

Well, yes. You could become well versed in Unix, boot into Single User mode, log on, and start entering line after line of commands. This procedure may sound like oodles of fun to you, but it doesn't to me. Unless I know that the right Unix command is going to put my Mac in the pink in short order, I'll double-check that my important files and applications are backed up and reinstall a fresh copy of Mac OS X.

You have a couple of options when you reinstall Mac OS X. You can run a standard reinstall—one in which the installer places a new copy of Mac OS X on your drive but leaves almost everything else you've added since you've first installed OS (or it was installed on a new Mac by Apple). Or you can erase the Mac OS X volume and start fresh, thus erasing the data on the volume as well.

The point at which you must make the decision to perform a standard reinstall or wipe the drive comes in the Select a Destination window. In this window appear the mounted volumes—your Mac OS 9 and Mac OS X partitions and the Mac OS X Install CD, for example—and a little option at the bottom that reads Erase Destination and Format As. If you leave this option unchecked, the Installer installs a new copy of Mac OS X and leaves your Mac OS X volume relatively untouched. By *relatively*, I mean that your users are maintained, but certain applications may be replaced. If you've installed a copy of iTunes 2, for example, and the Installer includes the original iTunes as part of the installation, your copy of iTunes 2 is replaced with the earlier iteration of iTunes.

If you check the Erase Destination and Format As option, you'll have the opportunity to format the volume either as an Mac OS Extended volume or as a Unix File System volume. Unless you have a very good reason for doing otherwise, choose Mac OS Extended. When you click the Continue button, the Installer formats the selected volume and installs a clean copy of Mac OS X. When you restart your Mac, the Mac OS X Setup Assistant appears, and you go about the business of creating a new user.

As I mentioned previously in this chapter, you may not have the option to directly reinstall the version of Mac OS X on your hard drive. Instead, you may have to wipe the Mac OS X volume clean, install an earlier version of Mac OS X, and then apply a series of updates to bring the operating system up to the current version.

> **Create a Bootable Disc within Mac OS X**
>
> In Mac OS X 10.1, you can create a bootable CD with Apple's Disc Burner. Here's how:
>
> 1. Running Mac OS X 10.1, insert a bootable CD (your Mac's Software Install CD, for example) and launch Disk Copy, located in the Utilities folder inside Mac OS X's Applications folder.
> 2. Choose New Image from Device from the Image menu.
> 3. In the resulting dialog box, select your CD-ROM drive and click the Image button.
> 4. When you're asked, specify a location for the image as well as its format.
>   Place the image wherever you like, and choose CD/DVD Master from the Format pop-up menu.
> 5. Make sure that None is selected in the Encryption pop-up menu.
> 6. Click the Image button.
> 7. When Disk Copy finishes creating the image, choose Mount Image from Disk Copy's File menu.
>   When the image is mounted, you can modify it any way you like (add troubleshooting utilities, for example).
> 8. When you've finished modifying your disk, unmount the image by dragging it to the Trash; then choose Burn Image from the Image menu.
> 9. Select the image file you created and click Burn to create your bootable disc.

The Login Window Appears, But Your Username Is Nowhere to Be Seen

The Mac is able to boot into Mac OS X, but for some reason, the Mac isn't able to locate your User data. This situation could indicate a corrupt User folder or, if this happens after you've attempted to reinstall Mac OS X (or install an update), an incomplete install.

Unix can help with this problem in a couple of ways. The commands aren't terribly difficult, but if the following makes you queasy, feel free to reinstall Mac OS X.

Solution 1

When you start up your Mac, hold down Command-S to boot into Single User mode.

You'll see a black screen with white letters racing across it. Eventually, the Mac will stop with the letters. You should see the word `localhost#` (if you don't, press Return).

Type the following, pressing Return after each line. (Yes, spacing and capitalization are vitally important.)

Notice that as you press Return, `localhost#` returns. This situation is normal. Just continue to type the commands and press Return.

```
mount -uw /
cd /private/var/db/netinfo
mv local.nidb local.old
rm ../.AppleSetupDone
exit
```

Your Mac will continue to boot up. When it finishes, the Setup Assistant that appeared the first time you installed Mac OS X will appear again. Run through the Setup Assistant again to create your user identity.

If you're interested in knowing what you've just done, you've essentially instructed your Mac to move an invisible database file (one that keeps track of users) to another location. Then you told the Mac to remove the AppleSetupDone file—a file that tells the Mac that you've run the Setup Assistant successfully. With this file trashed, the Mac thinks you're setting Mac OS X up for the first time and so launches the Setup Assistant.

Please note that this works in Mac OS X 10.1, it may not work in any subsequent version of Mac OS X. When Apple issues an update to Mac OS X, it has been known to move directories around or introduce new elements into the operating system that can make tricks that worked beautifully under a previous version of the OS fall flat in the updated version.

Solution 2

Before you begin, I must issue two warnings.

- If you follow this procedure, you will lose your Documents, Movies, Music, Pictures, Public, and Sites folders. I strongly recommend that before you implement Way 2, you boot into Mac OS 9.2 or earlier, open your Mac OS X volume, and back up these folders onto your Mac OS 9.2 volume.
- For this technique to work, you will have had to change the way Mac OS X displays the Login window.

By default, the Mac OS X Login window carries a list of users who are allowed to use the Mac and an icon that represents each user. To log in, you click the icon associated with your username and then enter your password in the text box that appears. There is an alternate way to login, however.

As an Administrator user, open the Login system preference and click the Login Window tab. Following the words Display Login Window As you'll see that the List of Users with Accounts on This Computer option is selected. Change this option to Name and Password Entry Fields.

Now when you log in to your Mac, you'll see two blank text boxes: one for your username and one for your password.

With this setup, you can finally proceed to Solution 2:

1. In the Login window, type `>console` in the username text box and click Log In.

   Don't enter anything in the Password field.

   A command-line console will appear, and you'll see the login prompt.

2. Enter your username and, when asked for it, your password.

3. Type `cd /Users` and then press Return.

4. Type `ls` and then press Return.

   You'll see a list of all the users who are authorized to use your Mac and the shared folder. You might see shared, chris, bubba, and biff, for example.

5. Type sudo rm -R *home* (*home* is the name of your Home directory—chris, in my case), and press Return.

   You'll see a warning and then will be asked for your password again.

6. Enter the password and press Return.

   You've just killed your old Home directory—the one that wouldn't allow you to log on. If you want to confirm that the director is gone, repeat the cd and ls commands. You should no longer see your Home directory in the list.

   Now you'll create a new Home directory.

7. Type sudo mkdir /Users/*home* (*home* is the name of the directory you just killed), and press Return.

8. Type sudo chown *theshortname*:staff *home* (*theshortname* is the short username you used, and *home*, as I think you know by now, is the name of your Home directory), and press Return.

   Were I to be entering this command, I would type sudo chown chris:staff chris.

9. Type exit and press Return.

   Your Mac will now boot to the Login window.

Phew! OK, what did that exercise do for you?

When you next log in, you should be able to enter your old username and password and log into Mac OS X. You will notice, however, when you open your Home directory that it contains only two folders: Desktop and Library.

As I warned you earlier, your Documents, Movies, Music, Pictures, Public, and Sites folders are gone. Fortunately, you followed my advice and backed up their contents. To restore them (but not their former contents), just open your Home directory, press Shift-Command-N to create a new folder, and name the folder Documents. When you press Return, the Documents folder will assume its custom icon and will be ready for business. Repeat this procedure for the other missing folders. Finally, copy the files you backed up into their respective replacement folders.

Your Mac "Freezes"

In Mac OS X, Macs don't freeze in the "I'm-so-totally-dead-I-can-hardly-stand-my-bad-self" way that they do in Mac OS 9.2. Instead, Mac OS X has picked up a little trick that's familiar to anyone who's used America Online: the Spinning Beach Ball of Death.

You know how it is. You're whiling away your time on AOL, and suddenly, everything grinds to a halt—save the spinning beach ball, which offers the vain hope that in a short while, the AOL application will actually do something more productive than make you wait for five minutes before telling you that you've been uncerimoniously booted off the system (*Goodbye!*).

Mac OS X performs this same trick from time to time. You're in an application, or even the Finder, and a rainbow-colored beach ball begins to spin—and spin and spin and spin and spin. (It's not a bad idea to let it spin for a while, particularly when your Mac is first booting, to make sure that your Mac really isn't busy with an important chore.) But after waiting for three minutes for this digital dervish to conclude its performance, you realize that this little ball is going to keep spinning until a ski resort opens in one of the hillier districts of Hades.

Solution 1: The Force Quit command

Because of Mac OS X's protected-memory scheme, you usually can unfreeze your Mac by demanding that the Mac forcibly quit the application (yes, even the Finder) that's causing the freeze. Unlike the case in Mac OS 9.2 and earlier, you have a reasonable hope of emerging from that Force Quit unscathed. The command works this way.

1. When you see the spinning beach ball, and you're sure that it's not going to stop, click an application (System Preferences will do) in the Dock to launch that application.

2. When the new application launches, choose Force Quit from the Apple menu.

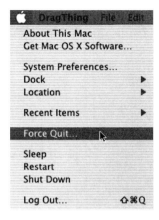

Bounce the Ball.
The Force Quit can put an end to an endlessly spinning beach-ball pointer.

3. In the Force Quit Applications window, click the name of the offending application and then click the Force Quit button.

4. Confirm your decision to Force Quit the application in the sheet that appears.

5. If you're force-quitting the Finder the Force Quit button will change to Relaunch; click this button without fear.

   You'll once again be asked to confirm your choice.

6. Click the Relaunch button in the Do You Want to Force Finder to Quit? sheet.

   After a couple of moments, the Finder will reappear, *sans* spinning beach ball.

Finder's Weepers.
Although you can't make the Finder quit permanently, you can force it to relaunch.

When you Force Quit an application, any open documents will be closed without changes being saved. Although a Force Quit won't bring your Mac to its knees, it's not an elegant way to quit an application. For this reason, it's a good idea to save early and often.

Solution 2: Quit with Process Viewer

You can also quit an application or background process from the Process Viewer utility (which you'll find in the Utilities folder inside the Applications folder). To do so:

1. Launch Process Viewer.

    You'll see a list of all the processes slogging along on your Mac. You'll note that only a few of these processes are applications you've launched; most of them are processes that Mac OS X requires to keep the OS up and running.

2. Scan the list of processes until you find the process you'd like to quit, select it, and choose Quit Process from the Processes menu.

3. When you're asked to do so, confirm your command.

    The process will quit.

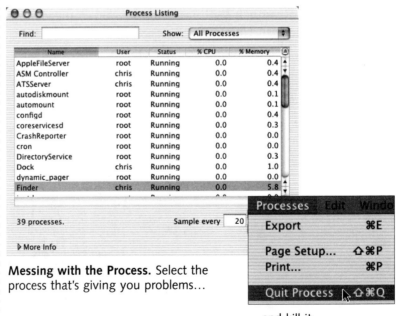

Messing with the Process. Select the process that's giving you problems...

...and kill it.

Now, why would you perform this action when using the Apple menu's Force Quit command is so much easier? Well, that Force Quit command lists only applications you've opened. If something else is gumming up the works—the Dock, for example—you can't quit it with Force Quit. Process Viewer offers you the option to quit background tasks. (The Dock, by the way, relaunches automatically when you quit it with Process Viewer, so you can't use this technique to kill the Dock.)

I need to issue a warning here: If you don't know what a particular process does, don't shut it off. You won't harm anything permanently if you do, but your Mac may not function properly again until you log out.

> **Process Viewer Escape Hatch**
>
> At times, the Finder locks up, the Force Quit keyboard command won't work, you can't get to the Force Quit menu command, and you can't open applications and utilities from the Finder (because, as I said, it's locked up). Here's a way to use the Process Viewer as an easy out.
>
> In the Utilities folder, locate Process Viewer, and drag its icon to the Dock. When the Finder next locks up, you should be able to launch Process Viewer from the Dock. When that utility is up and running, just select Finder in the list of processes and choose the Quit Process command from the Processes menu.

Solution 3: Log out

If this force-quitting business doesn't seem to be doing the trick, you can try logging out and then logging back in again. Doing so should take care of whatever was mucking up your Mac.

Solution 4: Restart

At times, you can't get away from that spinning beach ball; you try to launch another application to access the Force Quit command, and the Mac just won't cooperate. In such cases, it's best to just restart the Mac. You can accomplish this task on some Macs by pressing Command-Control-power key and on other Macs by pressing the Reset button. Your Mac's manual will tell you the proper way to restart your computer.

When you restart in this manner, none of your work will be saved, so use it only as a last resort.

Your Mac Panics

Mac OS X Macs don't crash; they panic. Specifically, the kernel—the essence of Mac OS X upon which everything else is built—panics. A kernel panic is akin to the Mac OS's being walloped by a 2-by-4. It can't recover from such a blow. Just as it goes down for the count, it issues a string of text that you're unlikely to understand and then gently breathes its last.

Solution 1: Restart

There's nothing else for it. A kernel panic is as bad as a complete crash in Mac OS 9.2 and earlier, and the only way to resuscitate you Mac is to restart. And because the Mac has panicked, the only way to restart is to use that Command-Control-power key or Reset button business I mentioned earlier in this chapter.

Solution 2: Check your hardware

I asked you earlier in this chapter to disconnect any external hardware if you're having problems with Mac OS X, but if your Mac panics, more than an errant USB printer could be causing the problem. The SCSI card inside your Power Mac G4 may not have a compatible driver, for example. The processor upgrade card may not function under Mac OS X. Or your add-on graphics card may drive Mac OS X crazy. If your Mac panics repeatedly and you've tried everything you can think of, start removing PCI cards. If you've replaced your original AGP graphics card with another, swap the new card out for the old one.

Solution 3: Check your firmware

Your Mac may need a firmware update to work reliably with Mac OS X. Boot into Mac OS 9.2 or earlier and run Software Update. If Software Update reports that a firmware update is available for your Mac, download and install it.

Solution 4: Think back

You don't recall moving certain folders (such as the Applications, System, or Library folder), do you? Moving those folders is a no-no in Mac OS X. Mac OS X expects certain folders to be in certain places, and if you move them, the Mac won't start up or will panic. If you did attempt a little housecleaning of your Mac OS X volume after booting into Mac OS 9.2

and earlier, go back to Mac OS 9.2 and earlier, and undo the changes you made. The Applications, Library, and System folders belong at the root level of your Mac OS X volume.

Solution 5: Reinstall Mac OS X

If your Mac continues to panic after each restart, and you can't trace the cause, it could be that something down deep has become corrupted. You can try to repair that corruption with Disk First Aid or a third-party troubleshooting utility, but you may find it easier simply to reinstall Mac OS X.

You've Lost Your Password

It happens sometimes. You're so excited about running this new OS that you hurriedly type a password when you first set up Mac OS X and are called away for a seven-month pleasure cruise. When you return, you draw a complete blank when Mac OS X asks for your password. Here's how to enter a new one:

1. Boot your Mac from the Mac OS X install CD.

    When the Installer application is up and running, choose Reset Password from the Installer menu.

2. Select your Mac OS X volume in the resulting window.

3. Choose your username from the Select a User pop-up menu.

4. Enter and confirm a new password in the text boxes.

5. Click Save.

    You're ready to log in with that new password.

You'll notice that in this window, you can also create a password for the System Administrator (root) user. I will take this opportunity to issue this stern warning: *Logging in as the root user provides you the opportunity to perform countless helpful and destructive actions. Delete, move, or inappropriately alter the wrong file, and your Mac could become inoperable—at least until you install a fresh copy of Mac OS X. If you don't know what you're doing, don't log in as root!*

For those of you who can boot into Mac OS X, have Administrator privileges, and would like to change your password, launch the Terminal application and type sudo passwd *username* (username is your, well, username). You'll see a warning to respect the privacy of others and to think before you type. After taking this advice to heart, type your old password at the prompt. When you are further prompted, type a new password of at least five characters and confirm that password.

Device X Doesn't Seem to Work with Your Mac

You've slipped a CompactFlash PC card adapter into your PowerBook's PC Card slot, and no business results. You attach a printer to your Power Mac G4, yet the printer doesn't appear in Print Center. You attach your Palm Pilot's HotSync cradle to your iBook, but Mac OS X doesn't offer a way to sync your handheld.

The solution is to be patient. Lousy solution, I know. But this is where you start to feel the sting of the unfinished state of Mac OS X.

The problem is twofold. The first part can be pinned on third-party vendors who are dragging their feet when it comes to creating Mac OS X-compatible drivers. They'll eventually get around to creating drivers for their recent creations but may never come up with drivers for older gear—thinking, perhaps, that there just aren't enough of these things around to justify the development cost. (The cynical Chris might also suggest that if you can't use that older gear with Mac OS X, you might be tempted to chuck it and purchase a new doodad from this company.)

But Apple plays a part in the problem as well. As much as a vendor may want to develop an Mac OS X driver for such-and-such thingamabob, the underlying structure of Mac OS X may not support it. As I write this chapter, the PC Card slot on PowerBooks is woefully undersupported. Considering that Apple continues to include this slot on its PowerBooks, there's every reason to believe that devices intended for this slot will one day be given their due. But Apple, understandably enough, has to prioritize. Image the uproar if Apple implemented support for a slot that few of its customers use, yet failed to allow all but a couple of printers to work with its computers.

The Mail App Won't...

Here we go again. *As I write this chapter,* the Mail application that ships with Mac OS X is pretty junky. You ask it to delete messages from the server, and it won't. You want to set up extensive mail filtering, and it can't. You want it to stop flashing some weird error when it starts up, and the error reoccurs every time you launch Mail.

Unless Apple rolls up its sleeves and creates a really worthwhile email client, I strongly recommend that you look elsewhere. Eudora (www.eudora.com), Qualcomm's email client, is currently shipping in a Mac OS X beta version. Eudora is wonderfully full-featured but the beta is a little flaky. It's my fervent hope that by the time you read this, Qualcomm will have released a solid shipping version of Eudora for Mac OS X. The down side of Eudora is that if you want to use it for free, you have to put up with a little window that displays advertisements. If you're willing to pungle up $50, you can make those ads go away.

The Mac OS X version of Microsoft Office includes an Mac OS X-native version of Entourage, an email client/personal information manager. It, too, is more capable than Mail.

Application X Got Weird!

SuperWhizzoPaint Pro for Mac OS X has been charging along like a champ, yet one day, it goes haywire. All your preferences seem to have been set back to the defaults, and the program behaves in a generally funky fashion.

A bad preference file in Mac OS X can give an application a bad case of the shakes, just as much as it can in Mac OS 9.2 and earlier, and tossing a miscreant preferences file can be just as helpful.

To locate the preferences file, open your Home directory, the Library folder within it, and then the Preferences folder. Inside, you'll find the preferences file that you seek. Just quit the misbehaving application and drag its preferences file to the Trash. When you relaunch the application, a new preferences file will be created. If the application's sunny disposition seems to have been restored, feel free to empty the Trash.

More !!!
For Less $$$

Upgrading Your Mac

Although Apple employees would, as one, don lampshades and strew confetti from one end of Cupertino to the other if you pungled up for a brand-new Mac whenever you became disenchanted with your computer's performance, few of us can afford to drop these kinds of dollars with any regularity. Fortunately, there are ways other than buying a new computer to appease your penchant for performance. All Macs manufactured in the past several years can be upgraded to include more RAM and higher-capacity hard drives. And many of these Macs also accommodate new processors and more-capable graphics cards. Given a little knowledge and a certain outlay of funds, you can turn many an older Mac into a computer capable of going head to head with Apple's latest offerings.

Upgrade Options

Given that you can upgrade many parts of your Mac, you may have a few questions. Such as:

- What should I upgrade first?
- Which upgrade is going to pay off in the greatest performance boost?
- How much money are we talking here?
- How difficult are these things to install?

Maybe the following sections will help.

RAM

Provided that RAM prices remain as low as they are as I write these words, increasing RAM is the most inexpensive upgrade you can perform. It's absolutely true that you can never be too beautiful or have enough RAM, and for this reason, upgrading RAM is the first thing I'd do. Increasing the Mac's memory allows you to open more applications at the same time, throw tons of memory at RAM-hungry applications such as Photoshop, speed your Mac by allowing you to turn off virtual memory, and create enormous RAM disks. (RAM disks is an option in the Mac OS 9 Memory control panel that lets you move applications—even the System Folder, if you have a bucketload of RAM—into a virtual hard disk created entirely of RAM.)

Although installing RAM in early iMacs and some PowerBooks is a bit tricky, it's a cinch on most Macs made in the past 10 years.

Hard drive

About a year after I started using a Mac, I purchased a 100 MB hard drive—one of the most expansive drives available at the time—for around $1,000. I'm pleased to report that since 1988, hard-drive prices have dropped somewhat. Today, that same G-note would earn me a couple of hundred gigabytes of storage. Not that you have to spend that kind of money, of course. For around $100, you can add an internal 20 to 40 GB drive to any desktop Mac, including an iMac. If you desire a drive that you can move from one Mac to another, a fast FireWire drive will run about double that price. And portable users can place a 20 GB drive inside a PowerBook or iBook for around $150.

Upgrading to a roomer hard drive allows you to be fairly free and easy about installing massive game data files and downloading thousands of MP3s. Upgrading to a faster hard drive allows data to move more quickly to and from RAM, thus speeding your computer. For these reasons, a more-expansive and faster hard drive is my second upgrade choice.

Installing a new hard drive is more difficult than shoving a couple of RAM modules into your Mac, but on most Macs it's hardly rocket science.

Processor

Sorry to bore you with another story from the old days, but somewhere during the Bush Sr. administration, I had occasion to upgrade the processor—the Mac's brain—in a Mac that started life as an original 128 KB model (later turned into a Mac Plus). Although I've tried to blot out the horrible memory of the installation process, I recall that a soldering iron, a small hacksaw, and a six-pack of beer were required to complete the job.

Fortunately, the bad old days of such gruesome surgeries have passed. All Power Mac models made in the past several years include slots that make it easy to remove and replace the Mac's central processing unit (*CPU*, for those of you who care to sprinkle your cocktail conversation with such heady acronyms). Processor upgrades are available even for such "nonupgradeable" Macs as certain PowerBooks and iMacs.

The price of processor upgrades depends on the Mac model you're upgrading and on the variety and speed of the new processor. As I clack away here, Sonnet Technology (www.sonnettech.com) offers a 500 MHz Power Macintosh G3 upgrade for around $300, a 500 MHz G3 upgrade for a Wall Street PowerBook costs $400, and a 500 MHz G3 upgrade for the original Bondi Blue iMac can be had for $300. PowerPC G4 processor upgrades are a couple of hundred dollars more.

I rate a processor upgrade as the third most-important upgrade you can perform. Processors are worthwhile upgrades but may be too expensive for some folks. Also, some people may be disappointed when they discover that a new processor doesn't speed their Macs as much as they expected it to (see the sidebar "The Proof Isn't Necessarily in the Processor" in this section).

> **The Proof Isn't Necessarily in the Processor**
>
> One might assume that when you place two Macs with similar processors side by side, they'd perform similarly. Slapping a 400 MHz PowerPC G3 processor into a Power Mac 7500 should make it just as fast as a Blue & White Power Mac G3 with the same processor, right?
>
> Wrong.
>
> Processing speed depends not only on the speed of the processor but also on the speed of the Mac's *system bus*. I swore that I wasn't going to get overly techy in this tome, but you should be familiar with this term. Basically, the system bus determines how quickly data can move between the processor and your Mac's RAM. Imagine two dams. Both hold back the same amount of water, but one has a release opening the size of a cantaloupe, whereas the other sports an opening that comfortably accommodates the pitching staff of the 1993 San Francisco Giants arrayed in a human pyramid. That opening is the system bus.
>
> Which opening will deliver more water? Right—the Giants opening. That's the basic idea behind the system bus. Assuming the same pressure behind the stream, the wider (faster) the opening, the more data can pour through. As you might imagine, the system bus on a Power Mac 7500 allows a lot less data through than the bus on a Blue & White.

Graphics card

The Mac's graphic card is responsible not only for displaying a variety of colors and monitor resolutions but also for handling such chores as screen redrawing and 3D hardware acceleration. When you place a faster graphics card in your Mac, you'll notice that windows open in a zippier fashion and documents scroll more quickly. You'll also discover that many modern games play more smoothly.

Graphics cards in iMacs, PowerBooks, and iBooks cannot be upgraded; these suckers are soldered in place. You can upgrade desktop Macs that carry PCI and AGP slots, however. Although everyone can benefit from a graphics-card upgrade, I commonly recommend this variety of upgrade only to gamers. Graphics cards cost upward of $200, which is more than most people care to pay just for spreadsheets that scroll more swiftly. For those who play games, however, a new graphics card can make the difference between a game that's an exercise in frustration and one that kicks serious patoot.

There's one other compelling reason to add another graphics card to your Mac: multiple monitors. When you've spread your work space across two monitors, shoving palettes and extraneous windows off to the right, you may never go back to a single monitor.

Graphics-card upgrades are a breeze in any PCI or AGP Power Mac, excluding the cramped Power Mac G4 Cube.

Other cards and adapters

Thanks to the Mac's many ports and slots, you have other upgrade options. You can, for example, add an AirPort-compatible card to a PC Card-slot-bearing PowerBook. Or you can allow a Power Mac that lacks a sound input port to record audio with an add-in PCI sound card or USB sound adapter. You can even downgrade your Mac so that you can use your old SCSI, serial, and ADB peripherals. In the following pages, I show you how.

Upgrading Your RAM

The steps in upgrading your RAM are as follows:

1. Determine what kind of RAM your Mac uses.
2. Determine how much RAM your Mac will hold and how it's configured.

   Do you need to install RAM in groups of two, for example, or can your Mac accommodate a single RAM module?
3. Determine how much you can afford.
4. Determine where to get the best RAM for the best price.
5. Determine how to install it.
6. Order it, pay for it, and install it.

The good news is that you can do just about all of this online. The even better news is that you don't have to dig down through Apple's Web site to learn which RAM works where.

Purchasing RAM

I rely on two resources when I buy RAM: TechWorks and RAMSeeker.

TechWorks (www.techworks.com, 800-688-7466) is a RAM dealer in Texas that offers reasonable prices and guarantees that its RAM meets or exceeds Apple's specifications. (The company has, at one time or another, actually supplied RAM to Apple.) Its Web site has a searchable database that includes all Mac models. When you call up the Web page appropriate to the Mac you want to upgrade, you'll find information regarding the number of open RAM slots in your Mac, the maximum amount of RAM it will hold, the type of RAM it takes, and part numbers and prices for the RAM that's compatible with your Mac.

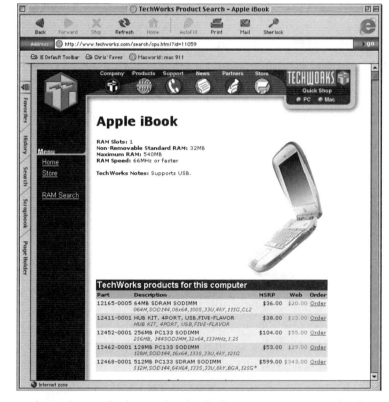

Tech Works! To find out what kind of RAM your Mac needs, drop by TechWorks' Web site.

If this process sounds a bit daunting, you're welcome to call TechWorks toll-free. Just tell the representative what kind of Mac you have and the amount of memory you'd like (or ask for a recommendation), and the company will see to it that you get what you need. I've dealt with TechWorks for years and have had nothing but positive experiences with the company.

The RAMSeeker site is a portal to other sites that sell RAM. On RAMSeeker, you can comparison-shop for RAM among several vendors. If you're seeking the lowest prices on RAM, RAMSeeker is the way to find them. I can't vouch for the quality of RAM from all these vendors, however. So it's not a bad idea to ask around on Mac-centric bulletin boards (*Macworld*'s forums, for example) and see how others have fared with these companies. And of course, you should always use a credit card when shopping for any computer component. That way, if you have trouble with the vendor, you can have the credit-card company intercede on your behalf until things are settled to your satisfaction.

> *I've given you a couple of tips on where to find RAM. Now here's one on where* not *to get it: from Apple or just about any warehouse mail-order outlet. The fact is that unless Apple is giving the stuff away for free (it sometimes bundles additional RAM with a new Mac), prices on RAM at the Apple Store are no bargain. Likewise, companies such as MacConnection, MacWarehouse, and MacZone charge a premium for RAM. Also beware of any of these outlets that give you RAM for "free" yet charge you an installation fee (which often, coincidentally enough, is high enough to pay for the RAM itself and then some). Honestly, unless you lack opposable thumbs, you can install RAM yourself.*

> **Better Safe Than Sorry: Static Electricity**
>
> If you've ever shuffled across a high-pile carpet, touched a metal object, and proclaimed "Youch!" when a tiny spark arced from your finger to that object, you know that the human body is capable of accumulating static electricity. This static buildup is more than just a problem for laundry. Electronic components—like those inside your Mac—can be affected adversely when subjected to these tiny jolts.
>
> For this reason, you should discharge any static electricity before working on your Mac. If you want to be safe as milk in this regard, you'll wear something called a *grounding strap*. This doohickey wraps around your wrist and is attached to a grounded piece of metal: the grounding screw on a power outlet or the power supply of your Mac. Grounding straps are often included when you purchase RAM or other internal Mac components. If your component arrives *sans* grounding strap, you can buy one for less than a buck at any electronics boutique.
>
> If you won't or can't use a grounding strap, you should be sure to touch the power supply inside your Mac before removing a component from its staticproof bag or touching any components inside your Mac. The power supply is the biggest, boxiest hunk of metal inside your Mac. (Don't confuse it with the processor's heat sink!)

Installing RAM

Most new Mac users have a quite-understandable fear of opening their computers. Given that I'm about as hopeless an auto mechanic as anyone who's ever trod this earth, I completely sympathize with this sentiment. Opening boxes full of circuit boards and wires *is* daunting. I want to assure you, however, that with most Mac models made in the past few years, this procedure is not a big deal. Unlike in the bad old days, Apple *wants* you to you upgrade your own RAM and has done everything it can in the design of the Macintosh—yup, even the PowerBook and iBook—to make this process easy.

If you have a Blue & White Power Mac G3 or Power Mac G4, PowerBook G3 (Bronze keyboard or later), iBook, or slot-loading iMac, installing RAM is a snap.

Blue & White Power Mac G3 and Power Mac G4

The Blue & White G3 and Power Mac G4 are the most easily accessible Macs every created. To get inside these babies, turn the power off, insert your finger into the ring in the top panel of the right side of the computer, and pull down. Like a medieval drawbridge, the side door—and the motherboard assembly attached to it—fold down.

With the motherboard exposed, you can spy the empty RAM slots on the right side of the machine. To install new RAM, make sure that you're grounded, check that the cutouts in the RAM match the dividers in the RAM slot, insert the RAM, and push until the retaining brackets snap into place. Close it up, and you're done.

RAM-a-Lam-a-Ding-Dong. The Blue & White Power Mac G3's RAM slots.

Slot-Loading iMac

The original tray-loading iMacs were, quite frankly, a bear to get into. Fortunately, when the folks at Apple redesigned the iMac to include slot-loading CD-ROM drives, they also made it much easier to upgrade the iMac's RAM.

To add more RAM, switch the iMac off, and place it monitor-side down on a soft surface (a towel or baby blanket, for example). Turn it so that the bottom (the side with the kickstand) faces you, and look for the first doorlike thingie above the kickstand. This opening provides access to the iMac's RAM slots and AirPort slot.

Using the coinage of your choice, twist the plastic locking mechanism so that the indentation runs from left to right. When the door is unlocked, fold it open. You'll see one occupied RAM slot (the one above, by default) and one empty one. That empty slot above is for the AirPort card. Touch the metal grill at the top of the door to discharge static electricity, remove the new RAM from its staticproof bag, insert the RAM, and push until the retaining brackets snap into place. Close it up, and you're done.

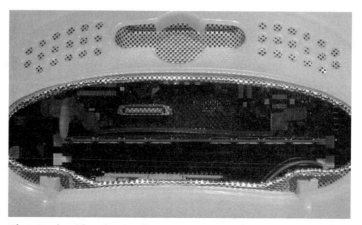

Slot Cards. The slot-loading iMac's RAM slots are located in the top rear of the computer.

PowerBook and iBook

Apple's late-model portables sport an easy-as-pie design that allows you to add RAM simply by removing the keyboard. No, really, this procedure is much easier than it sounds.

With the Mac off, look for a couple of plastic tabs at the top of the iBook or PowerBook. Sliding a fingernail under the top of each of these tabs, push the tabs toward you and fold the keyboard back. Don't try to pull the keyboard away from the Mac; a ribbon cable there is attached to the innards. Just fold it over the hand rest.

With the keyboard gone, you'll see an empty RAM slot below. (The RAM slot on these things is white.) To install new RAM—and stop me if you've heard this one before—touch an innocent-looking piece of metal to discharge static electricity, remove the new RAM from its staticproof bag, insert it at a 45-degree angle, shove it in, and push it down until the retaining brackets snap into place. Close it up, and you're done.

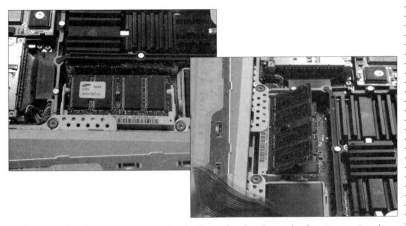

Before and After. The RAM slot below the keyboard of a PowerBook G4 before installation of additional RAM and with the RAM at the proper insertion angle.

Other Macs

Just because you don't have one of these late-model Macs doesn't mean that installing RAM is an impossible chore. Adding RAM to just about any desktop Mac made in the past 10 years is no more difficult than removing the Mac's cover, locating the RAM slots, and jacking new RAM modules into place. Older PowerBooks can be more difficult to work with, because everything inside them is jammed close together. Also, to be honest, Apple didn't really want you to break open these portable puppies, so it didn't make RAM slots easily accessible.

If the manual that came with your older Mac tells you how to add more RAM, I strongly recommend that you give it a try. If instructions aren't included in your manual, give TechWorks a call and see whether the company can send you instructions along with your new RAM.

If the task seems to be too daunting, you can take your Mac to a Apple Authorized Dealer and have the RAM installed there (after you purchase the RAM on your own, natch). Or you might call the local junior college or high school and see whether some Mac-savvy student would like to come over and lend you a hand for a few bucks. Maybe you can get him or her to mow your lawn, too, while you're at it.

Upgrading Your Hard Drive

There's no reason on earth why you should forgo the simple pleasures of computing life just because you've maxed out the hard drive that originally shipped with your Mac. After all, aren't you getting just a little bit tired of sacrificing the digital snapshots of the family to make room for the that massive 500 MB 3-D shoot-'em-up?

Of the four product lines of the Macintosh family—Power Mac, iMac, PowerBook, and iBook—only the Power Mac (excluding the Cube) allows you to add internal hard drives. If you want to put a new hard drive in an iMac or one of the Mac portables, you must either replace the internal drive or add an external hard drive.

Types of Hard Drives

At one time, all Macs shipped with SCSI (Small Computer System Interface) drives. These drives were, at the time, faster than the IDE (Integrated Drive Electronics) drives that shipped with most PCs. They were also more expensive. Apple later ditched these SCSI drives for less-expensive IDE drives, which are still used in all Mac models released today. IDE drives are now nearly as fast as SCSI drives.

> **Jumper Jumble**
>
> You probably thought that a jumper was a kicky little garment worn by Marlo Thomas in "That Girl." Not necessarily so. A jumper is also a little plastic doodad that you place on a pair of the hard drive's tiny data pins that tells the hard drive where it fits into the scheme of things. It works like this...
>
> SCSI and IDE drives have addresses. These addresses tell the computer where to locate a hard drive or other peripheral device.
>
> SCSI has eight addresses: ID 0 – 7. On a Mac that ships with an internal SCSI drive, ID 7 is reserved for the Mac itself, ID 0 is the internal hard drive, and ID 3 is the CD-ROM drive. The other SCSI IDs are available for other SCSI devices, such as additional hard drives, removable drives, and scanners. If you assign the same address to more than one SCSI device, all sorts of horrible things can happen. Don't do it.
>
> *continues on next page*

IDE drives have two addresses: Master and Slave. The internal drive on an IDE-bearing Mac is a Master drive. If you add a second IDE drive (presuming that your Mac supports it; not all Macs do), that drive would be the Slave drive. You can't have two Master or two Slave drives.

Now back to jumpers. The way you set the address on an IDE or SCSI drive is through the strategic placement of jumpers on the data pins. On an IDE drive, you simply have to place a single jumper over the Slave data pins to turn that drive into a Slave drive. Remove that jumper, and you have a Master drive.

IDE Jumpers. This IDE drive is jumpered as a Master drive.

SCSI is trickier, because with those eight addresses, you have to deal with more than a single jumper. Rather, SCSI drives ask that you deal with three pairs of data pins. Here's how the jumper assignments shake out for SCSI IDs 0 – 6 on most SCSI drives (you're never going to use ID 7, so you don't need to know):

ID 0 = no jumpers

ID 1 = jumper on the first pair of pins

ID 2 = jumper on the second pair

ID 3 = jumper on the first and second pair

ID 4 = jumper on the third pair

ID 5 = jumper on the first and third pair

ID 6 = jumper on the second and third pair

continues on next page

SCSI Jumpers. This SCSI drive, with no jumpers on the first three sets of pins, is set to SCSI ID 0.

> **Jumper Jumble** *continued*
>
> Fortunately, this information isn't the kind you need to memorize. When you purchase a new hard drive, a reputable drive manufacturer will include not only the jumpers you need but also a diagram that explains where to put those jumpers to configure your drive properly.
>
> If you get an external SCSI device, you needn't worry about these jumper settings. External SCSI devices carry some kind of selector that allows you to set SCSI ID without the use of jumpers. If you opt for a USB or FireWire drive, this whole jumper business is moot; those drives don't have ID jumpers at all.

Power Macs made in recent years, since the beige Power Mac G3 and beyond, have internal IDE drives (and yes, a few models before that have IDE drives as well). Some also have both internal and external SCSI connectors. Most Power Macs G3s and all Power Mac G4s will accept two internal IDE drives (the beige G3 and first revision of the Blue & White Power Mac G3 don't), and all provide enough space internally to add at least one more drive. Most Macs released before the Power Mac G3 have internal SCSI drives and carry an external connector for attaching SCSI peripherals. If your PCI-bearing Power Mac lacks a SCSI port, you can add a SCSI adapter card. You can also add IDE drives to your Mac with the help of a PCI IDE adapter card, such as ProMax's (www.promax.com) TurboMax card.

Rather than make you dash over to Apple's Spec Database (www.info.apple.com/applespec/applespec.taf) to learn exactly what flavor drive your Mac has, run the Apple System Profiler. (You can find it in the Apple menu in Mac OS 9.2 and earlier and in the Utilities folder in Mac OS X.) Click the Devices and Volumes tab, and look at the left side of the window to see which variety of drives your Mac has. An ATA entry indicates an IDE drive.

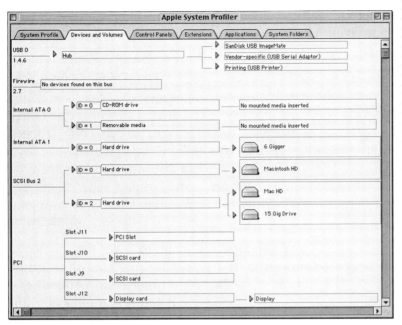

Impressive Profile. The Apple System Profiler tells me that my Blue & White Power Mac G3 is packed with drives, containing one IDE hard drive and two SCSI adapter cards.

What to Look for in a Drive

Naturally, you should find a drive that's compatible with your Mac. That means that if you have a Mac with an internal SCSI drive, you should purchase a SCSI drive. If you have an IDE drive—well, you know.

If you are after a SCSI drive, get one whose pins match those of the drive you're replacing or the cable or connector to which you want to attach the drive. If you're replacing the internal SCSI drive on your Power Mac 7100, for example, get a SCSI drive with a 50-pin connector, just like the one on your old drive, rather than a drive with a 68-pin connector. Yes, adapters are available for these things, but space can be tight inside your Mac, and you might not have enough room for both the drive and adapter. Likewise, if you've added a SCSI PCI card to your Mac, get an external SCSI drive whose pins match those on the card.

IDE is a bit easier. You can purchase any old IDE drive and biff it into your Mac if it will fit. This fit thing is important. You'll never squeeze a 3.5-inch IDE drive into your iBook.

If you do the kind of work that requires data to move from your drive to your Mac and back again as swiftly as possible (video and audio work, for example), get a drive with a high rpm rating. All but the least-expensive drives are rated at 7,200 rpm. If speed is ultra-important, get an Ultra SCSI drive and adapter. Ultra2 SCSI and Ultra160 SCSI are wicked fast, transferring data at 80 MB per second and 160 MB per second, respectively. Or look into an external FireWire drive. If, on the other hand, you want your data to move at a snail's pace, consider an external USB drive.

As for brands and vendors, I'm going to leave that choice to the experts. One of the best places for this kind of information is XLR8YourMac (www.xlr8yourmac.com). This site is devoted to Macintosh upgrades, and you'll find reliable information on which drives are worth purchasing (as well as a general idea of how much you can expect to pay for them).

Installing the Hard Drive

Installing a new hard drive isn't as easy as adding more RAM to your Mac, but in most cases, it's less taxing than, say, simple brain surgery. Again, because I don't have the time or patience to run through every Mac model made, I'll concentrate on those Macs made in the past few years.

Power Macs

If you read the "Installing RAM" section earlier in this chapter, you know how to open your Blue & White Power Mac G3 or Power Mac G4. Those with earlier Macs will have to remove the outside cover.

If you're replacing the original hard drive, you might first want to back up the data on that old drive—unless it's DOA, of course. After the backup, open the Mac's case with the power off, and locate the drive. Fortunately, it's nearly impossible to mistake the hard drive for any other component inside your Mac. Carefully remove the data and power connectors. Detach these cables by pulling on the connectors rather than on the cables themselves. Jerking on a cable can lead to a broken connection—generally considered to be a bad thing to all but those in the Mac-repair business.

Now you must try to suss out how the drive is anchored to the Mac. In many cases, the drive is attached to some kind of bracket with four Phillips-head screws, and that bracket is in turn screwed to the Mac. Remove the bracket screws, and pull the bracket out of the Mac. Now unscrew the old drive from the bracket, and screw in the new drive. Reattach the bracket and cables.

To complete the process, initialize the drive, install a new system, and restart your Mac (see the "Starting Fresh" sidebar for more details).

Starting Fresh

Your new hard drive is in place, yet your Mac won't start up. Why not? Because the drive is unformatted and lacks a System Folder. Here's how to complete the process.

Mac OS 9.2 and Earlier

1. Boot your Mac from a System install CD by inserting the disc into the CD-ROM drive and holding down the C key while the Mac starts up.

   When you see the Happy Mac icon, you can let go of the C key.

2. Launch Drive Setup (located in the Utilities folder inside the Applications folder in Mac OS 9.1 and 9.2).

3. Select the hard drive in the Drive Setup window, and click the Initialize button.

4. If you want to partition the drive (turn it into more than one volume) click the Custom Setup button, and from the Partitioning Scheme pop-up menu, choose the number of partitions you'd like to create.

   After the drive is formatted, it will appear on the desktop.

5. Launch the Mac OS Install application, and install a new System on the hard drive.

Mac OS X

1. Boot from the Mac OS X installation CD, using the C-key trick mentioned in earlier in this sidebar.

2. When the Mac boots, you'll find yourself inside the Mac OS X Installer application.

3. Choose Disk Utility from the Installer menu.

4. Click the hard-drive icon on the left side of the Disk Utility; then click the Erase tab.

5. Click Erase to format the drive.

6. If you want to partition the drive, click the Partition tab, choose from the Volume Scheme pop-up menu the number of partitions you'd like to create, and click OK.

7. When the drive is formatted, quit Disk Utility and proceed with the installation of Mac OS X.

iMac

I may have hinted earlier that cracking open an iMac is a bit of a chore. It can be, but unfortunately, that's the only way to get at the hard drive (and the RAM, in the tray-loading iMacs). But please don't let me scare you off. Opening an iMac isn't all that difficult; it just takes time and patience. With little more than a Phillips-head screwdriver and a towel, you can have your iMac apart and back together in less than an hour. (I've managed to cut my disassembly/reassembly time down to less than 10 minutes on a tray-loading iMac.)

So take a deep breath and get started.

The Tray-Loading iMac

Apple's original iMacs can be divided into two body-types. The original Bondi-blue and fruit-flavored iMacs carried a tray-loading CD-ROM drive. Later models replaced this drive with a slot-loading media drive. We start with the tray-loading models.

Back up your data

As a conscientious computer user, you undoubtedly backup your data on a regular basis. *Don't you!?* If not, now's the time. Even if you intend only to upgrade your iMac's RAM, something could go wrong, and your data could go the way of the dodo.

Before you can back up, you must have a device to back up to. The early iMacs don't carry the CD-RW drives in modern iMacs, so you must use an external means to back up your data. FireWire is also out, as these iMacs don't carry such a port. You must, therefore, seek a USB or Ethernet connection. If you have access to an Ethernet network, simply copy your files from your iMac to another drive on the network. You can also back up your data to the Internet (your iDisk, for example), but Internet backup is painfully slow, so plan to back up a limited amount of data. If you need to back up a fairly substantial amount of data, consider purchasing a USB CD-RW drive.

Regardless of how much data you back up, at the very least, you must back up the documents you've created and such important files as your email messages, address books, and browser bookmarks.

If you use Outlook Express, back up the Microsoft User Data folder inside your Documents folder to save your email and email addresses. You can find your Internet Explorer bookmarks (contained in the Favorites.html file inside the Explorer folder, which in turn is inside your System Folder's Preference folder). Netscape users should back up the Netscape Bookmarks.html file, located inside the Netscape User's folder inside the System Folder's Preferences folder. In Mac OS X you'll find your Internet Explorer favorites inside the Explorer folder inside the Preferences folder inside the Library folder inside your users folder (or, using the parlance of Mac OS X in ~/Library/Preferences/Explorer, where " ~ " equals your users folder). With Netscape, you'll find the bookmarks file by following this path: ~/Library/Mozilla/Profiles/yourprofilename/*someoddlynamedfolder* (where *someoddlynamedfolder* bears a name like <<4ezedmal.slt).

Prepare the iMac and crack the case
Working in a comfortable, well-lit location, begin by unplugging any cables attached to your iMac, including USB, modem, Ethernet, sound, and power cables.

To access the innards of your iMac, you must place it monitor-side down. To protect the monitor from scratches, lift the iMac and place its face on a soft surface such as a pillow, blanket, or plush towel. If you use a pillow, make sure it's flat enough so that the iMac doesn't rock from side to side when you're working on it.

With the iMac face-down, turn it so that you can see the bottom (the white side). There, you'll see a handle with a Phillips-head screw in the middle. Remove this screw, and put it somewhere for safekeeping.

Easily Handled. Remove this screw to unleash the iMac's cover.

Retract the handle, and give it a gentle tug to remove the white plastic cover. Because the cover is secured in some places with plastic tabs, you'll hear an unsnapping sound. Don't worry; this sound is a normal part of the operation. Put the cover aside.

Inside the iMac

Remember what I said about static buildup? It can damage your iMac, too. Before touching any internal components, touch the iMac's metal case to discharge static.

You'll see four cables attached to a rectangular metal box: two large clumps of multicolor wires and two gray cables. Remove the round gray cable to the right. Then, using a Phillips-head screwdriver, unscrew the two screws that keep the larger gray cable clamped to the case. Next, remove the large multicolor cable by pressing down on the tab inside the metal cutout and pulling firmly on the connector. Now pull straight up on the small multicolor cable's connector to disconnect it. Finally, remove the small screw that holds the small multicolor cable in place.

Now You See Them... Before you can remove the iMac's innards, these cables have to go.

Remove the two screws below the clear plastic handle near the top of the case, just below the serial-number sticker.

Two to Go. Removing these two screws below the inner handle will allow you to extract the motherboard assembly.

The motherboard/drive assembly is ready to be extracted. Move the cables out of the way, and pull straight up on the plastic handle.

Upgrade the RAM

I know you're supposed to be upgrading the hard drive, but since you have the iMac open, you might as well upgrade the RAM too. These iMacs carry a scant 32 MB of RAM. You can add as much as 256 MB of RAM (144-pin, PC100 SO-DIMM) to the empty RAM slot.

The Hidden, Revealed.
So *that's* what the inside of a tray-loading iMac looks like.

Place the motherboard/drive assembly so that the CD-ROM is closest to you. Near the top of the motherboard, you'll see a shiny metal cover. To access the iMac's spare RAM slot, remove this cover. *Warning: The cover's edges are sharp! To avoid injury, don't handle the edges.* Instead, pry up the side of the cover with a flat-blade screwdriver.

Below the cover, you'll spy a white plastic bracket. This bracket is where the RAM goes.

Empty Cage.
Below the RAM cage is a RAM slot waiting to be filled.

Remove the RAM module from its bag, line up the notches in the RAM module with those in the RAM slot, and press the RAM into the slot at a 45-degree angle until it's seated securely. Now press down on the top of the RAM module until it snaps into place.

What's Your Angle? Why, 45 degrees, of course.

If you have a Rev. A iMac, you'll see a similar empty RAM socket on the left side of the motherboard. This socket is the video RAM (VRAM) socket. While you're inside, it's not a bad idea to max out this iMac's VRAM by adding a 4 MB SGRAM SO-DIMM (around $20).

Upgrade the hard drive

You must remove the CD-ROM drive to expose the hard drive below it. The CD-ROM drive is held in place by a couple of hooks on the front of the drive mounting that slip through slots in the drive cage. To remove the CD-ROM drive, push in the face of the CD-ROM drive to slip these hooks out of the slots; then lift the drive up and over the top of the cage. When the drive is clear, disconnect the CD-ROM drive's ribbon cable, and put the drive aside.

In and Out. The CD-ROM drive hides the hard drive. After you move the CD-ROM drive aside, you can unfasten the data cable, remove the hard drive from its bracket, and replace the drive.

With the hard drive exposed, remove the metal clip over the drive and the two Phillips-head screws on the top of the cage—on the left and right sides of the hard drive. These screws secure the hard drive's bracket to the cage.

Pull the bracket from the cage, and disconnect the drive's data and power cables. Unscrew the bracket screws, and remove the old drive.

On the new drive, reverse this process by attaching the bracket and cables, slipping the bracket back into the cage, screwing the bracket to the cage, reinstalling the clip over the drive, and replacing the CD-ROM drive.

Putting it back together

Putting Humpty-iMac back together again is largely a process of following the preceding steps in reverse order. In one or two places, however, the process isn't as simple as it seems. To put things right, follow these steps:

1. Before reinserting the motherboard, make sure that all connectors and chips are firmly seated.

   You'd prefer not to return to the scene of this crime.

2. Grasp the motherboard/drive assembly by the plastic handle, and slide it back into place.

   To do so, push the four cables aside, making sure that they're clear of the assembly. You'll see metal pins on the side of the drive cage. These pins must slide behind the iMac case's plastic rails. Finally, be sure that the front of the CD-ROM drive is flush with the front of the iMac.

3. Replace the two screws below the plastic handle.

   These screws will go in easier if you tilt the iMac away from you.

4. Reattach the large multicolor cable first, then the small multicolor cable, then the screw that holds the small multicolor cable in place, then the large gray cable, and finally the smaller gray cable.

5. Replace the cover by slipping the plastic lip at the bottom of the cover under the rim of the iMac's case.

6. Snap the rest of the cover into place, and replace the single screw below the handle.

7. Replace your iMac's cables, and switch it on.

That wasn't so bad, was it? To finish the job, you must format the new hard drive and install a new System on it (see the "Starting Fresh" sidebar earlier in this chapter).

You must partition drives larger than 8 GB. Apple says that on tray-loading iMacs, you must partition a hard drive that exceeds 8 GB, the reason being is that the iMac expects to find a bootable partition within the first 8 GB of the drive. If it doesn't, it may not start up. When you're partitioning a high-capacity drive—say, a 60 GB drive—create at least two partitions (the first one no larger than 8 GB), and be sure to install your System software on this partition.

The Slot-Loading iMac

Upgrading a slot-loading iMac is far less of a chore. Here's how to go about it:

Back up your data

You've been over this, yes? Do it.

Prepare the iMac and crack the case

You've been here before as well. The shorthand version: Mac off, disconnect cables, Mac on face on soft surface, turn so you can see the bottom.

New stuff: Open the door above the kickstand that covers the RAM and AirPort slots. Touch the metal grill to discharge any static electricity. Then remove any RAM and, if present, the AirPort card; these cards get in the way of the hard-drive cables.

Now remove the next panel up: the perforated one that hides the VGA connector. Pry it off with a flat-blade screwdriver. Below this cover, remove the two outer screws.

Next, remove the two screws at the bottom of the iMac's bottom—the ones near the kickstand's front feet.

The First Two. Begin by removing the two screws on the side of the VGA port.

The Next Two. Remove the two screws near the iMac's front feet.

Now, starting at the top, pull the plastic cover off the iMac. The plastic cover will resist and may even make a cracking sound. Don't worry; this sound is perfectly normal. Be patient, pull and push, and the cover eventually will come off.

You'll see a metal screen below the plastic cover. You must dislodge this screen by removing the six screws that hold it in place. Four of the screws are at the bottom of the screen, and two are at the top. A couple of the bottom screws are really tucked away, and I've been known to drop them into the innards of the iMac. To avoid my mistake, use a screwdriver with a magnetic tip.

Pull the screen away when the six screws are out.

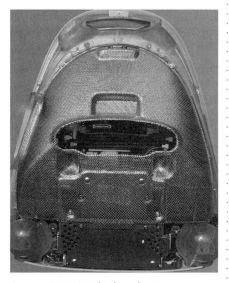

Screen Test. With the plastic cover gone, you must remove the six screws that hold the metal screen in place.

Upgrade the hard drive

No need to monkey about with extracting the motherboard. On these iMacs, the hard drive is easy to reach after the cover and screen are gone.

You'll see the hard-drive bracket at the bottom of the case, between the round speakers. Remove the four screws that hold the hard drive in place. Now dislodge the data and power cables, and slide the hard drive out.

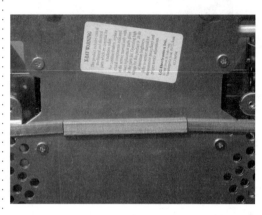

Screws Again.
These four bracket screws hold the hard drive in place.

Replace the hard drive, and reverse these steps to put your iMac back together again. To finish the job, you must format the new hard drive and install a new System on it (see the "Starting Fresh" sidebar earlier in the chapter).

Ah, Success!
See, you really can take the drive out without destroying the iMac.

PowerBook and iBook

After that seemingly endless description of pulling an iMac apart, I imagine that you're expecting great things from me in regard to disassembling a PowerBook and iBook. I'm afraid I must disappoint you and meekly suggest that in the case of PowerBooks, you read the manual or check Apple's Web site if you'd like specific instructions.

I offer this cowardly suggestion because, over the years, Apple has jammed hard drives into every conceivable PowerBook nook and cranny. On some models, getting to the hard drive is as simple as lifting the keyboard, removing a couple of screws, and plucking the drive out. These models include the PowerBook G3s. On others (the 1xx series), extracting the hard drive is about as easy as removing your own kidney.

The Titanium PowerBook G4 is somewhere in between. To pull this PowerBook's drive, you must remove the battery and bottom cover of the PowerBook, detach the data cable, and pry the drive out after removing a couple of retaining screws. Not an impossible job by any means, but one that requires you to work with eensie-weensie parts and screws.

As for iBooks, Apple does not include the iBook's hard drive among its list of user-upgradeable components for a good reason: Upgrading the bloody thing is a dreadful experience. I've spent a lot of years pulling Macs apart, and quite honestly, this is one upgrade I wouldn't attempt. The least of your worries is that you'll void your warranty. The worst is that you'll mess up your iBook so badly that it becomes a useless pile of high-density plastic and metal scrap. Somewhere in between is the embarrassment of trudging into your local Apple Authorized Dealer with a grocery sack full of parts, mumbling, "Um, do you think you could put this back together?"

Upgrading Your Processor

If you've scanned the system requirements of most new Mac products, you've seen that many would like some variety of PowerPC G3 processor running under Mac OS 9 or later, thank you very much. If you're still chugging along with System 7.1 and a PowerPC 601 processor, that software has zero chance of running on your Mac. With a processor upgrade, your Mac could welcome that software with open arms.

And don't forget Mac OS X. Apple's new operating system has very strict requirements—some variety of PowerPC G3 processor at the very least. (A G4 is even better.) Without that PowerPC G3 or G4, you can forget all about Mac OS X's throbbing, lickable interface. Processor upgrade cards that carry G3 and G4 processors are not officially supported by Apple for Mac OS X but the cards' manufacturers have created patches that will allow some of these upgrades to work under Apple's new OS. If you seek Mac OS X compatibility, check with the upgrade manufacturer's Web site before purchasing the upgrade.

Types of Processor Upgrades

The type of processor upgrade you choose depends entirely on the kind of Mac you want to upgrade. Processor upgrades come in the form of processor replacements that fit directly into a slot or socket designed for the Mac's CPU or some kind of expansion card that fits into another slot—a processor direct slot (PDS), L2, or PCI slot, for example.

Big and Small. Don't let its size fool you; that little ZIF processor is 10 times faster than the larger PDS one.

Although I could provide you an exhaustive list of which Macs will accept which kinds of processor upgrades, I have more helpful ways to spend the pages allotted to me (and don't tables give you the worst sort of headache?).

Instead, I'd like to provide you the URLs for the Web sites of the three major processor-upgrade companies: Sonnet (www.sonnettech.com), XLR8 (www.xlr8.com), and Power-Logix (www.powerlogix.com). All three of these outfits make darned-speedy processor upgrades that work in most Macs made in the past several years. And each company provides an easy-to-read list of its products and which Macs those products work with.

Sonnet offers the widest variety of processor upgrades, including upgrades that fit Macs as old as the Color Classic and Mac II. (Now, *why* would you want to upgrade one of these old beasts when you can buy an early Power Mac on eBay for, like, the price of a premium can of cat food?) Sonnet has also hired many of the former employees and acquired the technology of the late, great Newer Technology, which was my favorite processor-upgrade outfit.

XLR8 makes some very compelling processor upgrades and is on the forefront of releasing dual-processor upgrades. XLR8's processor upgrades are also fairly configurable. Thanks to a few switches on these things, you can make them run faster than they're rated to run.

PowerLogix often has the least-expensive processor upgrades around, though prices on these things usually are fairly competitive, particularly when you're reviewing a slew of them for a magazine such as, oh, *Macworld,* and you're trying to track down pricing information for publication. (*"What's that? You're a reviewer for* Macworld? *Our price? Oh, ah, well, what are the other guys charging? Really? Hmm. Well, we're $20 cheaper. Did I say $20? I meant $40. Is that good enough? Cuz, ya know....."*)

> Sonnet isn't your only resource for processor upgrades for ancient Macs. MicroMac (www.micromac.com), a company that made processor upgrades waaaaay back in the old days, is still alive and kicking, offering upgrades for Macs as ancient as the Mac Plus. Again, why you'd want to upgrade such a geriatric Mac is completely beyond me.

Installing a New Processor

How you install a processor upgrade depends on the type of upgrade you're installing. If you're upgrading an earlier Mac model, such as a Mac II or Quadra that includes a 680x0 processor, you'll likely have to shove the processor upgrade into a slot of some kind (although some early models had socketed processors).

Most Power Macintosh models since the Power Mac 7300 (including the Mac clones from such companies as Power Computing and Umax) and up to the Power Mac G3 include a processor card that fits directly into a processor direct slot (PDS). These cards can be lifted out of the Mac easily when the cover's off.

With the Power Mac G3s, Apple discarded this design in favor of the even-easier-to-upgradeable Zero Insertion Force (ZIF) socket design. Swapping a ZIF-based processor requires no more effort than pulling up on a small handle, removing the processor, inserting the new processor, and cranking the handle back down.

A Major ZIF.
The Zero Insertion Force (ZIF) socket in Power Mac G3 and G4 computers.

Power Macs and earlier 680x0-based models aren't Apple's only upgradeable computers. Both Sonnet and PowerLogix make processor upgrades for the slot-loading iMacs and some PowerBook G3 models (the Wall Street models specifically). Although I've provided you instructions for gaining access to your iMac and hinted how to get into your Wall Street PowerBook, you needn't have this book close at hand when you perform one of these upgrades. Both Sonnet and PowerLogix provide detailed installation instructions.

Regardless of the kind of Mac or processor upgrade you have, you'll likely have to install a driver to make the processor work to its full potential. Generally, it's a good idea to install the driver before the upgrade, shut down the Mac, install the upgrade, and then boot up.

Along with the driver, some upgrades include a control panel that allows you to muck around with the upgrade's backside cache settings. I've had little success with configuring these things via control panel, but you're welcome to give it a go.

As I mentioned in regard to XLR8's upgrades, some processor upgrades include switches or dials that allow you to adjust their speed. The idea behind these switches is that the processors are rated to work at a certain speed—400 MHz, for example. But just because a processor is rated at a certain speed doesn't mean that it can't exceed that speed comfortably. That 400 MHz processor may be able to function perfectly well at 450 MHz, for example. These switches and dials allow you to experiment with faster speeds. If, after you adjust the speed up, the Mac routinely crashes, you know that the processor doesn't care to operated at the increased speed. If the Mac behaves, you may be in luck.

But is it a good idea to run a processor faster than it's rated to run? Maybe yes; maybe no. Some upgrade vendors tell you straight out that if you muck with the processor speed, your warranty is kaput (yet they still include the switches; go figure). Others, such as XLR8, not only welcome the idea but also provide you with instructions on how to proceed.

Personally, I think it's a perfectly peachy proposal to push a processor as long as your Mac can stand it and your computer is properly cooled. *Whuzzat?* When you jack up the processor's speed, it produces greater heat. Because that excess heat can shorten the life of the processor, I make sure that it stays nice and cool by adding a fan to my Mac. Yes, Power Macs already include fans, but because I've asked my processor to live on the edge, I give it a little extra help by mounting a fan on the front of the case that blows air across its heat sink.

However, I make my living by pushing Macs around. A more level-headed person who simply wants his or her Mac to work would refrain from pushing the processor.

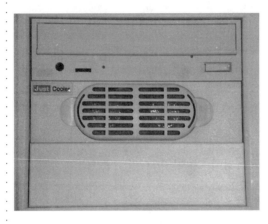

Fan Appreciation. This front-panel fan helps keep my Power Computing PowerTower 180e (and its slightly pumped-up G3 processor card) cool.

When upgrading some Blue & White Power Macs with PowerPC G4 processor upgrades, you first must update the firmware: *a set of upgradeable instructions held in a Mac's ROM chip. Processor-upgrade vendors supply these firmware upgrades on a disc that ships with the upgrade. One catch to keep in mind: As this book goes to press, not all these firmware updates are reversible. This means that if you want to pull the G4 upgrade and go back to your original G3 processor, you may be unable to do so (at least if you hope for your Mac to work with that G3 processor).*

Upgrading Your Graphics Card

If you have an underpowered graphics card—and by that, I mean any card that came with a Mac made before the Blue & White Power Mac G3—inside your Power Mac, you might give some thought to plunking a new one into a free PCI slot. The Apple and early ATI graphics chipsets that shipped with earlier Macs are painfully slow compared with products currently released by ATI. As I write this chapter, ATI offers the Radeon, a 16 MB, 3D graphics card that goes for about $200 for the PCI edition. It's a fine graphics card and runs games beautifully.

If you have a Mac that carries an AGP (Accelerated Graphics Port) slot—all but the earliest Power Mac G4s have AGP slots—you can do better than the already pretty-fine graphics card within. nVidia (www.nvidia.com) offers the GeForce 3, a distinctly perky graphics card designed mainly for gamers with deep pockets (the card costs $500!) who seek the faster 3D hardware acceleration around.

The process of upgrading your card is fairly simple. Install the drivers for the card, shut down the Mac and disconnect its monitor cable, open the Mac, locate a free PCI slot (or pull your current video card from its PCI or AGP slot), insert the card, attach the monitor cable to the new card, and fire up the Mac.

Alternatively, you can keep your current video card and attach a second monitor to the new video card. With the two cards in place and a monitor attached to each one, you configure the multiple monitors this way:

1. Open the Monitors control panel, and click the Arrange button.
2. Click the Identify the Startup Screen option.

   This option places the icon of the Mac on one of the monitor icons that appears in this window. The monitor with the icon is the monitor that holds the menu bar and displays the march of icons at startup.

3. If you want to extend your Desktop, drag the other monitor icon to the right, left, above, or below the startup icon.

   The position of this icon indicates the direction in which you want the Desktop to extend. If you place it to the right, for example, when you drag the mouse pointer to the right edge of the first monitor's screen, it next appears on the left side of the second monitor.

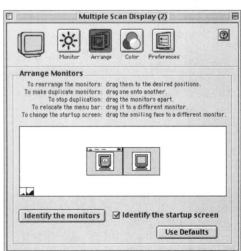

Double Vision. Use the Monitors control panel to configure multiple monitors.

You don't have to extend the Desktop in a multiple-monitor setup. Instead, you can *mirror* (duplicate) the first monitor's image on the second monitor. To do so, just drag the second monitor's icon on top of the first monitor. Identical images will now be displayed on both monitors.

One more tip: You needn't display the same number of colors or even the same resolution on both monitors. You can set a resolution of 1024 x 768 on the first monitor and 800 x 600 on the second, if you like.

Adding Other Cards and Adapters

But wait—there's more!

Sorry to sound like a television huckster, but you can do other things to your Mac to make it more capable.

Add a Sound Input Device

In this day, when MP3 audio files rule the roost, many Mac users are getting interested in sound. Regrettably, Apple picked this time to strip the sound input port from its Power Mac and PowerBook computers. Anyone who owns a PowerBook G4 or Power Mac G4 must rely on third-party sound input devices to get quality sound. (No, I don't count the cheesy internal mic on the Titanium PowerBook.)

Fortunately, you can add this capability in several ways. Power-Book users can bring sound into their Mac via the USB and FireWire ports. Currently, the least expensive USB input device is Griffin Technology's (www.griffintechnology.com) $35 iMic adapter. This stereo input device allows line level (the kind of signal sent by your home stereo amplifier) and microphone input. The same company also offers the $100 PowerWave USB adapter. The Power-Wave includes a stereo amplifier and digital signal processing.

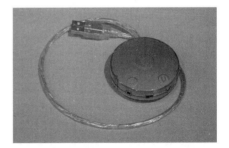

Round Sound. No, it's not a Duncan yo-yo. It's Griffin's iMic USB audio adapter.

FireWire audio input devices such as Mark of the Unicorn's (www.motu.com) $795 Motu 828 for FireWire are intended for audio professionals. Such devices include multiple inputs and outputs and high audio resolution, and work with professional recording applications.

Owners of PCI Macs can add a PCI sound card. Currently, Creative Technology (www.creative.com) offers the $100 SoundBlaster Live! audio card, but the company has yet to upgrade the card's drivers so that the audio input works with currently available Power Mac G4 models, and the future of Mac OS X drivers is iffy. If you have an older Power Mac, this card is an attractive option, but given Creative's lackluster support for the Mac, I wouldn't hold out much hope for updated drivers.

Fortunately, other PCI-based sound devices are available. Like the Motu 828, these devices are largely intended for the professional market—and therefore carry professional prices of several hundred dollars and more.

Add an ADB Device

I know that this sounds like a step backward, but I adore my ADB Apple Extended Keyboard II and will stop using it when they pry it from my cold, dead hands. Although Apple hasn't put an ADB port on a Mac in years, I can still use this keyboard along with my trusty Kensington Thinking Mouse, thanks to Griffin Technology's iMate adapter. This $39 device bears an ADB port on one end and plugs into the Mac's USB port. The iMate supports loads of ADB input devices, and I wouldn't compute without it.

Add a Serial Port

While I'm on the subject of Griffin Technology, I should mention that its gPort, g4Port, and CubePort adapters ($49 each) allow you to use serial devices such as printers, modems, and MIDI interfaces with any Blue & White Power Mac G3, Power Mac G4, and Power Mac G4 Cube. To use one of these things, you must give up the Mac's internal modem. If you have a Rev. A or Rev. B iMac, you can use Griffin's $79 iPort adapter to add a serial and external monitor connection to your iMac.

Serial Box.
Griffin's CubePort allows you to use serial devices with your collectible Power Mac G4 Cube.

Several other serial-port adapters will work with your Mac. Of those, I'm particularly keen on Belkin's (www.belkin.com) and Keyspan's (www.keyspan.com) products.

Add a Network Printer

If you have a printer that can be networked via LocalTalk yet bears only a serial-style connector, you may think that you're out of luck. Not so. With the help of Asante's (www.asante.com) $95 EtherTalk-to-LocalTalk Bridge or Proxim's (www.proxim.com) $93 EtherMac iPrint Adapter LT, you can add that printer to your network. These adapters include a 10Base-T Ethernet connector on one end and a serial port on the other. Just string a serial cable between the printer and the adapter and an Ethernet cable between the adapter and your Mac's network (an Ethernet hub, for example). Then make the proper network connections (I'll show you how in Chapter 8), and you're in business.

Talk to Me.
You can make your LocalTalk printer communicate with your network with Asante's EtherTalk-to-LocalTalk Bridge.

Add a SCSI Device

Although SCSI ports no longer grace modern Macs, you can still use your old SCSI devices with the help of a SCSI adapter, provided that you have the right kind of Mac or the right kind of SCSI peripherals.

If you have a Power Mac, your best option is to purchase a PCI SCSI card adapter from a company such as Adaptec (www.adaptec.com) or Orange Micro (www.orangemicro.com). With such an adapter, you'll be able to use any SCSI device that's ever graced the earth (barring the usual SCSI problems, of course).

Getting SCSI.
No need to trash your old SCSI peripherals with a PCI SCSI adapter card in your Power Mac.

If you have a slotless Macintosh—an iMac, PowerBook, or iBook—things get trickier, because USB-to-SCSI adapters are limited. To begin with, they work only with the simplest SCSI devices: external hard drives and removable media drives such as Zip drives. Attempting to attach a SCSI scanner to one of these things is an exercise in futility. In addition, they're slow. USB wasn't designed to deliver data quickly.

If I had an old SCSI scanner and a new iBook, rather than get one of these adapters, I'd think seriously about replacing the scanner. USB scanners are cheap, cheap, cheap, and unlike their SCSI counterparts, they will work, work, work.

Share and Share Alike

The Networked Mac

If there's a skill that divides the casual Mac user from one who has plunged in—fully-clothed, with shoes tied and hair combed—that skill is networking. Nah, I don't mean flashing your business card with aplomb or delivering the perfect handshake. I mean connecting two or more computers and configuring same to swap information.

It's understandable, of course. When the subject of networking is introduced into general conversation, you can be assured that before three minutes have elapsed, dozens of arcane acronyms—TCP/IP, SMTP, POP, Cat-5, and the like—will have fluttered about the room. Is it any wonder that most people believe networking is something best left to the professionals?

Aside from the perceived difficulty of setting up a network, people also avoided thinking about networks because it wasn't necessary to do so. With a single Mac connected to the Internet via modem, what was the point in learning how to configure a network? Fortunately, those one-Mac/one-modem days are over. Many people now have multiple Macs (or a mixed group of Macs and PCs) and access the Internet via fast cable and DSL connections. Given such a multicomputer environment and the potential to share a fast Internet connection, learning to network your computers has become a necessity.

And here's the best part: It's not difficult.
And the even better part: I'll show you how.
Now. (Brown cow.)

A Little History

Macs have been able to talk to one another for years and years. They did so via something called *AppleTalk*—a networking scheme devised by Apple that allowed a few Macs and printers to chat with one another via cable stung between the various Macs' and printers' Printer ports. The cables and connectors used at this time were branded with the name *LocalTalk*. (Yeah, I know, all this "talk" stuff is confusing.) For its time, this AppleTalk/LocalTalk duo was a perfectly fine way for Macs to communicate. Unfortunately, AppleTalk isn't supported natively by PCs, and LocalTalk is, by today's standards, deathly slow.

Round about the time Apple released the first Power Macs, a new port graced the back of the Mac: the Ethernet port. Unlike the Printer port, which was forced to serve two masters (networking and printer connections), the Ethernet port was designed for one purpose only: networking.

All Macs made today include an Ethernet port. Ethernet ports come in a variety of styles and are rated at different speeds. All Macs made in the past few years carry an RJ-45 connector, which looks like a big phone jack. This connector is by far the most common Ethernet connector you're likely to come across (see the sidebar "Daddy, I've Got an AAUI!" later in the chapter).

Older Macs include 10Base-T Ethernet ports. More recently, Apple has released Macs that support 100Base-T and even Gigabit Ethernet. The difference? 10Base-T can move data as fast as 10 megabits per second (Mbps), 100Base-T up to 100 Mbps, and Gigabit Ethernet as fast as 1 Gbps (or 1,000 Mbps). To take advantage of these faster standards, the computers talking to one another and any intervening devices must support them. If you have two QuickSilver Power Macs that include Gigabit Ethernet, and they are connected via a direct cable, you should get mighty zippy communications between the two.

If, on the other hand, you have a QuickSilver Power Mac that includes Gigabit Ethernet and an older Blue & White Power Mac G3 that supports only 10Base-T, transfer rates will be limited to 10Base-T speeds.

> **Daddy, I've Got an AAUI!**
>
> On early Power Macs, Ethernet ports were of the AAUI (Apple Attachment Unit Interface) variety. An AAUI port is a trapezoidal thing with a <•••> designation next to it. (That <•••> is the symbol for Ethernet.) To incorporate an AAUI port into a standard Ethernet network, you must use something called an Ethernet *transceiver*. The transceiver is a go-between device with a male AAUI connector on one end and one or more female Ethernet (RJ-45) connectors on the other. Ethernet transceivers are available from companies such as Proxim (www.proxim.com) and MacSense (www.macsense.com) and cost less than $30.

Even with modern Ethernet connectors on Macs, the Mac OS continued to support only AppleTalk connections. Realizing that it was unlikely that the rest of the computing world was finally going to adopt AppleTalk, Apple got hip and began supporting networking via TCP/IP (Transmission Control Protocol/Internet Protocol), a communication standard designed to work across networks and the Internet on a wide variety of computers. Mac OS 9.2 and Mac OS X support both AppleTalk and TCP/IP.

Making Connections

Before you can begin networking, you have to provide the means for your Macs to talk with one another. Traditionally, this means has been provided by stringing cable between a couple of Macs. But thanks to Apple's AirPort technology, you can do this sort of thing without wires.

Coming to Terms

Before you begin, I'll get a few more terms out of the way:

> **Category 5, or Cat 5, cable.** This cable is the kind used to create Ethernet cables.
>
> **Ethernet hub.** This box contains Ethernet ports (usually, four or more). The hub acts as a traffic cop for Ethernet signals, directing data sent from one computer (or the

Internet) to another. Ethernet hubs cost less than $50 and are made by such companies as NetGear (www.netgear.com), LinkSys (www.linksys.com), and Asante (www.asante.com).

Router. Similar to an Ethernet hub, a router performs all the chores of a hub but can also act as the gateway between the Internet and your network of Macs. A router can also protect your network from intruders, allow access only to those computers you want to let in. This protection feature is called a *firewall.* LinkSys makes a fine four-port router for around $85.

Crossover cable. This cable is an Ethernet cable wired in such a way that two Macs can talk to one another directly without an intervening device such as an Ethernet hub. Crossover cables cost less than $10 for a 6-foot cable and are available at any computer-supply shop.

Straight-through cable. This cable is standard Ethernet cable. It's wired in such a way that if you want to connect a couple of Macs, you first have to run the cable through an Ethernet hub. (Note: Certain Macs, such as recent PowerBooks, allow you to use a straight-through cable to make a direct connection to another cable. No cross-over cable is necessary.) Straight-through cables are dirt-cheap and available at any computer-supply shop.

Ethernet-to-LocalTalk adapter. This device allows you to establish a network connection between an Ethernet network and a LocalTalk device (such as a printer). Such adapters are made by Proxim and Asante and cost less than $100.

AirPort. AirPort is Apple's implementation of the IEEE 802.11 standard. (Yeah, I know, *that's* a big help.) IEEE 802.11 is a standard agreed upon by people who agree upon such things that details how wireless computer networks should run. Another acronym you might see thrown around in this regard is *Wi-Fi*, a certification that indicates that a certain device can communicate with other Wi-Fi devices. AirPort has been Wi-Fi certified.

AirPort Base Station. This podlike device not only receives and transmits wireless connections between your network and any AirPort-compatible devices but also can act as a router. With an AirPort Base Station, you can connect wirelessly to a wired network. AirPort cards cost $99, and the AirPort Base Station will set you back $299.

Typical Physical Connections

Now that you have the terms out of the way, you're ready to wire a few networks. You'll begin with a simple two-Mac network and progress from there.

The Two-Macs network

Mac No. 1 is a Blue & White Power Mac G3. Mac No. 2 is a Bondi Blue iMac. To connect the two, grab an Ethernet crossover cable, and shove one end into the Ethernet port on the Power Mac and the other end into the iMac's Ethernet port.

You're done. Tough, ain't it?

The two-Macs with a DSL/cable connection network

Run the two Macs and modem (DSL or cable) into an Ethernet hub with straight-through Ethernet cables.

The two-Macs with a printer and a DSL/cable connection network

You can make this connection in a few ways, depending on the kind of printer you have.

> **If you have an Ethernet printer:** String straight-through Ethernet cables from the Macs, modem, and the printer into an Ethernet hub.
>
> **If you have a LocalTalk printer:** String straight-through Ethernet cables from the Macs and the modem into an Ethernet hub. Attach an Ethernet-to-LocalTalk adapter to the hub with a straight-through Ethernet cable, and run a LocalTalk (serial) cable to the printer.
>
> **If you have a USB printer:** String straight-through Ethernet cables from the Macs and modem into an Ethernet hub. Attach the printer to one of the Macs with a USB cable. Run USB Printer Sharing (see the sidebar "Sharing USB Printers" later in this chapter).

The multiple Macs and DSL/cable connection without AirPort network

Run straight-through cables from all the Macs and the modem into an Ethernet hub. Add a printer as suggested in the setup for two Macs and a printer.

The multiple Macs and DSL/cable connection with AirPort network

Run straight-through cables from all the Macs and the modem into an Ethernet hub. Connect an AirPort Base Station to the hub with a straight-through Ethernet cable. Add a printer as suggested in the setup for two Macs and a printer.

Sharing USB Printers

There's no need to spend hundreds upon hundreds of dollars for a fancy-shmancy laser printer to enjoy the benefits of printer sharing. Thanks to Apple's USB Printer Sharing control panel and extension, you can print to a compatible USB printer from any Mac running Mac OS 9.x on your network (regrettably, USB Printer Sharing isn't supported under Mac OS X as we go to press). Here's how:

1. If USB Printer Sharing isn't installed by default on all your Macs running Mac OS 9.x and you don't find it in the Control Panels folder, download it from Apple's Web site (http://www.info.apple.com/support/downloads.html) or perform a custom install of your System software (part of the Mac OS 9.x package).

2. Install the USB printer's software on any Mac that will print to this printer.

    Yes, that means your networked Macs as well.

3. On the Mac that's connected directly to the printer, open the USB Printer Sharing control panel, and in the Start/Stop window, click the Start button.

4. Click the My Printers tab, and make sure that the USB printer appears in this window and that the Share option is selected.

5. Open the File Sharing control panel, and enable the Enable File Sharing Clients to Connect Over TCP/IP option.

    USB Printer Sharing won't work over AppleTalk.

6. On the networked Macs, open the USB Printer Sharing control panel, and click the Start button in the Start/Stop pane.

7. Select the Network Printers tab, and click the triangle next to Local Services.

    The networked USB printer should appear in the list of networked printers.

8. Finally, to use the printer, open the Chooser and select its driver.

Software Setup: Mac OS 9.2 and Earlier

Now that the Macs and other network devices are linked physically, it's time to make them talk to one another. In either Mac OS 9.2 and earlier or Mac OS X, you do this by configuring the Mac's software. The following sections show you how to do so in Mac OS 9.

Configure AppleTalk

The first thing you need to do is make sure that your Mac is prepared to talk to other Macs on the network through the right port. To prepare your Mac, open the AppleTalk control panel, and if you're running an Ethernet network, choose Ethernet from the Connect Via pop-up menu. If you're using AirPort, choose AirPort from this menu.

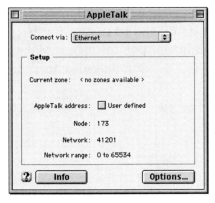

Talk the Talk.
Choose the method by which your Mac talks to the rest of the network in the AppleTalk control panel.

Selecting Volumes and Files

Before you can put your Mac on the network, you have to decide which files you want to grant access to. Depending on your needs, you may want to share every drive attached to your Mac or just a single folder. Here's how to do both.

Single-User access

If you're the only person who plans to share the Macs on your network and you want to share every drive on your Mac, open the File Sharing control panel, click the Users & Groups tab, select the Owner user (that would be you), and click the Open button. In the resulting dialog box, choose Sharing from the pop-up menu, and click the Allow User to See All Disks option.

Owner-ous Behavior. As the owner of your Mac, you get to see everything on your network.

Multiple-user access

If you want to grant access to other users, go back to that Users & Group tab, and click the New User button. In the window that appears, assign a name and password for that user and then choose Sharing from the pop-up menu. Make sure that Allow User to Connect to This Computer is checked, and click the close box.

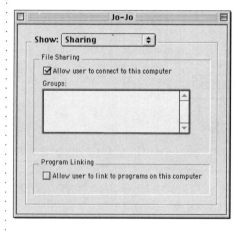

Open-Door Policy. New users must be granted entry to your Mac.

To grant access to a single drive, click that drive and press Command-I to bring up the Get Info window. Now choose Sharing from the pop-up menu, and click the Share This Item and Its Contents option. After you do, you can determine what kinds of privileges other users have: read, read and write, or write only.

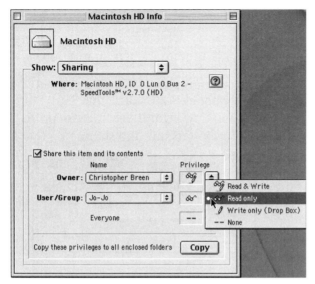

The Privileged Class. Granting privileges allows you to control what other users see on your network.

This Write Only option is worth a closer look for this reason: By creating a folder with Write Only privileges, you can provide a place for other users on your network to drop their work without being able to see what else is in that folder. This option is wonderful if you want to create a household suggestion box, and your cousin Jo-Jo drops a file titled "Sister Betty makes lousy Irish Stew" into that box. You'll see the title of that message, but Sister Betty won't.

Another thing to note in the Users & Groups tab is the privileges area for something called Everyone. By granting privileges to everyone, you enable Guest access to your Mac, meaning that any user who can see your Mac on the network has whatever access you grant to Everyone when he clicks the Guest option in the Network Browser or Apple-Share section of the Chooser. (Don't worry; I'll discuss those topics later in this chapter.)

Turn on Sharing

Now that you've configured which volumes or folders are accessible for sharing, it's time to switch sharing on.

On each Mac that you'd like to appear in your network, open the File Sharing control panel, and select the Start/Stop tab. In this portion of the window, you'll see the option to Start File Sharing. Click that option to start file sharing on that Mac.

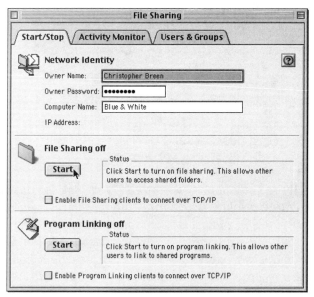

Please Share. Click the Start button to enable file sharing.

This window carries another option worth mentioning: Enable File Sharing Clients to Connect Over TCP/IP. As the name implies, with this option on, anyone with the right privileges can log on from any Mac over TCP/IP—and by any Mac, I do mean those connected via the Internet as well as those across your home network. Because your Mac can be accessed from the Web when this option is on, you're better off leaving this option off if you're concerned about security.

Alternative Access. You can also allow users to connect via TCP/IP.

Accessing the Network

After you click the Start button in File Sharing, your Mac is available to the other Macs on your network. That's half the battle. Now, how do you access other Macs on your network?

The Chooser

Since before the beginning of time—or at least since the early days of the Macintosh—the way to access networked Macs was through the Chooser. This is still one way to do so.

Open the Chooser and select AppleShare. When you do, the Macs on your network that have File Sharing enabled should appear in the window to the right. Select one of these Macs, and click OK.

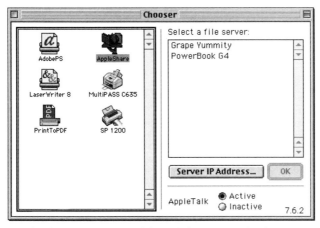

AppleShare and Share Alike. Click a networked computer to begin the login process.

In the resulting window, you enter your user name and password if you're a registered user, or you click the Guest option if the networked Mac offers guest privileges. Now click Connect.

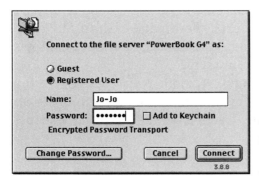

What's the Password? Enter your name and password here.

Select the volumes to which you want to connect. Shift-click the volumes you want to mount on your Desktop, and click OK.

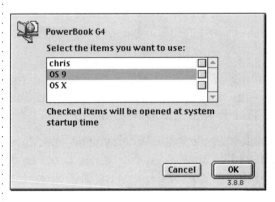

Choose Wisely.
Click the volume you want to mount.

If you want to connect to another Mac via TCP/IP from the Chooser, click the Server IP Address button, and enter the IP address for the Mac you'd like to access.

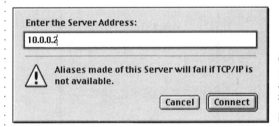

Other Means of Entry.
If another Mac allows you to connect via TCP/IP, you can enter its IP address here.

Network Browser

In the past few years, Apple has introduced another way to access network volumes in Mac OS 9.2 and earlier, via something called the Network Browser. To use Network Browser, choose it from the Apple menu, and click the triangle next to AppleTalk. When you do, the Macs connected to your network will appear in the list below. To log onto one of these networked computers, click the triangle next to the computer's name. Doing so produces the Connect To dialog box. You should know what to do from there.

If you want to connect to another Mac via TCP/IP from the Network Browser, choose Connect To Server from the Shortcut Button and type the IP address of the Mac you'd like to access.

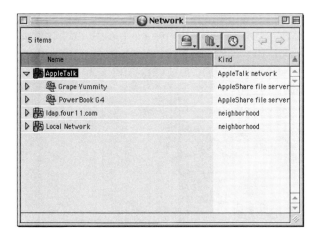

Just Browsing. The Network Browser is another way to access volumes on the network.

May I Serve You? Use the Connect To Server button to access other Macs at home or on the Web via TCP/IP.

Adding AirPort

If you have an AirPort-compatible Mac—just about any Mac released in the past couple of years fills the bill—it's worth thinking about using AirPort to connect to your network rather than cable. In particular, AirPort makes sense for PowerBooks and iBooks, which are Macs that you're likely to drag from place to place, as well as for any Macs that are far away from your computing nerve center. Do you really want to risk the bites sure to be inflicted by the countless venomous critters that live under your house and behind its walls to string the cable necessary to grant Junior's iMac easier access to the Web? No way. In such cases, wireless is the only way to go.

To use AirPort, your Mac must have an AirPort card. Apple currently bundles AirPort cards only with its top-of-the-line PowerBooks, so if you have a lesser AirPort-compatible Mac, you'll have to plunk down $99 and buy one. Fortunately, AirPort cards generally are fairly easy to install (I say *generally* because to get one into a Titanium PowerBook G4, you have to remove the bottom of the PowerBook—not a terrible chore but tiresome nonetheless.)

For the AirPort card to work with your wired network, you also must have an AirPort Base Station—a separate device that contains its own AirPort card and Ethernet port. As I mentioned earlier in this chapter, you connect the Base Station to the wired network by stringing a standard Ethernet cable between your hub and the Base Station.

A Pod, Not iPod.
An AirPort Base Station.

Now that the easy part's over, you're ready to set up the Base Station and your AirPort-equipped Macs.

Configuration

Because Internet service providers offer differing ways to configure your Mac to access the Internet, I can't guide you through the specific way to enter your TCP/IP settings; your ISP can provide this information. I can, however, tell you the easiest way to set up your Base Station. First, configure a Mac to log onto your ISP; then use the AirPort Setup Assistant (located in the AirPort folder inside the Apple Extras folder, which in turn is inside the Applications folder of your Mac OS 9.x volume) to copy those settings to the Base Station.

For the sake of argument, suppose that you'd like to connect an AirPort-bearing iBook to the network, and on this network are a Blue & White Power Mac G3 and an iMac. You'll use the iBook to configure the Base Station.

Copy Internet settings

Launch the AirPort Setup Assistant on the iMac, and click the Set Up an AirPort Base Station option. In the Internet Choice window, click Yes to indicate that the iMac is configured to access the Internet. If your ISP requires the Point-to-Point protocol over Ethernet (PPPoE), click Yes in the next window; otherwise, click No.

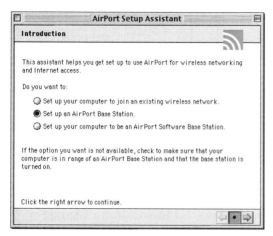

Lending Assistance.
The AirPort Setup Assistant allows you to configure an AirPort network easily.

In the Internet Access window, select the TCP/IP settings that you want to copy to the Base Station, and click the right arrow. In the next window, name your network and provide a password. Finally, click Go Ahead to install these settings on the Base Station. Wait while the settings are transferred to the Base Station.

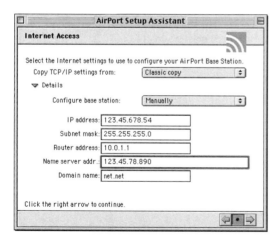

AirPort Shuttle.
Use the AirPort Setup Assistant to copy Internet settings to your AirPort Base Station.

Configure Base Station as a router

The AirPort Base Station can operate as a DHCP (Dynamic Host Configuration Protocol) server, a device that shares a single Internet address (IP address) among numerous computers. This service is vital if your ISP allows you only a single static IP address or a dynamic IP address. To configure your Base Station as a DHCP server, follow these steps:

1. Launch the AirPort Admin Utility (also located in the AirPort folder), select your AirPort network, and click Configure.

2. Enter the Base Station password to access the Configuration window, and click the Network tab.

3. Click the Distribute IP Addresses option and the Share a Single IP Address (Using DHCP & NAT) option.

   When you switch on these options, your Base Station acts as the contact point between your network and the Internet. As far as your ISP knows, you're using the single IP address allotted to you from a single computer. In reality, the Base Station creates an internal network, distributing IP addresses to each computer within that network (such addresses fall into the 10.0.1.2–10.0.1.50 range) that can share the IP address provided by your ISP.

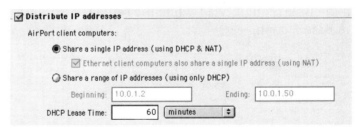

Distribution Center. Use these settings to share an IP address across your AirPort network.

In this example network, you have a Mac connected to the network via Ethernet. Because you want to use this Mac to access the Internet and your wireless network, you also must check the Enable DHCP on Ethernet and Enable AirPort to Ethernet bridging options. These options allow computers connected via Ethernet to join the network. If your network lacks such a wired connection, leave these two options switched off.

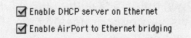

Get It Wired. These additional settings allow you to share the network between wired and wireless devices.

Configure Macs for the network

Although your Base Station is ready to share an IP address, this fact does you little good if your Macs aren't prepared to use the Base Station and its settings. Here's how to set up the Macs on your network to share that single IP address:

1. Open the AppleTalk control panel, and from the Connect via pop-up menu, choose the method by which your Mac is connected to the Base Station (AirPort, if your Mac has an AirPort card, and Ethernet, if your Mac is wired to the hub).

2. Close the AppleTalk control panel and click Save when prompted to do so.

3. Open the TCP/IP control panel, and choose Configurations from the File menu to create a new set of TCP/IP settings.

4. Select any configuration in the resulting window, click Duplicate, name your new configuration, and click the Make Active button.

5. In the TCP/IP window, be sure that the Connect Via pop-up menu displays the connection protocol appropriate for your Mac (AirPort or Ethernet).

6. From the Configure pop-up menu, choose Using DHCP Server.

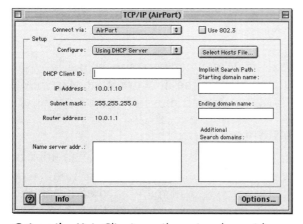

Get on the Net. Clients on the network must be configured to grab their IP addresses from the Base Station.

Don't be concerned with the DHCP Client ID field or any other empty fields. The information necessary to establish your Internet connection—IP address, name server address, and domain name—is stored in your Base Station. (To confirm, open the AirPort Admin Utility and click the Internet tab.) As you log onto the Internet with each Mac, the IP Address, Subnet Mask, and Router Address fields will be completed in the TCP/IP control panel automatically.

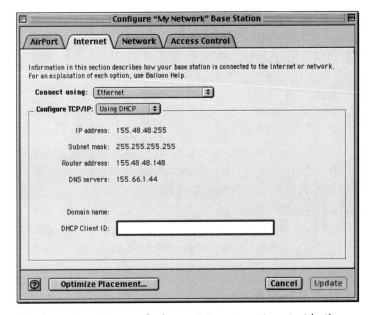

Confirmation. You can find your Internet settings inside the AirPort Admin Utility.

And you're done. Now when you launch your browser or email client from any Mac on the network, that Mac should be able to get to the Web with no muss or fuss.

Adding a Router

If you don't require AirPort's wireless capabilities but would still like to share a single IP address with a bunch of Macs, a router is the way to go. As I mentioned earlier in the chapter, these devices aren't terribly expensive (less than $100). Regrettably, they're not as easy to configure as an AirPort Base Station. You see, unlike the Base Station, routers don't come with easy-to-use, Mac-compatible configuration programs. The fact is, they don't come with Mac software at all. Rather, you must configure them from your browser.

Fortunately, I'm prepared to lend a helping hand. Here's how to set up that router.

Make connections

The router is likely to have a port labeled WAN (for Wide Area Network) or Internet. This port is your way to the Web. String a straight-through Ethernet cable between your DSL or cable modem and this port. The router will carry at least one other port. Use this port to connect to your Ethernet hub or, if the router carries multiple ports, to the other Macs on your network (again using straight-through cables). Your router may carry an *uplink* port, which is for stringing multiple routers together. Don't plug anything into this port unless you intend to gang a couple of routers.

Configure your Macs

If you haven't already done so, open the AppleTalk control panel, and make sure that the Connect Via menu reads Ethernet. Close and, if necessary, save.

For the Macs on your network to share a single IP address, you must ask them to search the network for a DHCP server (the router will act as this DHCP server). To do so, open the TCP/IP control panel on each Mac, and choose Ethernet from the Connect Via pop-up menu and Using DHCP Server from the Configure pop-up menu. Don't worry about the other settings in this window; they'll be filled in automatically after the Mac connects to the router. Close and save.

Configure the router

On one of the networked Macs, launch a Web browser, such as Internet Explorer or Netscape Navigator. In the address bar of your browser, enter the IP address for your router. (You can find this address in the router's manual.) For the sake of argument, suppose that address is 192.168.1.1 (a common address for these things).

You'll be asked for your name and password. This information is also contained in the manual. Don't worry; you can change both the user name and password later.

Set addresses

How you proceed depends on the kind of Internet address you have. You can have either a *dynamic* or *static* IP address. A *dynamic* IP address is one that changes each time you log onto the Internet, and a *static* address is one that doesn't change. Unless you're paying a premium, you likely have a dynamic IP address. Here's how to set up the router for either.

Dynamic IP. Look for something called PPPoE in the Configuration window. Choose the Enable option, and enter the user name and password you use with your Internet account (the information you use to log onto your email account, for example). You should also see the Connect on Demand option. When switched on, this option tells the router to glom on to the last IP address it was assigned. Otherwise, it lets go of the address when it's finished with its Internet chores and grabs another address when it next needs one.

Enable this option unless your ISP tells you to do otherwise.

Static IP. If you have a static IP address, look for the WAN IP Address area, and enter your IP address, subnet mask, gateway address, and DNS server address or addresses. All this information should be provided to you by your ISP.

Restart. That's it. Quit your browser, and restart your Macs for your router to start doing its job.

Software Setup: Mac OS X

As you might expect, Mac OS X supports file sharing as well. In this section, I show you how to configure Mac OS X for file sharing.

Turn on Sharing

Choose System Preferences from Mac OS X's Apple menu or from the Dock, and select the Sharing system preference. In the File Sharing section of the resulting window, click the Start button. Unless you want to share Web pages in your Sites folder (an option I leave off), keep Web Sharing off.

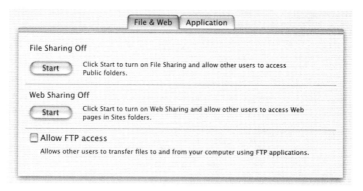

Sharing X-ercise. To share your Mac OS X machine, switch on Sharing.

I'd also leave Allow Remote Login and Allow Remote Apple Events off in the Application pane. These options allow other users to get to your computer from the Internet and, therefore, pose a greater security risk. If you know that you want to grant other users access to your Mac (or to grant yourself access, if you plan to dial in to your home Mac from the road), feel free to switch these options on.

If you haven't taken the opportunity to give your Mac a more descriptive name than Billy-Bob's Computer now's the time. At the bottom of the Sharing window, you'll find the Computer Name text box. Rename your computer (something like "BB's SuperDuper iMac" might be nice).

Switch on AppleTalk

Although Mac OS X was designed to communicate via the TCP/IP protocol, it hasn't completely abandoned the venerable AppleTalk. If you'd like your Mac OS X machine to see other Macs or printers on the network that support AppleTalk, open the Network system preference, choose the method you use to connect to that network from the Show menu (Built-in Ethernet or AirPort, for example), click the AppleTalk tab, and enable the Make AppleTalk Active option. You can leave Automatically selected in the Configure menu unless your network is so complex as to include different AppleTalk zones. If it is this complex, you or your IT person probably knows how to configure this option.

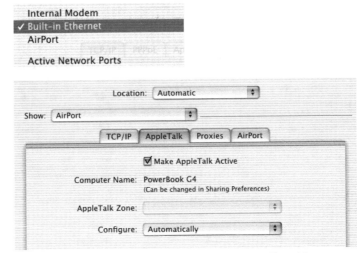

Ways and Means. If you'd like to connect to other Macs over AppleTalk, select the way your Mac connects to the network and then enable AppleTalk.

Add Users

As in Mac OS 9.2 and earlier, you grant access by creating users and determining what those users can do with your computer. Unlike in Mac OS 9.2, when you grant access to a networked user, you're granting much the same access to that user when he or she physically sits down in front of your Mac OS X machine. In terms of sharing, Mac OS X doesn't distinguish between a networked user and one who pounds on your Mac's keyboard.

To add users, simply launch System Preferences and click Users. In the resulting window, click the New User button. In the New User window, enter a name for the user in the Name text box. (Remember, this is the name *they'll* use and see on the login screen of your Mac, so choosing a name like Old Stinky-Pants probably isn't a good idea—unless that person's name really is Old Stinky-Pants, of course.) When you complete the name and press Return or Tab, an eight-character version of the person's name will appear in the Short Name text box. (Abraham Lincoln becomes abrahaml, for example.) You can make this name even shorter, if you like, but it can be no longer than eight characters.

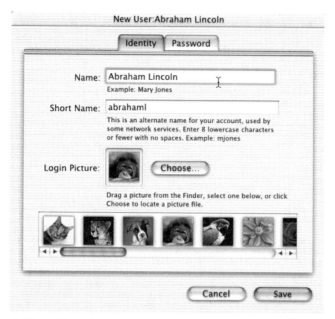

Adding Abe. The New Users window.

If you care to add an editorial element, feel free to pick a particularly unflattering picture to accompany the user's name at login. I prefer the orangutan when configuring my Mac for loathsome relatives. Regrettably, users can change their login picture if they're sitting at your Mac (drat it!).

Now click the Password tab, enter a password for this user, and confirm it in the text box below. There's even a place to put a hint for the password, should you forget it.

In this same window, you'll see the Allow User to Administer This Computer option. Enabling this option won't do much for people who log in across the network—Mac OS X confines their travels to their own User folders—but should such a person hunker down at your computer with such privileges, he or she can make all kinds of changes. Unless you're sure that you want this person to control all aspects of your Mac, leave this option off.

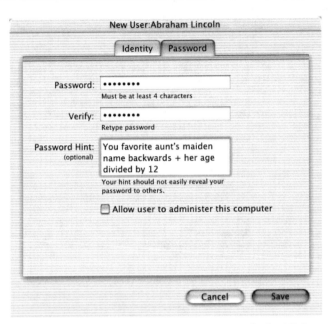

Give Me a Hint. If you forget your password, the Hint box can come in handy.

This point may seem to be evident, but it's my duty to make it: Don't choose really obvious passwords and hints. Using the word password *for your password, for example, is not smart. My cat could figure that out, for heaven's sake. A secure password is one that contains a jumble of letters and numbers—ycp98a38vm, for example. Your birthday, phone number, or street address are also high on the list of poor password ideas.*

Oh, and don't kill yourself coming up with the uncrackable 24-digit password. Mac OS X recognizes only the first eight characters of a password.

When it comes to the Hint text box, please try to come up with something broad. If your password is chicken, for example (a bad password, by the way), and the Hint box says Kentucky fried or cluck-cluck, you deserve the erased hard drive you'll gain when a passing 6-year-old hacks into your Mac.

Assign Privileges

When you talk about sharing files in a networked environment under Mac OS X, you're talking about sharing only a user's folder. Mac OS X doesn't provide access to any folders except those within the user's folder unless you're an administrator. A user's folder contains the Documents, Library, Movies, Music, Pictures, Public, and Sites folders. By default, users have read and write access to all these folders within their personal User folder.

As administrator, you can limit access to all these folders. You can keep Bubba from opening even the Documents, Library, Movies, Music, and Pictures files in his User folder. Bubba will, however, still be able to open his Public and Sites folders, though you can keep him from writing anything to them.

To bridle poor Bubba, just click a folder—the Movies folder, for example—and choose Show Info (Command-I) from the Finder's File menu. When you do so, up pops the Show Info window. Click the pop-up menu and choose Privileges. Three additional menus marked Owner, Group, and Everyone appear below. These menus allow you to assign privileges.

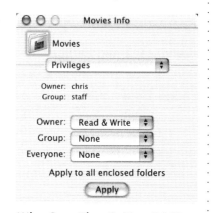

Who Goes There? Mac OS X's privileges allow you to determine who gets in and who stays out.

Owner is Bubba. To grant Bubba all access to this folder, be sure that Read & Write is selected in the pop-up menu (as it is by default). If you want to allow him to open files in this folder but not save new files here, choose Read Only. If you care to allow him to save files to this folder but not see what else is in the folder, choose Write Only. And if you want to deny the poor sap all access to the folder—meaning that he can't even open the blasted thing—choose None. (Poor Bubba!)

The Group menu is where you assign privileges for a particular group. Mac OS X is far less flexible about groups than Mac OS 9.2 and earlier. You can't create new groups of users easily—the accountancy pool, for example. Rather, Mac OS X creates a couple of its own groups: one group with administrative privileges and another without, for example. Until Mac OS X allows you to create your own groups, don't bother mucking with this menu.

Finally, the Everyone pop-up menu lets you set privileges for those who log on as guests. In a networked environment, this option does you little good, because guests logging in over the network can see only a user's Public folder and the items within it (unless you choose None or Write from the Everyone pop-up menu).

Logging On

With file sharing on, users created, and privileges assigned, your Mac is open for business. For other users to log onto your Mac, they'd do the following.

Mac OS 9.2 and earlier

1. Open the Chooser, and select AppleShare.

   In the pane to the right, the networked Mac should appear if you switched AppleTalk on in the Network portion of the Mac OS X machine. (If you haven't switched on AppleTalk, click the Server IP Address button, and enter the IP address for the Mac OS X machine.)

2. Select the Mac's name, and click the OK button (or double-click the Mac's name).

   The sign-in window appears.

3. Enter your usename and password, and click OK.

   If you've signed in as an administrator, the resulting window will grant you access to every volume on the Mac OS X machine. Select the volumes you want to mount on your Desktop, and click OK.

   If you've signed in as a user, by default you'll be given access to your User folder as well as to the Public folders of other users.

Alternatively, you can log onto the Mac OS X machine via the Network Browser (located in the Apple menu). Click the triangle next to the Local Network entry and then click the triangle next to Local Services. Your Mac OS X machine should appear below. Double-click the Mac's name to view the sign-in window. After entering your user name and password, you'll be able to select which volumes or folders you'd like to access.

Mac OS X

To connect to another Mac when running Mac OS X, choose Connect to Server (Command-K) from the Finder's Go menu. In the resulting window, you'll see entries for AppleTalk and Local Network. Any AppleTalk-compatible Macs with File Sharing switched on will appear when you click AppleTalk. Those Macs that have sharing over TCP/IP enabled will appear when you click Local Network.

Go, Mac, Go. The Finder's Go menu is the means of accessing your network under Mac OS X.

To log onto a Mac, just click its name in the right side of the window and click Connect (or double-click its name). When you do, you'll be prompted for your user name and password. (You can also choose to log on as a guest, if that Mac permits.) Enter your name and password, and click Connect. In the next window, choose the volumes or folders you want to access.

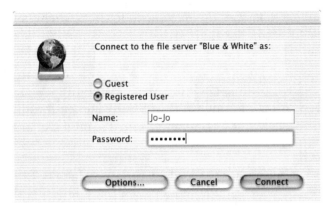

Déjà Vu. Mac OS X's user name and password window looks eerily familiar.

If you don't see the Mac to which you want to connect—it's a Mac located on the Internet somewhere, for example—you can attempt to connect to it by entering its IP address in the Connect to Server's Address text box.

IP Freely. Yes, Mac OS X allows you to access other computers by IP address as well.

If you routinely log onto a particular networked Mac, there's no need to go through this whole rigmarole. Instead, you can mount the volume or folder one time and then drag that volume or folder into the Dock. The next time you want to connect to that Mac, just click its icon in the Dock. When you do, the sign-in window pops to the fore. Enter your user name and password, and the networked item mounts.

Practical Networking Projects

I blame you not one smidge if the preceding pages of this chapter have elicited a reaction no stronger than a stifled yawn. Sure, being able to move files between Macs and to share printers and an Internet connection is important, but *sheesh*, what a bore. There's just no way around it; networking *qua* networking is a dull affair.

To repay you for your patience, I'd like to present a couple of networking projects that will make your Mac even more productive and—dare I say it?—fun to use.

The Backup Server

By now, you realize the benefits of backing up your data. If you have more than one Mac, you can make the process even easier by setting up one of your Macs as a backup server—a computer that manages the backup process for every other Mac on your network.

What you need

A Mac to act as server. A backup server needn't be a particularly powerful computer; just about any Mac made in the past 10 years will do. But there are advantages to using more recent Macintosh models. Because you can back up your data more quickly via a TCP/IP connection than via AppleTalk, you should try to use a Power Macintosh; 680x0 Macs don't support network connections via TCP/IP. The earliest Power Macintosh computers were the 6100, 7100, and 8100 models.

There are advantages to using even more recent Macs than these early PowerPC models. Having a PCI slot, for example, will allow you to add a fast SCSI card, which (if your backup medium supports this faster transfer protocol) could make your backups zip along much more quickly. You'll also see some performance gain from a network that supports 100Base-T Ethernet rather than the slower 10Base-T. Adding a faster processor can also speed backups. Software compression and encryption, for example, take less time with a faster processor.

Retrospect and Retrospect clients. For network backups, Dantz's Retrospect (www.dantz.com) is the only software I recommend; there just isn't a better way to back up your data. Retrospect Desktop Backup (the flavor of Retrospect that supports network backup) costs $175. A five-pack of network clients, which supports both Macs and PCs, costs $120. If you need to back up lots of computers, the workgroup edition of the program, which supports as many as 20 clients, is a good deal at $340.

Retrospect requires your Mac to have at least 16 MB of memory and your hard drive to have 50 MB of free space. Dantz recommends that your Mac run Mac OS 7.6.1 or later. Open Transport (included with System 7.5.3 and later) is required for backups via TCP/IP.

As this book goes to press, Dantz is readying a version of Retrospect for Mac OS X, but I haven't seen it yet. My guess is that it will work very much like the Mac OS 9 version, so the instructions in the following sections should apply to Mac OS X as well.

Something to back up to. Three factors will influence the backup medium you choose: the amount of data you need to back up, how reliable you'd like your backup to be, and your budget.

If your network is made up of Macs whose hard drives hold dozens of gigabytes of data, you should look at a high-capacity tape drive. Tape is one of the more reliable media types around, and although a tape drive can be expensive (at more than $1,000), you can store a lot of data on an inexpensive tape. DVD-RAM is another fine high-capacity option.

Some folks favor an external hard drive for backups. I'm on the fence on this one. Yes, fast external drives are not terribly expensive, and thanks to FireWire, they can be quite portable. But unlike a removable-media drive, an external drive gives you only one piece of media to back up to: the external drive. If that drive dies, your backup is hosed.

A CD-RW drive is a good option for medium-to-large backups. CD-R discs cost less than 50 cents apiece when purchased in bulk and hold 640 MB reliably. The disadvantage of CD-RW is that for multigigabyte backups, you'll spend a lot of time swapping media.

Removable-cartridge drives—such as Iomega's Jaz and Castlewood's Orb—that hold a couple of gigabytes of data per cartridge can be unreliable and are not good long-term storage solutions. Iomega's Zip drive has been known to have reliability problems as well. Also, each cartridge holds less than 100 MB of data, necessitating dozens of disk swaps for even a small network of modern Macs.

And only a masochist would consider backing up a network of Macs on floppy disks.

How to do it

Configure your network.

1. If your Macs are already configured for TCP/IP and are set up to access the Web via the Ethernet port or AirPort, you can skip to the next step; your Mac is configured for network backup. If you access the Internet via modem or if this is your first outing with TCP/IP, here's how to set up your Mac.

   Open the AppleTalk control panel, and Choose Ethernet from the Connect Via pop-up menu. Now open the TCP/IP control panel. Choose Ethernet from the pop-up menu and Manually from the Configure pop-up menu. In the IP Address text box, enter 192.168.6.1 on the first Mac you configure. On subsequent Macs, increase the last number by one (192.168.6.2, 192.168.6.3, and so on). These IP addresses are reserved for internal networks and won't conflict with any Internet IP addresses. In the Subnet Mask text box, enter 255.255.255.0 on each of the Macs. Close the TCP/IP window, and click Save when prompted. Your Macs are now ready to talk across the network.

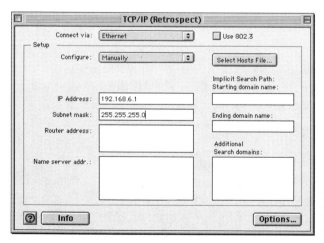

Getting Addressed. If your network isn't yet set up with IP addresses, configure it this way.

2. Install Retrospect and configure clients.

   Installing the Retrospect application is dead easy, so I won't bore you with the details. You do have to click through a few windows to configure Retrospect's clients, however.

   After installing the client software on each networked computer, launch Retrospect from the backup server. Click Retrospect's Configure tab and then click the Clients button in the resulting pane. In the Client Database window that appears, click the Network button.

   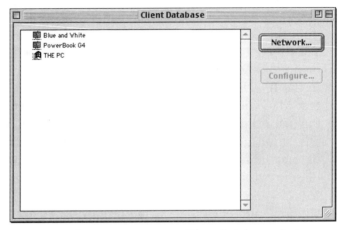

   Attracting Clients. Retrospect's Client Database window shows you the computers on your network running copies of Retrospect Client.

   In the Clients on Network window, you'll see AppleTalk and TCP/IP listed as network protocols. Click TCP/IP and Mac OS to see all the running Macs on your network. (If you have AppleTalk clients, clicking AppleTalk reveals them.) Clicking Windows 95/98/NT shows all PCs on the network.

   Now select a client computer, and click the Configure button. The resulting client window includes options for selecting volumes for backup as well as for changing the client's network protocol from TCP/IP to AppleTalk or vice versa. Click OK to confirm your choices.

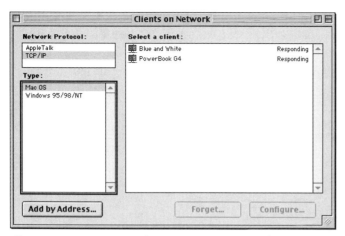

Client Connections. See how your Retrospect clients are connected to the network in this window.

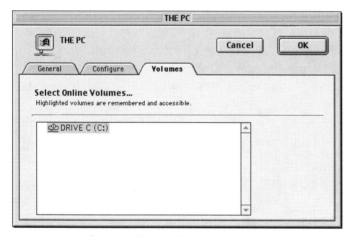

Turning up Volumes. Clicking the Volumes tab reveals the drives and volumes on a particular computer.

3. Pick and choose.

   Now you should think about what kind of files you want to back up. Sure, you could fire up Retrospect and ask the program to back up every item on your network, but do you really need to back up that massive 632 MB game installation? Of course not.

   Retrospect allows you to filter out files you don't care to back up. After clicking the Backup button, click the Selecting button in Retrospect's main window. In the next window, you have the option to select a subset of the files on your Macs. You can back up everything except cache files, for example. Or you can back up all your documents but no applications. Or you can back up only those files marked with the Hot label.

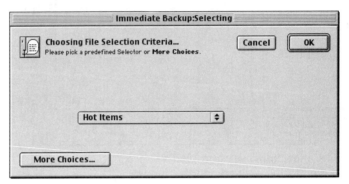

Be Choosy. With Retrospect's filters, you don't need to back up all your files.

If you click the More Options button, you can narrow your selection by, among other things, file type (your Microsoft Word files, for example), size, and date.

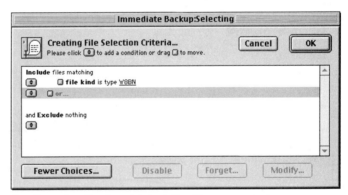

Be Choosier. Really, pick just the files you want.

4. Create a schedule.

   The key to successfully backing up your data is *consistency*—making sure that your data is backed up often enough that, should a Mac's hard drive take leave of its senses, you can recover as much of your data as possible. And the secret to a consistent backup is scheduling, creating a script that automates your backups.

Fortunately, Retrospect includes EasyScript, an easy-to-use scheduling assistant. To create a backup script, just click the Automate button in the main Retrospect window; click the EasyScript button; and click through a series of windows that ask you which volumes you'd like to back up, what variety of storage media you'll use, how often you'd like to back up, how often you want to rotate your backup media, and what time you'd like the backup to begin.

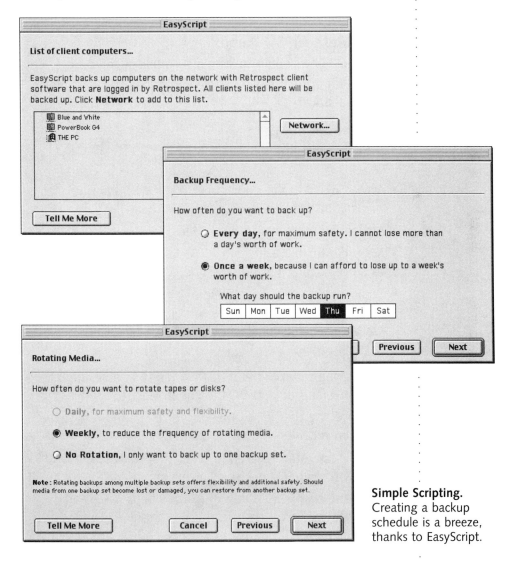

Simple Scripting. Creating a backup schedule is a breeze, thanks to EasyScript.

After you answer these questions, Retrospect creates a backup script for you and automatically runs the script at the time you designated in EasyScript. If you want to edit a script you've created, simply choose Scripts in the Automate portion of the main Retrospect window, select the script you'd like to edit, click the Edit button, and alter the script to your heart's content.

To complete your backup, leave your Macs running, load the media into your backup device, and turn out the lights; your Macs and Retrospect will do the rest.

The Wireless MP3 Jukebox

This project allows you to stream MP3 music files from a remote Mac through your home stereo. I think this wireless jukebox is terribly cool. After you've set it up, you will, too!

What you need

- A Mac that holds a mess of MP3 files. I'll call this the *server*.
- A Mac placed near your home stereo. I'll call this the *client*.
- AirPort connections in both Macs.
- A stereo Y-cable with two RCA plugs on one end and a stereo miniplug (Walkman-style connector) on the other.
- Copies of Apple's free music player/encoder, iTunes, on each Mac. If you don't have a copy, you can download it at www.apple.com/itunes.

How to do it

1. Plug the miniplug end of the stereo Y-cable into the Sound Output port on the client Mac.
2. Shove the two RCA plugs into a free input on your stereo receiver (AUX, for example).
3. Flick on your receiver, and set the input selector to AUX (or whatever input you used).
4. On the server Mac, log onto the client Mac, and mount its hard drive on the Desktop.

5. On the server Mac (the one that holds the MP3 files), copy the iTunes Music Library file to the client Mac's hard drive.

   This file is located inside the iTunes folder inside the Documents folder at the root level of your startup drive.

6. On the client Mac, place the iTunes Music Library file that you just copied in this same location (Hard Drive: Documents: iTunes).

   Moving the file to this location on the client Mac will overwrite any iTunes Music Library file already present, so store the old file in a safe place if you want to save it.

7. Launch iTunes on the client Mac.

   When you do, you'll see that the library contains a list of the iTunes audio files contained on the server Mac. Click the iTunes Play button, and a dialog box appears, asking you to connect to the server Mac. If necessary, enter your user name and password, and click OK. After you do, the iTunes files stored on the server Mac will be played over your AirPort network, to the client Mac, through the client Mac's Sound Output port, and into your stereo.

8. Rock out.

You can perform this trick on a wired network as well, and if you'd rather not plug your iBook into the family stereo, you're welcome to listen through the Mac's speakers or through headphones jacked into the Mac instead. But come on, the whole wireless element makes it that much ginchier. Wouldn't you agree?

Digital Hubbub

Music, Movies, and More on Your Mac

Not so long ago, Steve Jobs took the stage at a gathering of the Mac faithful and proclaimed that the Macintosh was, from this day forward, more than just a computer. Unbeknownst to legions of Mac users, the stylish box sitting on their desktops or in their laps was not a mere thinking machine. It was, in fact, a digital hub—a go-between box for such multimedia thingamabobs as digital cameras and camcorders, portable MP3 players, home DVD players, and external speakers.

OK, so such a proclamation likely originated in Apple's marketing department rather than in R & D. Despite the hype, there's a fair dollop of truth in the statement. The Mac has long been the platform of choice for those professionals who work with audio, video, and graphic design. Jobs could have made this same statement long ago.

The difference here is that content creation is no longer strictly the purview of the pros. Thanks to such cool Apple tools as iMovie, iTunes, and iDVD (and the underlying QuickTime technology that makes these tools work), *every* Mac user can muck with multimedia.

But *how?*

That's exactly what I'd like to spend time doing in this chapter: showing you how to make the most of your Mac and multimedia. To do so, I'll offer up a few of my favorite tips and tricks. To gain the most benefit from these tips, you should have a general working knowledge of how iMovie, iTunes, and QuickTime go about their business.

I'll begin with one of my favorites.

Recording LPs and Cassettes on Your Mac

If, like me, you've trod this planet long enough to know what an LP is—and actually have a few in your possession—you've likely been struck by how inconvenient these vinyl discs are compared with CDs. To begin with, they play for only about 18 minutes, and then you have to turn the dratted things over to hear the other side. And, of course, there's the disturbing knowledge that each time you play one of your precious records, the turntable's needle scratches away another tiny layer of its life.

Tape cassettes are little better. Over time, tape stretches and eventually breaks, ruining your precious bootleg copy of the Dead playing a seemingly endless rendition of "Puddin' Head Jones" at Winterland in 1973.

Wouldn't it be swell if you could preserve your precious analog recording in digital form? You can (if you couldn't, would I lead you on this way?). Here's how.

Hardware Connections

For this trick to work, you'll need:

- A turntable or cassette deck.
- A stereo receiver.
- A cable for moving sound from the stereo receiver to the Mac. This cable likely will feature two mono RCA plugs on one end (the kind of plugs on your stereo receiver) and a stereo miniplug (Walkman-style plug) on the other. You can obtain it at any Radio Shack.
- A Mac with some kind of sound-input port.

No Sound Input on Your Mac?

If you're a seasoned Mac user with a recent Mac model—a Power Mac or PowerBook—you'll notice that your computer shipped *sans* sound-input port. "Chris," you might be saying, "why is that?"

I haven't a clue.

Mac users who are interested in audio have asked that question numerous times at various volumes in public as well as in private, and Apple has never deigned to provide an answer. But here's my theory: Built-in audio ports won't work under Mac OS X, and rather than make those ports a higher priority for the Mac OS X development team, Apple simply stopped including them on new Mac models.

From Apple's point of view, doing so makes some sense. How would it look if Apple continued to plunk this port into its computers, only to have customers discover that built-in sound input was a nonoption under Mac OS X? Rather than suffer those complaints (and thus taint its sparkling-new operating system), Apple opted to take the heat from a few cantankerous audio users.

Shortsighted? I think so, particularly given this whole "digital hub" thing. But who asked me?

Given that Apple has bailed on the audio-input front, you must look to third parties to get sound into your Mac. Such vendors provide USB, FireWire, and PCI audio-in options. Of these, USB and PCI are the least expensive. FireWire audio-input devices are largely intended for the professional market.

Griffin Technology (www.griffintechnology.com) makes a couple of USB audio devices for the Mac. The iMic is a $35 USB device that accepts line-level (the signal sent from your stereo amplifier) and mic-level (a signal from a microphone) input through a stereo miniplug jack. The company's $100 PowerWave includes RCA jacks (the kind of jacks used on home stereos), boasts higher-quality audio, and incorporates a USB hub.

USB sound-input devices are fine if you're doing simple audio work, but they're not a good solution for audio professionals. Because of the relatively slow speed of USB, timing can be thrown off when you're recording one audio track on top of another, making it difficult to sync a multitrack recording. If you'd rather sync than swim in a sea of ill-aligned audio tracks, look to a PCI or FireWire input device instead.

Creative Technology (www.creative.com) offers the $100 SoundBlaster Live for Macintosh PCI audio card. This card is a fine choice if you have an older Macintosh. Regrettably, as this book goes to press, it's not compatible with Power Macs manufactured since January 2000 (sound input doesn't work reliably).

(Tiny rant: How the company could fail to write updated drivers to make this card compatible with newer Power Macs is beyond me. I mean, criminy, this card is the perfect solution for thousands of Mac users who mourn the loss of the sound-input port, and Creative can't be bothered to hire a Mac-savvy programmer for a couple of weeks!? What are these people thinking!? Let's pray that Creative delivers on its hints that a Mac OS X driver for this card is in the works.)

Beyond this card, you start dabbling in the professional lines of audio cards and input devices. Such companies as Yamaha, Mark of the Unicorn, MidiMan, Roland, Emagic, and Digidesign make audio-input devices for the semiprofessional market; these devices can run around $1,000.

To make the proper connections, string the adapter cable between the Mac and your stereo receiver. The miniplug will go into your Mac's sound-input port (or the input port on your soundcard or audio adapter, if your Mac doesn't have a sound-input port), and the RCA plugs will go into some variety of audio-output ports on your receiver (Tape Out, for example).

Nearly all the ports on your stereo receiver are for input—for devices that send audio into the receiver. If you plug your Mac into the receiver's AUX jacks, for example, you'll get no sound into your Mac. You need output ports, such as the receiver's Tape Out ports.

Your turntable or cassette deck should already be connected to your receiver. If it isn't, hook it up now.

You can plug the outputs of your cassette deck directly into the sound-input port of your Mac and adjust the input level of the tape in the Mac's audio editing application (I'll get to that later in this chapter). You cannot, however, plug a turntable directly into the Mac's input port. A turntable's audio signal is too weak for the Mac's input and needs to be amplified first.

Software and Recording

Sound can now get into your Mac, but you still need software to record that sound. You have several options here.

Option 1

If you plan to do this kind of thing on a regular basis, I strongly suggest that you purchase a copy of Roxio's (www.roxio.com) Toast Titanium, a CD writing application that costs around $80. Toast Titanium includes an application called CD Spin Doctor that was designed for exactly this kind of project.

To record your tracks with CD Spin Doctor, just launch the program, select the input source for the audio (the Mac's sound-input port), click the program's Record button, and drop the needle or start the tape. CD Spin Doctor begins recording your record or tape. You don't need to start and stop the record or tape for each song. When you finish recording, you can direct the program to look for audio gaps and divide the album into cuts based on those gaps.

The Doctor Is In. CD Spin Doctor makes it easy to dub LPs and tapes to your Mac.

But wait—the program's not done. CD Spin Doctor also includes a feature that filters out the pops, clicks, and hum that are an inherent part of records. Normally, this kind of filtering would cost you $99 in the form of Ray Gun from Arboretum Systems (www.arboretum.com). Ray Gun is a plug-in filter that is the basis of CD Spin Doctor's noise-reduction system.

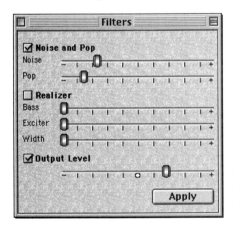

Hiss, Boom, Bah. Clean up pops, rumble, and hiss with CD Spin Doctor's built-in noise-reduction feature.

After your tracks have been brought into CD Spin Doctor, you can save them in a format that's ready for burning into a CD-R.

As I write this chapter, Toast Titanium is still in beta under Mac OS X, and the beta version does not include CD Spin Doctor. If you plan to run Mac OS X exclusively, check Roxio's Web site to see whether CD Spin Doctor is included; it likely won't be until Apple can work out sound input under Mac OS X.

Option 2

If you don't care about noise reduction or you're on a serious budget, you can grab an inexpensive audio editing application. My current favorite is Felt Tip Software's (www.felttip.com) $35 Sound Studio, a simple yet elegant two-track audio editor.

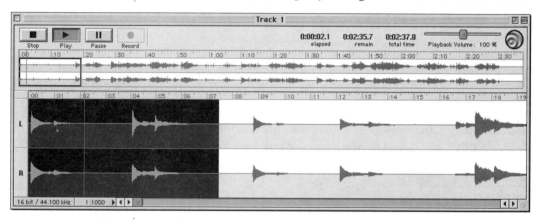

Easy Editor. Sound Studio packs enough punch for simple two-track audio editing.

To use Sound Studio or any other two-track editor, choose the proper input source on the Mac (the sound-input jack, for example), and open a new stereo sound file. Before recording, drop the needle or start the tape, and check the input meters in the software.

Input What!?

Most audio editors allow you to adjust the *gain* (or volume) of an audio signal, which is a good thing unless it's done to excess. You may find that your recording is awfully quiet. To make it less so, you adjust the input higher in your audio editor. If you adjust it too high, however, you're in for trouble. An audio signal that's too hot will overdrive the input and distort. Distortion in the analog "Jimi Hendrix guitar sound" distortion sense can be a cool thing. Digital "input gain too high on my Mac" distortion is not a cool thing. It's an incredibly ugly sound and will ruin a recording. To guard against such distortion, play the loudest portion of your tune, and make sure that the meters stay at the top of the green and out of the upper reaches of the red.

It Goes to 11! Use the input gain controls of your audio editor to prevent digital distortion.

After you've set the input gain properly, click the Record button, and start the record or tape. Although you can record one track at a time, I find it easier to record an entire side of a record or tape and then open the audio file and chop the file into individual tracks. This task is easy because audio editors display sound in the form of waveforms on a timeline. You can find gaps in the recording quickly by looking for periods of no waveform activity. Just cut and paste the areas between these periods of inactivity into new tracks.

> *You don't have to divide tracks if you don't care to. You can leave your recording as one long file. The problem with this approach is that after you burn this long track to a CD, you won't be able to navigate to individual tracks when you play the CD. As far as the CD player is concerned, you have just a single, incredibly long track.*

With the music recorded, save your files in AIFF format (44.1KHz, 16-bit, stereo). This audio format is the one used for audio CDs and one that your CD-burning application will readily recognize.

Sound Studio comes in an Mac OS X version, but as this book goes to press, it can't record audio (that Mac OS X audio-input problem again). Check Felt Tip's Web site for more details on Mac OS X compatibility.

Option 3

If you want more control of your recordings and noise reduction, go with a professional audio editing application and more complete noise filtering. Bias (www.bias-inc.com) makes a fine audio editing application called Peak LE that I like quite a bit.

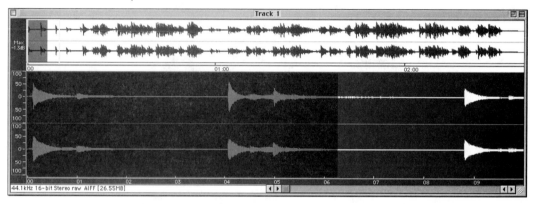

A Peek at Peak. This shot is of the professional version of Peak, but Peak LE has many of the same features.

Peak LE costs $99 and provides you extensive control of your audio files, allowing you to fade one track into another and increase the overall sound of a track to a level just below distortion (a feature called *normalizing*). Peak LE also supports audio plug-ins in the Premiere format, for adding effects such as *reverb* and *chorusing*.

Ray Gun, the noise-filtering software I mentioned earlier in this chapter, is one such Premiere plug-in that works with Peak LE. If you care enough about your audio files to purchase Peak LE, you should pick up a copy of Ray Gun as well to filter out pops, hum, and clicks.

To get audio into Peak LE, follow the same procedure as you might for recording audio with Sound Studio: Set levels with the input gain control, record, and segment your files.

Zap!
Get rid of noise with Arboretum's Ray Gun plug-in.

Audio files that are compatible with CD-burning applications require about 10 MB of space for each minute of audio. Make sure that your hard drive has enough space before plunging ahead with a long recording.

Burning

You've recorded your music into your Mac. Now all that's left to do is bring the audio files into your CD-burning application, arrange the tunes, and let 'er rip. Right?

Well, you can make one more teensy change within your CD-burning application before you commit to the burn: You can change the gap.

In the music biz, they say that silence is as important as sound. If you pay careful attention to the silence between tracks on an album or CD, you'll see how true this saying is. Go ahead—throw on your favorite CD and listen to the gaps. Notice anything? That's right; the gaps between songs are different. Some are quite drawn out; others are over in a instant. Variable gaps are used for dramatic effect. A slow, evocative piece may be followed by a long gap to allow the listener time to recover from the emotional journey. Short gaps may be used to give a recording a sense of urgency. In short, using variable gaps can make your home-grown CDs sound more professional.

Unfortunately, iTunes doesn't easily allow you to use variable gaps. Although you can vary the length of gaps, that length is set for every song in the playlist. To set this gap, choose Preferences from the Edit menu (or, in Mac OS X, choose Preferences from the iTunes menu), click the Advanced tab, and make a choice from the Gap Between Tracks pop-up menu (None to 5 seconds). If variable gaps are important to you, you can cheat by adding more or less silence to the beginning of your audio track in your audio editor.

If you have the patience of a saint you can also add to and remove silence from tracks in iTunes by Control-clicking a track, choosing Get Info from the contextual menu, clicking the Options tab in the Song Information window, and adjusting the Start and Stop Playback time. But, as I mentioned to my editor, Cliff (who offered up this technique for your consideration), "Yeesh! What a chore!"

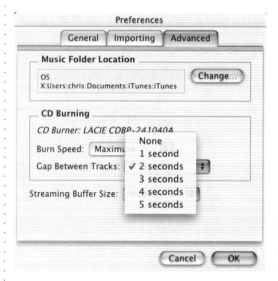

Inflexible iTunes. Regrettably, iTunes doesn't make it easy for you to set a different gap for each tune in your playlist.

Roxio's Toast Lite and Toast Titanium do allow you to set gaps for individual tracks. Just click the area below the Pause heading, and select the gap your prefer. Toast allows you to choose no gap on up to an 8-second gap.

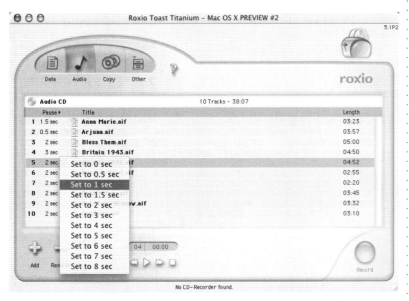

Tolerant Toast. Roxio's Toast, on the other hand, not only allows you to place gaps of different lengths between songs but also allows gaps as long as 8 seconds.

Make a Video CD

The top-of-the-line Power Macs boast a terrific feature: the capability to create discs that will play in most commercial DVD players. The means to this end is Apple's iDVD, an easy-does-it application for creating DVDs of about an hour's length.

The only fly in this ointment is that you have to drop a couple of thousand clams on a Power Mac that carries a SuperDrive (a drive capable of burning DVDs) to make such DVDs. Isn't there another way?

Why, yes, there is—sort of. Although there isn't a less expensive way to create DVDs (other than adding a third-party DVD recorder to your existing Mac), you can create discs that will play movies on many DVD players. And get this: You don't need to purchase expensive DVD discs. You can use standard CD-R and CD-RW media.

The kind of disc you'll create is called a Video CD. Video CD is a format popular in Japan and Hong Kong but not common in the United States. Video CDs can hold about an hour's worth of video and have a quality that's a little less spectacular than a VHS tape. (In other words, we're not talking about pristine video or audio here.)

Finding Mac-compatible tools to create Video CDs was nigh on impossible until 2001, when Roxio released Toast Titanium—the CD-burning application that allows you to create such discs easily. Here's how to go about it in Mac OS 9.2 and earlier:

1. Create a QuickTime movie of the material you want on your video CD (please respect copyright laws), and place the movie on the Desktop.

2. Open the Roxio Toast Titanium folder and then the Roxio Video folder.

3. Drag the Toast Video CD Support file to your closed System Folder, and allow the Mac to place that file in your Extensions folder.

4. Restart your Mac.

5. Launch Toast Titanium.

6. Click the Other button in the main window and hold down the mouse button.

7. Choose Video CD from the resulting menu.

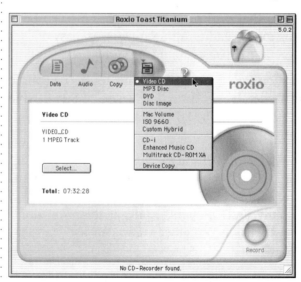

Making Movies. Toast Titanium allows you to create Video CDs that will play on many commercial DVD players.

8. Drag your movie from the Desktop into Toast's main window.

   A dialog box will appear, asking you to approve Toast's default settings (29.97 frames per second, NTSC). These settings should be fine for North America; you can select the PAL settings if your movie will be played back on European or Australian gear.

9. In the dialog box, click OK.

   Wait, wait, and wait some more while Toast encodes your movie.

   For Toast to perform this minor miracle, it must encode the movie in MPEG-1 format (as well as change the audio format), and this job can take a hefty hunk of time. Be patient.

10. Burn your disc.

    After the disc is burned, pray that it will actually play back in your home DVD player.

    That's right—there's a catch. Some older DVD players wouldn't know a Video CD if it came up and bit them. It's possible that you own one of those players and will be disappointed when you insert the disc, your DVD churns and churns in a vain attempt to mount it, and finally spits the poor thing out. For this reason, it's not a bad idea to flip through your DVD player's manual to see whether it's VCD-compatible before you purchase a copy of Toast Titanium.

Make a Slide Show

During my college years, my friend Kent was always gallivanting off to Europe (ostensibly to "study abroad"—yeah, right...) and invariably returned home with hundreds of slides of his travels. Swell Joe that I am, I sat through countless slide shows with something approaching an appreciative smile plastered to my puss, all the while secretly swearing that one day, I'd return the favor. After a recent monthlong trip Down Under, snapping photos at every turn, I decided that the time was ripe to exact my revenge.

I dropped by Kent's home one afternoon, and when he asked about my trip, I casually mentioned that I had some slides I could show him. Sensing the trap, he quickly responded that his slide projector was on the fritz.

"No worries there, mate," I replied as I opened my backpack, "I've prepared a slide show on my PowerBook. Make yourself comfortable. What with a little color commentary, my guess is we'll be done around midnight."

Whether your goal is to entertain or simply annoy, it's easy to create slide shows on your Macintosh. Although a wealth of tools are available for creating slide shows, I'd like to limit my discussion to a scant (and inexpensive) few.

The (Probably) Free Solutions

Your Mac may hold all the software you need to create your own slide shows.

AppleWorks

If you have an iMac, you have a copy of AppleWorks, Apple's all-in-one productivity suite. Unless you routinely sit your kin down for a monthly discussion of the family finances, you've likely never used AppleWorks' presentation component. Now's the time.

And Now Presenting... Add new slides in AppleWorks' Control window.

1. Place the pictures you want to use in your slide show in a folder on your Desktop; then open that folder so you can see your pictures in a window.

2. Launch AppleWorks 6, and click the Presentations icon in the Starting Points window.

3. If the Controls window isn't open, choose Show Presentations Controls from the Windows menu; then click the second tab on the bottom of the Controls window (the one with the picture of a slide).

4. Drag the first picture you want to use in your slide show into the open presentation window (called Untitled until you save it).

   You've just created your first slide.

5. Save your slide show.

6. In the Controls window, click the Plus button to add another slide.

7. Drag a picture into the blank window that appears.

8. Repeat for all your pictures.

9. Save the slide show.

   To specify how your slide show will be played back, click the Play tab in the Controls window (the last tab on the bottom).

   To make slides advance automatically, click the Auto-Advance Every checkbox and enter the number of seconds you want the slide to appear.

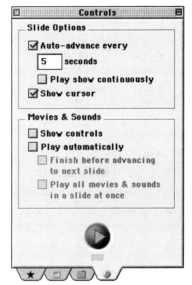

And Now Playing... In the Play portion of AppleWorks' Control window, you determine how long each slide will be displayed.

To present a slide show with AppleWorks, you need to have the AppleWorks application. This requirement is fine for your home computer, but it may not be so terrific if you want to send your slide show to someone else. That person would need a copy of AppleWorks as well.

AppleWorks' Presentation module displays slide shows at a default resolution of 640 by 480. What this fact means to you is that if your picture is larger than 640 by 480, portions of it will be cut off. To address this problem, scale the picture when you bring it into the presentation (click the picture and then choose Scale by Percent from the Arrange menu).

257

Alternatively, you can try holding down the Option key when you click the Play button. This technique keeps Apple-Works from changing the resolution. Regrettably, I routinely get Out of Memory errors when trying this trick.

You can do some fancy stuff with AppleWorks—draw a decorative frame to surround your pictures or annotate each slide—with AppleWorks' draw tools. You can also add transitions between slides. You can find these transitions in the Slides portion of the Control window.

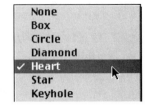

Have a Heart. AppleWorks allows you to place transitions between your slides.

iMovie

If you've purchased any Mac recently, you have a copy of iMovie. Now, I understand that iMovie is supposed to be for moving pictures, but nothing keeps you from using it to create slide shows as well. Here's how:

1. For the sake of convenience, gather your pictures in a single folder.

   You'll be able to insert the pictures more easily if you aren't tearing around your hard drive trying to find them.

2. Launch a copy of iMovie, and when the opening screen appears, click New Project.

3. Name your project and save it.

4. Choose Import File from iMovie's File menu (Command-I), and navigate to a picture you'd like to appear in your slide show.

5. Click Import to bring the picture into iMovie.

   To import multiple pictures from the same folder, Shift-click each picture.

6. Repeat steps 1 through 5 as necessary.

7. After you have your pictures in the iMovie shelf (that binlike area on the right), drag them into the timeline at the bottom of the screen.

8. To specify how long each image will appear, click an image and then change the time in the Image Selection area just above the timeline (it's set for 5 seconds by default).

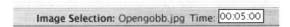

Seconds Count. Enter values in this text box to determine how long a picture remains on-screen.

9. When you've assembled your iMovie, choose Export Movie from the File menu.
10. When the Export window appears, choose To QuickTime from the Export pop-up menu.
11. Make a choice from the Formats pop-up menu.

Choose Full Quality, Large if you intend to display your slide show on your Mac. If, on the other hand, you want to save your slide show to a CD (and subsequently play it from the CD), choose CD-ROM Movie, Medium. Full Quality, Large burned to CD is likely to cause the movie to play back in a choppy fashion.

Export Business. To prepare your iMovie slide show for delivery, use the Export Movie command.

As my mother would say, "Hold on a second, Mr. Blister! I thought we were making a slide show. What's all this 'Quick-Time' and 'movie' stuff?"

OK, I tricked you. Instead of creating a slide show, you created a *movie* of a slide show. Considering that such resulting movie files are much larger than the kind of slide-show files you'd create with AppleWorks or a bonafide slide-show utility, why would you want to use iMovie?

Two reason: Transitions and background music.

iMovie doesn't give a hoot that you're creating a movie out of static images. It's more than willing for you to place transitions between those images and add a musical score to your movie. Just imagine the possibilities. Instead of cobbling together a slide show that clacks from one image to the next, you can create slides that dissolve into one another with a heroic score blasting away in the background.

Also, because you can save the slide show as a QuickTime movie, you can make a copy of it and send it to your friends and family, who need only a copy of QuickTime Player to view it. If you like, you can even post it on the Web via your iTools account.

But wait—it gets even better. If you have a digital camcorder with a FireWire connector, you can export your slide show to that camera via iMovie's Export Movie command, plug the camera into your TV, and watch your slide show on the Big Screen (well, as big as the TV screen in your rumpus room gets, anyway).

When you bring pictures into iMovie, make sure that they're saved in the JPEG format rather than PICT. PICT files look blurry when they're brought into iMovie.

The Not Free (But Very Cool) Solution

Despite what you may have heard, the best things in life aren't always free—this wonderful media management application, for example.

iView MediaPro

It's funny what people get excited about. Take, for example, the time I was at a Macworld Expo a year or so ago. I approached one of my pals to ask what he'd seen on the show floor that really turned his crank, and without hesitation, he replied, "iView MediaPro."

"Waidaminute," I responded. "You've tramped the length and breadth of this building, and the best you can come up with is a *digital asset manager!?*"

"Check it out. You'll see."

And he was right.

iView MediaPro is a $50 utility from iView Multimedia (www.iview-multimedia.com) that allows you to gather together and catalog the digital assets—graphics files, movies, sounds, fonts, PDF files, just about anything that displays a picture or text—on your Mac. In addition, you can use the utility to convert your assets to other formats—turn a JPEG into a TIFF file, for example—and sort your files 17 ways to Sunday. These capabilities alone make iView MediaPro worth the price of admission.

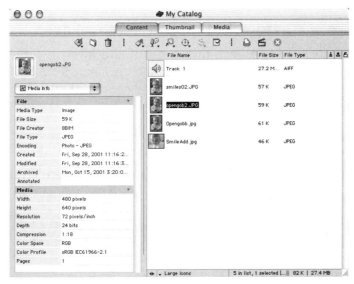

Watch Your Assets. iView MediaPro is the finest asset manager you can get for the price—and it makes slide shows, too!

But iView MediaPro also includes a very nice slide-show component. To add a background score to your slide show, simply drag a music file into the Content window and place it at the top of the list of contents. When you start the slide show, the music plays just as the first picture is displayed. The program scales all images for you, so there's no need to muck about with your pictures as you might have to in AppleWorks. As you can in iMovie, you can create a slide show with transitions.

You can also save your slide shows as QuickTime movies from within the program. Finally, you can create stand-alone slide shows. For your recipient to view your slide show, you must put the catalog file you create and the images in a folder together. The recipients must also have a copy of iView Media-Pro application (though they needn't pay for it, because this app works in "demo" mode).

To create a stand-alone slide show, assemble your slide-show element and save it. Then choose Catalog Info from the Edit menu and click the Slide Show stand-alone option in the resulting window.

iView MediaPro works with both Mac OS 9.2 and earlier and Mac OS X. Highly recommended!

Make a Custom Mac OS X Screen Saver

Screen savers were once things of infinite mystery (how *did* they make those toaster fly?). Thanks to Mac OS X, that's no longer the case. Anyone can create a cool customized screen saver easily. Here's how:

1. Place the pictures that you'd like the screen saver to display in a folder somewhere on your hard drive.
2. Launch System Preferences, and click Screen Saver.
3. In the resulting Screen Saver window, click Slide Show in the Screen Savers list.
4. Click the Configure button, and navigate to your folder full of pictures.
5. Click Open.
6. Close Screen Saver.

Now when your screen saver kicks in, the pictures in that folder will appear on-screen. If you have a fast Mac, those pictures will fade into each other smoothly, as well as zoom in and out.

Personalized Protection. Mac OS X includes a customizable screen saver.

We're all aware by now that the problem screen savers were supposed to address—the screen burn in that resulted from leaving the same image displayed on a monitor so long that the monitor's phosphor permanently displayed a ghostly hint of that image—is a thing of the past. Modern monitors don't suffer from this problem. Screen savers still serve a purpose, however (other than being visual diversions).

LCD screens—the screens on PowerBooks, iBooks, and those fancy flat-panel displays—wear out over time. The poor light-emitting units in the screen have just so much life in them. Using a screen saver with a dark image—a black screen, for example—may extend the life of that screen.

Also, some folks would like to give their monitor a rest without switching on Energy Saver, a feature that puts portions of your Mac to sleep. Mac OS X's Screen Saver is helpful in these situations. Just create a completely black image in a graphics program, place that image in its own little folder, and direct Screen Saver to that folder. When Screen Saver fires up, your monitor goes completely dark without causing your Mac's hard drive or processor to shut down.

Make Better iMovies

I don't need to provide you with a walk-through of iMovie; the iMovie tutorial and iMovie Help are wonderful resources for learning how to use the program. If you haven't scanned both, I suggest that you do.

I can, however, provide you a few tips that might make your iMovie experience more rewarding.

As You Shoot

Before you record a second of video, memorize the following hints.

- If your iMovie will have sound recorded by your camcorder, use an external mic. The microphones built into camcorders capture all kinds of ambient sound—wind, street noise, and so on. If you're filming a talking head, use a lavaliere microphone (one of those clip-on jobbies). You can get a lavaliere at Radio Shack for less than $30.

    If you need to shoot several people talking or a more general scene, consider using a camera-mounted shotgun mic. These mics have a more focused field, capturing what's in front of them rather than everything around them.

- Shoot a little extra footage at the front and back of a scene. This technique allows you enough space to insert a transition from scene to scene.

- Preview, preview, preview. It's very easy to shoot into the light, zoom too far into your subject, or shoot your subject from an unflattering angle. If you don't take a few test shots before rolling tape for real, you could wind up with some very funky raw footage. The few extra minutes you spend previewing may keep you from having to reshoot later.

    In particular, preview if you're thinking about using your camcorder's backlight control. This control—used when the background is quite a bit brighter than the subject—can be harmful as well as helpful. At times, I've switched on backlighting only to find my raw footage completely washed out. Had I previewed, I could have saved myself a reshoot.

- Use a tripod. I don't know about you, but my camera work isn't its best after I've had a couple of cups of coffee.
- Carry an extra, charged battery. How's your daughter going to feel when she discovers that you failed to catch her smashing cake into her new husband's gob because you used up your camcorder's battery shooting Uncle Gasbag's toast?
- Memorize. Unless you want to look like a particularly inept guest on "Saturday Night Live" (you know, the ones who search so frantically for their lines on the cue cards that they completely mess up the timing of the sketch), commit your speech to memory.

As You Edit

- The good Lord created exactly two useful transitions: dissolve and fade. Unless your goal is to produce or spoof a particularly cheesy infomercial, steer clear of barn-door, scale, wash, heart, and paging transitions. Effects such as Water Ripple and Mirror should likewise be avoided. Oh, and those zooming-letter titles? *Yeech!*
- If you've used iMovie's title feature, you know that it's not very flexible. Print may not be as big as you like it, or the text may be fuzzy. Fortunately, you can have titles in your iMovies without using this feature. Simply create your titles in a graphics program, save them as JPEGs, and import them into iMovie just like any other graphics file. Sure, the individual letters won't fly onto the screen, but I believe that I've already discussed the tastefulness of such an effect.
- Fix it in post-production. Even though you've followed my advice to the letter, it's possible that your raw footage is too dark or the color is washed out. Although there's no substitute for pristine footage, you can clean up some of your mistakes with iMovie's effects. If the video you shot is too dark, for example, use the Brightness/Contrast effect to lighten it. The Adjust Colors effect may help a washed-out scene. And if the footage is almost beyond repair, try the Black and White or Sepia Tone filter. Hey, if black-and-white was good enough for Chaplin, the

Three Stooges, and Woody Allen, it's good enough for you and your iMovies!

- You can add to the list of sound effects available in iMovie's Audio window. Just save an audio file in AIFF format and drag it into the Sound Effects folder, which is inside the Resources folder inside the iMovie folder inside the house that Jack built. When you next launch iMovie, that sound file is available for your use.

Sound Advice

I have a couple of cool sound tips and nowhere to put them. Why not here?

To add new alert sounds to Mac OS X, try this:

1. Open the Sounds folder inside the Library folder inside your Users folder.

   You can navigate to your Users folder quickly by clicking the Home button in a Finder window.

2. Drag an AIFF sound file from another Finder window or from the Desktop into your Sounds folder.

3. Choose System Preferences from the Apple menu and click the Sound icon.

4. Select your new sound in the Alert Sound window.

   Note: The sound file must bear the .AIFF suffix; .AIF won't do it. Also, if System Preferences was open before you moved the sound file to the Sounds folder, you might have to quit and relaunch System Preferences before the file is recognized.

Although Apple's iMovie now owns the entry-level Mac moviemaking market, plenty of people are still using Avid Cinema. And one of the most vexing problems with Avid Cinema is that although it carries two soundtracks—one for narration and another for music—these two soundtracks are unable to use the other's files. You can't, for example, drag a file intended for the music track into the narration track and vice versa. This can be a real problem when you have a background-music track that runs the length of your movie and want to insert a sound effect as well. Here's how to change a music or sound-effect file so that it will appear in the narration track.

1. Make sure that the file is an AIFF file.

   The file type and creator code for Avid Cinema's narration tracks must be AIFF and Mndy, respectively. So for this trick to work, you must start with an AIFF file. If your sound file isn't in AIFF format, use a tool such as SoundApp to convert it.

2. Using a utility such as ResEdit or FileTyper, change the creator code to Mndy, and save the file.

3. Now copy this changed file to the media folder of the movie in which you'd like the sound to appear.

   When you next open your movie, the sound will appear in the Library list in the Edit window, ready to be dragged into the narration track.

Exporting iMovies

One of the tricks to creating a decent-looking iMovie is using the Export Movie controls. Apple does its best to make exporting easy for you by including a few default export settings, such as CD-ROM, Medium and Email Movie, Small. But frankly, if you know your way around the Expert QuickTime Settings window, your results will be vastly superior to anything that iMovie generates by default.

What, exactly, is at stake? Oh, just the possibility that no one will ever bother watching your movie because it plays back so dreadfully or is far too large to download.

To get to the Expert QuickTime Settings window, choose Export Movie from iMovie's Edit menu. From the Export pop-up menu, choose QuickTime; then, from the Formats pop-up menu, choose Expert.

In the resulting window, you'll see an area for changing the width and height of your movie and a couple of Settings buttons: one for video settings and one for audio. Each of these settings has an effect on how your movie will look and perform.

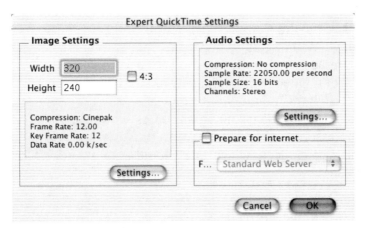

Export Overview. iMovie's Export Movie window is a key element in producing good-looking movies.

Image settings

The size of your QuickTime movie will have an effect on how smoothly it plays back on most computers. A large movie—say, 720 by 480—will likely stutter and skip when it's burned to a CD and played from that CD. CDs simply can't deliver that much data quickly enough for smooth playback.

Also, such a movie is going to tip the megabytes scale substantially. This situation should concern you if you're planning to post your movie on the Web. Even users who have ultrazippy broadband connections may think twice before downloading a 400 MB movie of your kid's soccer game.

Therefore, if you're concerned that an underpowered Mac might be tasked with playing your movie or that someone with a slow Web connection may want to download it, consider reducing the dimensions of your movie. 320 by 240 is a good size for a movie intended to be played directly from the hard drive, whereas 240 by 180 is a perfectly fine setting for CD-ROM playback.

Video settings

If you click the Settings button in the video section of the Expert QuickTime Settings window, you'll go to the Compression Settings window. Within this window lies the Compressor pop-up menu—the key to how your video will ultimately look. If you click this menu, you'll see scads of compressors, also known as *codecs* (compressor/decompressor). Given the number of choices, which one should you use?

Codec Collection. iMovie allows you to use the many video codecs bundled with QuickTime.

Fortunately, you really have to consider only a couple of codecs seriously: Cinepak and Sorenson Video.

Cinepak is the old standby for video compression. It compresses files to a reasonable size while maintaining decent quality. Its main drawback is that it compresses very slowly. Sorenson Video is the new kid on the block.

It not only boasts a good compression-to-quality ratio but also works far faster than Cinepak.

Those of you who have been paying attention to the doings in the QuickTime world are undoubtedly shouting, "Hey, just use Sorenson! That's what Apple uses for the splendid QuickTime movies on its site!"

Well, yes and no. You see, the versions of Sorenson Video (www.sorenson.com) bundled with iMovie (the Basic Editions of Sorenson Video and Sorenson Video 3) are not responsible for those crystalline videos you've seen on Apple's QuickTime site (www.apple.com/quicktime). Those videos was encoded with the Developer Edition of Sorenson Video—an edition that costs 500 simoleons.

It costs that much for good reason: The results it produces are umpteen times better than anything you'll squeeze out of the Basic Edition. Nonetheless, even the Basic Edition can provide a video that's perfectly watchable. But if you're deadly serious about your QuickTime movies, consider upgrading to the High-Priced Spread.

So which codec should you choose? Although you should make a test video and compress it with both options to see how you fare, I suggest that you opt for Sorenson first. If you're unhappy with the results, try Cinepak.

Sorenson compresses best when it's not bothered with a lot of keyframes—the reference frames that detail the state of each pixel in a frame. In the Key Frames Every text box, enter 150, and see how you fare.

Cinepak likes keyframes every second or so. Enter a number such as 12 in the Key Frame Every text box.

When you know that your final video will be heavily compressed (if you're creating an ultrasmushed video for the Web, for example), take some precautions while shooting. Fades and titles look particularly blocky when they're heavily compressed. If you have to use them, keep them short. Also, compressors can make smaller files when there's not a lot of motion. Try to shoot against a static background, and avoid unnecessary movement.

Sound settings

The Sound Settings window also contains a Compressor pop-up menu that contains a load of codecs. Again, you really have to consider only a couple of the options in this menu.

The first option is to consider using no compression whatsoever. *Huh!?* That's right—there are ways to reduce file size without having to resort to compression. Those ways include changing the resolution and number of channels—specifically, changing the resolution from 44.1 kHz to 22.05 kHz and changing the file to mono from stereo. Each of these actions cuts the audio file size in half. If you have 1 MB of audio in your file, for example, switching to a resolution of 22.05 kHz slims audio to 500 KB. Drop stereo for mono, and the file is further reduced to 250 KB.

Aural Sets. iMovie also includes a variety of audio codecs.

Before employing any compressor, consider using these settings. You'll be surprised at how much fidelity your file retains. I do not, however, counsel you to change the bit rate from 16 bit to 8 bit. 8-bit sound files are very noisy. If, at 22.05 kHz mono, your file is still too big, use a compressor rather than reduce bit rate.

And of those compressors, I'd choose either QDesign Music or IMA 4:1. Here's the dope on both:

- The QDesign Music codec compresses audio remarkably well—up to 1/50 of the original size—while maintaining reasonable fidelity. The knock on it is that it compresses slowly and plays back best on faster computers (but any Mac or PC made since 1999 should do the job). Also, like the Sorenson Video codec, QDesign Music comes in two flavors: the free Basic Edition and the anything-but-free-at-$400 Professional Edition (www.qdesign.com). It should come to no surprise to you that audio encoded with the Professional Edition sounds much better than audio files mashed by the Basic Edition. Again, you get what you pay for.

- IMA 4:1 is the old standby—a codec that people have been using for years. As the name implies, it compresses audio by a factor of 4. Although you won't gain the kind of file savings you get from the QDesign codec with this compressor, the results aren't bad, and encoding a file takes far less time. Also, modestly powerful computers can play back IMA 4:1-encoded files without breaking a sweat.

As for my druthers, I'd first try reducing resolution and number of channels. After that, QDesign Music is worth a shot. If you're unhappy with the sound of the resulting file or file size isn't of paramount importance to you, try IMA 4:1.

The Real Solution to Your Encoding Woes

I understand that tweaking these video and audio settings is a pain, particularly when the codecs that come with QuickTime (and, thus, iMovie) aren't as good as the professional versions. There is an easier way. But it will cost you.

That easier way is a product called Cleaner from Discreet (www.discreet.com). This $600 all-in-one compression/post-production utility can compress and clean up your QuickTime movies in more ways than you can imagine. It includes a host of preconfigured settings for preparing video for the Web and CD. It can also convert your QuickTime movies to other formats, including Windows Media and RealPlayer.

Regrettably, Cleaner doesn't include the Developer Edition of Sorenson Video or QDesign Music Professional Edition. QDesign sells such a bundle for $1,400. Expensive, I know, but if you're after the best-looking QuickTime movies you can produce, this application is the way.

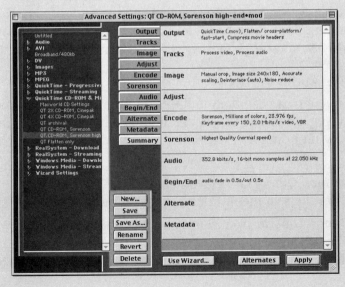

Get Cleaner.
Discreet's Cleaner is the end-all-and-be-all of postproduction QuickTime utilities.

QuickTime Player Pro Tips

Most of us take QuickTime Player for granted. Pop it open when you need to watch a movie and then show it the door when you're done. But if you have a copy of QuickTime Pro (a $30 upgrade available only through Apple), you can do much more. Like what? Well, how about...

MIDI to Audio

QuickTime Player includes a software synthesizer called QuickTime Musical Instruments. You can use this synthesizer to play files in the MIDI (Music Instrument Digital Interface) format. MIDI files contain instructions that tell the synthesizer what to play rather than audio data. Think of MIDI files as being the sheet music that a piano player reads to know what notes to play and an audio file as being a music CD.

You can find MIDI files all over the Web. One of my favorite sources is Classical Archives (www.classicalarchives.com), a rich repository of classical MIDI files. If you download one of these files to your Mac and open it in QuickTime Player, you'll hear the piece played back through the QuickTime synthesizer.

Nifty, eh? Ah, but wait—there's more. You can save that file as a stand-alone audio file. With the MIDI file open in QuickTime Player, choose the Export command from the File menu, and choose Music to AIFF from the Export pop-up menu in the resulting Save Exported File As window. In a flash, that MIDI file becomes an AIFF file, ready to burn to CD.

Multiple Audio Tracks

QuickTime movies can hold multiple audio tracks, and QuickTime Player Pro allows you to create those multiple tracks. In the following example, I show you how to do so by creating an audio montage of an approaching storm:

1. Launch QuickTime Player, and choose New Player from the File menu to create a new movie.

2. Choose Import from this same File menu, and select one of the sound effects that you'd like to hear throughout the sound track (a rain effect, for example).

If you want the sound to play longer, press Command-A to select the sound, Command-C to copy it, and then Command-V to paste that copy at the end of the sound track. Repeat as necessary.

3. Now import another sound file (a wind sound, for example) into a new Player window.

4. Select and copy this wind sound and then select the window with the rain soundtrack.

5. Click the point within the rain soundtrack where you'd like to insert the wind sound, and choose the Add command from the Edit menu.

   This command is hidden in versions of QuickTime before 5.0. To reveal it, hold down the Option key before clicking the Edit menu.

   The wind sound will now be layered on top of the rain sound. Repeat this process to layer on a thunder sound.

6. To change the volume of the three sounds individually, choose Get Info from the Movie menu.

7. From the left pull-down menu, in the Get Info window choose the first sound track (conveniently labeled Sound Track 1).

8. Choose Volume from the right pull-down menu.

9. Adjust the green Volume slider up or down.

10. Repeat steps 6 through 9 for the two other sound tracks until you have a pleasing mix.

11. Save the movie.

Play It Backward

If you'd like to replicate that late-Beatles-backward sound when you're playing back an audio or MIDI file, or if you want to watch a movie in reverse, just select a point in your movie or audio track within QuickTime Player, and press Command-left arrow. Command-right arrow will cause the track to play forward.

Add Effects

QuickTime includes a filters component that, in addition to a host of other things, allows you to play with the color balance, sharpness, and brightness of your movies. To take advantage of these filters, try this:

1. With your movie open, choose Export from QuickTime Player Pro's File menu.
2. From the Export pop-up menu in the Save Exported File As window, choose Movie to QuickTime Movie.
3. Click the Options button.
4. In the resulting Movie Settings window, click the Filter button.

   The Choose Video Settings window appears, displaying QuickTime's filters.

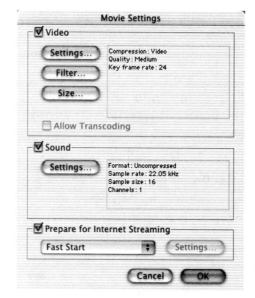

Effective Export. Click the Filter button to access QuickTime's many filters.

5. Choose the effect you like (Film Noise, for example), make any adjustments within that effect, and click the OK button.

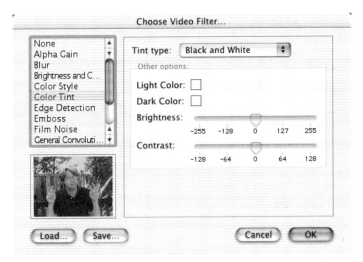

Filtered Content. Give your video that grainy educational-movie look with QuickTime's filters.

6. Click the OK button in the Movie Settings window and then the Save button in the Save Exported File As window to save your movie with the effect you've chosen.

   These effects are global, meaning that they will be applied to the entire movie. If you want to apply an effect to only a portion of a movie, copy to a new movie window the portion of the movie to which you want to apply the effect, apply the effect, save, and then paste the effected portion of the movie back into the original movie.

Add Annotations

During the 1950s, 1960s, and 1970s, some record producers made a practice of etching a little message into the inside bands of LPs. Phil Spector, Brian Wilson, and the folks at England's Stiff Records were famous for this practice. In a way, these messages were the equivalent of the hidden Easter eggs in software today.

I've long been intrigued by these messages, and as an homage to them, I make it a point to add my own little hidden messages to QuickTime movies that I release publicly—the videos I provide for the CD that's bundled with newsstand copies of *Macworld* magazine, for example. If this sort of thing tickles your funny bone as much as it does mine, here's how to add your own messages:

1. Open a QuickTime movie, and choose Get Movie Properties from the Movie menu.

    In QuickTime 4, choose Get Movie Info from this same menu.

2. When the Properties window appears, click the Add button.

3. In the resulting Add Annotation window, select the appropriate annotation—Album, Artist, Author, Description, or Disclaimer—and start typing in the text box.

Secret Messages. Plant your own Easter eggs in your QuickTime videos.

4. Click the Add button.
5. Close the Properties window.
6. Save your movie.

    The comments will be saved right along with it.

Helpful Resources

I'd love to claim that the 80,000 or so words in this book are all the help you'll ever need with your Mac. I'd be just as happy to claim that I can fly by flapping my arms in a vigorous manner. Regrettably, neither claim is valid.

The fact is that no single book can contain *all* the answers. For this reason, I include the following hints about where to find solid Macintosh information elsewhere—on the Web, on the phone, and in your local bookstore.

Apple Computer

You've heard of this company? It makes computers—specifically, Macintosh computers. As you might expect, it offers some fine information about the Mac. Check out the following.

AppleCare Knowledge Base
http://kbase.info.apple.com

They say that timing is everything and no more is the truth of this saying more evident than right here, right now. Y'see, the first draft of this appendix bore a scathing appraisal of version 2 of the AppleCare Knowledge Base—a repository for Apple technical documents. Version 2 was nearly impossible to search because Apple refused to allow you to search by date and provided no links to recent documents. Instead, the results of your search were based solely on what Apple deemed most relevant. Worse yet, Apple had a perfectly fine Web-based technical library—aptly called the Technical Information Library—and killed it in favor of this wretched waste of bandwidth.

But praise be, things have changed.

AppleCare Knowledge Base version 3 makes up for many of the failings of the previous version. Using the Expert Search function, you can now search for documents created or altered in the past 2, 7, 15, or 30 days. You can also narrow your search by keyword. And finally, Apple provides a document—Document 75185—that includes links to recently changed and published documents. You can find Document 75185 at http://docs.info.apple.com/article.html?artnum=75185.

So instead of brickbats, Apple earns a hearty slap on the back for Doing The Right Thing and making its technical documents once again easy to locate.

If you find the AppleCare Knowledge Base too daunting, Apple has provided support pages for specific products that contain links to common questions. The formula for finding these pages is:

www.info.apple.com/usen/*productname*/

productname is the particular product you want help with. www.info.apple.com/usen/imac/, for example, takes you to the iMac support page.

Product names that work with this scheme include:

g4	itunes	dvdstudiopro
g4cube	imovie	finalcutpro
imac	ibook	macosx
ipod	appleworks	macos9
itools	displays	

You can also download a Sherlock plug-in for the AppleCare Knowledge Base. It can't search by date, but it's much faster than a Web search. Last time I checked, you could download the plug-in here:

http://si.info.apple.com/updates/AppleKBase.src.hqx

Apple Discussions
http://discussions.info.apple.com

This area of Apple's Web site is where users can talk about the company's products. Apple representatives keep a pretty stern eye on what folks say in this area and have been known to delete posts that are perceived to be critical of the company and its policies or that dispense information that Apple would rather you didn't see (unsupported workarounds for problems, for example).

I don't mean to imply that Apple representatives watch over these areas simply to discourage discourse. These folks often offer helpful advice and insights that you won't find elsewhere.

This site is particularly useful when you want to know whether other people are having the same kinds of problems as you. If a new version of QuickTime comes out and some strange behavior results after you install it, this site is a good place to see whether your fellow Mac users are likewise suffering. You may find answers here long before Apple issues a Knowledge Base article.

Apple Spec Database
http://support.info.apple.com/applespec/applespec.taf

If you'd like to get the specifications on any Mac, Apple monitor, or Apple printer ever made, this database is the place to start. You'll find such information as the kind of processor the Mac uses, the variety of ports it has, the amount of memory and storage it has on-board, and the dates the model was introduced and discontinued.

Oddly enough, the information on this site isn't always accurate. The Maximum RAM specification is occasionally wrong, for example. It's a decent overview and easy to search, however.

Featured Software Downloads
www.info.apple.com/support/downloads.html

This site is your first stop for finding Apple software online. The page provides links to Apple's most popular updates and software. There's also a link to recent updates (software released in the previous five weeks) and product-specific links (such as QuickTime and AirPort links).

Software offered here often lags behind what's offered through the Software Update application included with the Mac OS, but I prefer this site to Software Update for a couple of reasons.

To begin with, after Software Update installs software, it deletes the installer. I like to have a copy of the installer should I care to install that software on another Mac or need to reinstall it later.

Also, I tend to be cautious about Software Update. On a few rare occasions, Apple has released updates that caused my Mac more harm than good. (A notorious iTunes 2 for Mac OS X installer wiped out some users' partitions, for example.) I prefer to wait to see whether other users have a hard time with an update before I commit to the update myself. By using this site, I'm forced to wait a while before I can get my hands on the latest and maybe-not-so-greatest updates.

Apple Tech Support Line
(800) 275-2273

Fat lot of good it does for me to rush you to the Web when, with a kaput Mac sitting before you, you have no way to reach it. At times, you simply have to place a call to Apple. It just so happens that I had occasion to call Apple very recently when my AirPort Base Station went on the fritz. There's a reasonably well-known problem with the capacitors on some of these babies, and mine was one of the unlucky units to succumb.

I dialed Apple, navigated through the phone tree, and waited on hold for perhaps five minutes. (The hold music was pretty good, by the way—recognizable tunes sung by the original artists rather than that canned jazzy junk so many places play.) The phone was answered by a fellow named Jason. After we established the basics—my name, email address, the product I was having difficulty with, and its serial number—he asked how he could be of service. I cut to the chase and told him that my Base Station appeared to be suffering from the capacitor problem.

He politely requested that we walk through the usual troubleshooting process to be sure that the product really was ailing. He issued the instructions clearly and politely, without rushing and without treating me like an idiot. Unlike tech-support reps from other companies I've spoken with, Jason actually seemed to know what he was talking about rather than reading from a script.

After we ascertained that the Base Station was dead, he explained that Apple would be pleased to provide a replacement (even though the product was out of warranty and didn't fall within the range of serial numbers that were targeted for replacement). He took my shipping information, asked that I return the failed unit (Apple refurbishes these things and ships them out to people whose Base Stations have likewise given up the ghost), and asked whether he could help me with anything else.

We parted with the promise that I would do everything I could to see that he got a raise.

Now, before you assume that I received some kind of special treatment, bear in mind that I am perhaps the least well-known, well-known Mac guru on earth. This guy didn't know me from Adam. I received courteous and professional service from the get-go, and I have no reason to believe that you won't receive the same treatment from any Apple support representative you speak with.

The moral of the story is that although I occasionally gripe about Apple's shortcomings, the company does most things very, very well. Phone support is one of those things.

Oh, and if anyone at Apple with the power to perform the service is reading, see what you can do about Jason's raise. Thanks.

Other Resources

Apple isn't your only source of information, of course.

Mac Publishing

Macworld

Disclaimer: I'm a contributing editor for *Macworld,* and much of my livelihood depends on my work for this publication.

Despite the obvious self-interest, I'd read *Macworld* from cover to cover whether I appeared in the masthead or not. The magazine has become a bit more technical and product-focused recently—a *very* good thing, in my book. You'll often see feature stories comparing a particular class of products, such as printers and digital cameras. The How-To section is also quite strong.

Macworld's reviews are second to none, thanks in large part to Macworld Labs, a state-of-the art facility for benchmarking (and beating the bejeezus out of) Macs, peripherals, and Mac software.

You'll also find my troubleshooting, tips, and tricks column, "Mac 911," cozily hunkered down within the pages of *Macworld*.

Macworld Online
www.macworld.com

Macworld focuses its online efforts where they do Mac users the most good. You'll find a searchable library of *Macworld*'s product reviews, links to stories that appeared in recent issues of the magazine, and content created specifically for the Web site. The home page often contains first looks at hot products and links to news stories from MacCentral, Mac Publishing's Mac news site.

Macworld forums
www.macworld.com/cgi-bin/ubb/Ultimate.cgi

Macworld's online forums are definitely worth a visit. The forums feature lively and extremely knowledgeable discussions of all things related to the Mac: troubleshooting, digital media, Mac OS 9 and Mac OS X, upgrades, games, and desktop publishing. If you have a question about your Mac, these forums are good places to ask it.

Macworld Weekly Newsletter
www.macworld.com/newsletters

Macworld also issues a newsletter each week. In this self-same newsletter, you'll find a mini-installment of my "Mac 911" column—where I answer one reader question, offer a helpful tip, and generally apply a healing balm to those troubled by their Mac's behavior.

MacFixIt
www.macfixit.com

I've mentioned MacFixIt in these pages more than a few times, for good reason: It's the best source for Mac troubleshooting information on the Web. When new Mac problems crop up, this site is the place to read about them and (usually) their solutions.

As I write this appendix, MacFixIt's main page is devoted to Mac OS 9.2 and earlier; a separate page deals with Mac OS X issues. By the time you read this book, the Mac OS X page should appear when you first enter the site. Don't worry; Mac OS 9.2 and earlier will continue to be covered for a long time to come.

MacFixIt's Recent Reports links are very helpful, as are the site's message boards. The site's search engine is reasonably speedy and very thorough.

MacInTouch

www.macintouch.com

Ric Ford's MacInTouch focuses more on news than MacFixIt does but devotes a fair amount of space to troubleshooting as well. The site includes reader reports—messages from readers on a particular topic—that are a terrific source of information from people who've had hands-on experience with products you're likely to be interested in.

Accelerate Your Mac

www.xlr8yourmac.com

Michael Breeden's Accelerate Your Mac is the Web's best source for information pertaining to Mac upgrades. If a piece of hardware can be upgraded, overclocked, or hacked, Mike or one of his readers has done it (and lived to tell the tale). This site is especially good if you're a Mac gamer looking for ways to squeeze the most performance out of your computer. Nearly all benchmark tests presented on the site also test frame rates for the latest 3D shooters.

My one complaint about the site is that it's often difficult to find the information you seek. With the help of the subject headings and search engine, you'll eventually find what you're looking for. It's well worth the inconvenience.

TidBITS

www.tidbits.com

Adam and Tonya Engst commenced publication of this venerable weekly Mac newsletter in April 1990. Although just about any Mac-related subject is up for grabs, the newsletters largely focus on Mac industry news, product reviews, analysis, and commentary. TidBITS is free, offered in seven languages (English, French, Spanish, German, Dutch, Japanese, and Russian), and is emailed to subscribers each Monday night.

Oh, and don't miss the April Fool's edition. It's a hoot.

Mac OS X Hints

www.macosxhints.com

If you yearn to learn more about Mac OS X, visit Rob Griffiths's Mac OS X Hints. This site is a collection of sometimes-useful, sometimes-obscure Mac OS X hints, tips, and techniques.

You needn't be a Unix geek to get the most out of this site, but it will help if you don't break out in hives whenever the phrase "command-line interface" is introduced in the course of conversation.

MacWindows

www.macwindows.com

Like it or not, we live in a world overflowing with PCs running Microsoft's Windows operating system. To learn how to make your Mac and PC see eye to eye, take a gander at John Rizzo's MacWindows site. John knows his way around both platforms and addresses such tricky issues as networking and emulation (running Windows on a Mac). Readers kick in a good load of information as well.

Ask Al

www.Alsoft.com

Alsoft, the company responsible for the superb troubleshooting utility Disk Warrior, offers a Mac question-and-answer forum called Ask Al. Although when I last looked, Al had published nothing new since June 2001, the site has a rich backlog of Mac troubleshooting material. It's definitely worth a look.

VersionTracker

www.versiontracker.com

If you seek Mac software, VersionTracker's your source. VersionTracker offers links to all the latest freeware, shareware, and updates, and it has an area where users can comment on the software. Except on the rare occasion when a user has an ax to grind or just doesn't get something, these comments are invaluable, giving you a glimpse of what is and what isn't worth downloading.

Inside Mac Games

www.insidemacgames.com

At one time, I wrote *Macworld's* "Game Room" column, which should give you a pretty fair idea that although I'm all grown up, I'm still a kid when it comes to computer games. Tuncer Deniz's Inside Mac Games is an outstanding Web site for those who are interested in Mac gaming. It includes stories from past issues of the Inside Mac Games CD-ROM (eight issues a year for $29), interviews, Mac gaming news, previews, and a forum.

If you're looking for freeware, shareware, and game demos, take a look at IMG's sister site, Mac Game Files (www.macgamefiles.com).

Game Ranger

www.gameranger.com

Speaking of games, if you want to play Mac games online against real live opponents, this site is the place. Aussie Scott Kevill created this terrific game server that allows players from all over the world to compete with one another. Unlike some other game servers, Game Ranger does not provide the games themselves. Rather, you play games that you already own: Quake III Arena, Risk, Unreal Tournament, and Scrabble, among many others. You can think of Game Ranger as being a place to meet, greet, and turn up the heat.

Andy Ihnatko's Temporary Waste of Bandwidth

www.cwob.com

What better way to close this portion of the book than with dessert? Describing Andy Ihnatko's home, home on the Web as a helpful Mac resource is stretching it a bit. I mean, there's a chance that you'll find *some* helpful Mac-related material on Andy's site—but it's just as likely that in a search for same, you'll click a link at random, find yourself ensnared by the tale of Andy and the Flying Karamazov Brothers, and be lost for the afternoon.

Andy Ihnatko is one of today's finest and funniest writers. If you enjoy his work on the back page of *Macworld* as much as I do, you must visit the TWoB.

Tips and Tricks

Although I've tried to plant helpful little tidbits throughout the book, finding places where the soil conditions are just right (and don't get me started on proper drainage) hasn't always been easy. For this reason, I've set aside the next few pages for tips and tricks just too cool to miss.

Mac OS 9.2 and Earlier

From AOL to Word, I've got a tip that will make you computing life easier.

Restoring from Software Restore

Those who received several Software Restore discs with their Macs may wonder how they can restore just a single application. These discs offer no option to custom-install applications; what choice do you have but to allow Software Restore to erase your hard drive and reinstall the applications it originally shipped with?

According to Apple, you can work around this dilemma. Here's how:

1. Pray that you have 2 GB of spare hard-drive space (you'll need it to perform this trick).
2. Create a new folder.
3. Copy the disk image files on each of the Software Restore discs into this new folder.

   You may find these disk images in a Configurations folder.
4. Launch the Disk Copy application.
5. Drag the first disk image file (it will be named something like PowerMac HD Disc 1.dmg) into the Disk Copy window.

   A disk image will appear on your Desktop. That disk image contains the software that originally shipped with your Mac.
6. Drag the software that you want to reinstall from the disk image to your hard drive to install it.

Open Sesame

The SuperDrive media drives on some QuickSilver Power Mac G4s have no manual eject button. If a disc gets stuck, you can no longer resort to the "shove a straightened paper clip into the little hole" trick to extract the disc. So how do you remove a stuck disc? Try these tricks:

- Hold down the mouse button at startup.
- Start up into open firmware (press Command-Option-O-F as the Mac starts up). and type `eject cd`. To continue booting your Mac, type `mac-boot`.
- Hold down the Option key at startup, and when the Select Startup screen appears, press Command-period.

Change Type and Creator Codes with ResEdit

Every so often, you'll hear some Mac pundit (someone like me, for example) cavalierly suggest that you change a file type or creator code with Apple's ResEdit. ResEdit is a utility that allows you to dig deep into the heart of a file and alter the file's properties in wonderful and (occasionally) frightening ways. Yet the person leaves out the all important instructions for doing so. Time to make amends, I say, and provide just those instructions.

Before you can begin, you need a copy of ResEdit, which can be tricky to find now that Apple's removed a listing for it from the Software Downloads library. Last time I looked, it still existed here:

http://download.info.apple.com/Apple_Support_Area/Apple_Software_Updates/English-North_American/Macintosh/Utilities/ResEdit_2.1.3.sea.bin

1. With ResEdit in hand, launch the program.
2. Choose Get File/Folder Info from the File menu.
3. In the resulting Open dialog box, navigate to the file you'd like to edit, and open it.

   In the Info window that appears, you'll see text boxes for changing the type and creator codes, as well as an option for making files visible or invisible.
4. Make your changes and then save.

The Usual Warning: Mucking about with ResEdit can be dangerous. Muck with the wrong file in the wrong way (particularly System files), and you could cause serious problems for your Mac. It's wise to make a duplicate of the file before you start mucking around in case things go bad.

Kill AOL's Sounds

You're probably aware that you can switch off AOL's chirpy announcements (such as "You've got mail!") by choosing Preferences from the My AOL menu and deselecting Play Event Sounds in the General tab. But because that's a global operation, you kill each and every one of AOL's sounds by following this procedure. Perhaps you would care to keep some sounds—the Instant Messenger alert, for example—and dispense with others.

To do that, open the America Online folder, then the Online Files folder, and finally the Sounds folder. Drag any files you don't want out of this Sounds folder, and those sounds will no longer play.

> *AOL determines which sound to play by the name of the sound. Therefore, you can use any System 7 sound file (the format used by the Mac version of AOL) and give it the name of a particular AOL event. You can record a snippet of Monty Python's famous Spam skit, save it as a System 7 sound, rename it You've Got Mail, and replace AOL's original You've Got Mail file with the new file. Now when you have AOL mail, you'll hear "Spam, Spam, Spam, Spam, Spam, Spam, Spam, Spam...."*

Common AOL Error

One of the most common errors Mac AOL users see is:

"To run an Internet application via America Online, you must sign on first. To run an Internet application via an ISP/LAN, you must restore your TCP configuration by clicking the Restore button in the AOL link panel within AOL's Preferences dialog."

A possible solution to this problem is to switch off Web Sharing. To do so, make sure that the Web Sharing Extension and Web Sharing control panel are both active (look in Extensions Manager), open the Web Sharing control panel, and switch Web Sharing off.

Next, open the TCP/IP control panel, and from the Connect Via pop-up menu, choose AOL Link Enhanced (or AOL Link, if that's what appears there). Then close the TCP/IP window, saving any changes.

USB Overdrive

Have a USB input device that lacks Mac OS drivers? Perhaps you should road-test Alessandro Levi Montalcini's USB Overdrive. This "two extensions and a control panel" package allows you to use a variety of USB mice, trackballs, and joysticks with your USB-capable Macintosh. USB Overdrive also allows you to assign different key combinations to multibutton input devices, as well as to employ game input devices that don't support Apple's InputSprockets. USB Overdrive is $20 and can be downloaded at www.macdownload.com.

Hide PowerPoint's Innards

In my other life, I'm a musician, and during a recent corporate gig, the folks in charge offered a PowerPoint presentation during one of my breaks. At the end of the slide show, the presenter clicked the last slide. Sure enough, there was the PowerPoint interface, complete with menus and toolbars; the man behind the curtain was revealed for all to see. I thought, "If I wasn't working in this other capacity, I'd recommend that these people press B on their keyboard so that the screen turns to black. It would surely be more elegant than leaving PowerPoint's interface strewn all over the screen while these folks finish their dessert. After the group has drained its collective glass and toddled off to their hotel rooms, the AV people simply need to press the Escape or B key to reveal PowerPoint's inner workings once again."

Netscape Calculations

Here's a neat Netscape Navigator trick. If you want to perform a quick mathematical calculation, simply type `javascript: eval (2+2)` in the location bar. (You can enter any values and operators you choose between the parentheses.) The answer will appear in the browser window.

Title-Bar Folder Icons

Those who are running Mac OS 9.x have undoubtedly noticed the folder icons that appear in windows' title bars. Some of you may not realize that these icons aren't merely decorative; in many ways, they operate like traditional folders. You can move these folders to the Desktop, to the Trash, or to another window by clicking the folder icon and then dragging it. You can also create an alias of the folder by pressing the Command and Option keys while dragging the icon to a new location. And as you might expect, duplicating the folder is as easy as holding down the Option key while clicking and dragging.

Rename Your Hard Drive

Suppose that you want to change the name of your hard drive from Macintosh HD to something more friendly, like Muffy's Mac. You click the name below your hard-drive icon once, and nothing happens. Unlike other files and folders, the hard drive won't let you enter new text. Why not?

The hard drive is being shared. To rename the drive, open the File Sharing control panel and turn off file sharing.

Remote Printout

If you're stuck on the road without a printer, and you desperately need a hard copy of one of your documents, try this trick: From your iBook, fax a copy of the document you want printed to the hotel's fax machine. Sure, it may cost you a buck or two to have a fax delivered, but if you really need a printout, it's an easy way to go.

Word Commands

Here's how to print a complete list of Microsoft Word's keyboard commands:

1. Choose Macro from the Tools menu, and then choose Macros from the Macro submenu.
2. In the resulting Macros window, choose Word Commands from the Macros In pop-up menu.
3. Scroll down the list of macros in this window, select ListCommands, and click Run.
4. In the next dialog box, choose Current Menu and Keyboard Settings or All Word Commands.

    Word will generate a Word file that lists all the keyboard commands. Print this list at your leisure.

AppleWorks Buttons

To change the size of the buttons in AppleWorks' Starting Points window, hold down the Control key; choose Starting Points Settings from the contextual menu; and then choose Small, Medium, or Large from the Thumbnail Size menu.

TCP/IP and Remote Access Settings

Here's a test: Without looking, write down all the numbers and domain names that appear in your Mac's TCP/IP control panel. Extra credit for also being able to scribble down the phone number entered in the Remote Access control panel.

Unless you have an extremely acute memory, you won't be able to do either of these things. (I certainly couldn't.) If you're like most people, you entered these numbers in the Internet Setup Assistant one time and promptly forgot them.

But ya know, you really should have a copy of this information, just in case you have to reenter it after a clean install or horrendous System crash. You could write all this information down on a grocery sack and then lose it, of course, but there's a better way.

Just open the TCP/IP control panel and press Command-Shift-3 to take a picture of the Mac's screen. Do the same for the Remote Access control panel. Open these pictures (you'll find them at the root level of your hard drive, labeled Picture 1 and Picture 2), and print them. Pin the printouts to your bulletin board and never, ever lose them.

Now when you need to reenter this information, you'll have an exact picture of the numbers and names you need, along with an illustration of where this information goes.

New Web Page

At times, it's convenient to open a Web page in a new window—when you want to switch between two Web sites quickly without resorting to the forward and back-arrow keys, for example. Sure, you could simply choose the New Page command from your browser's File menu, but you'll find it much easier simply to hold down the Command key while you click a link. When you do, that Web page opens in its own window.

Outlook Express to Word

If you'd like to move a collection of Outlook Express 5 messages to a single Microsoft Word document, take a look at Allen Watson's OE Many to Word v 2.2 AppleScript. Download this free script here:

ftp://ftp.macemail.com/oe/OE_Many_Word_2.2.hqx

Drop it into your Script Menu Items folder. When you next launch Outlook Express, the script will be available to you. To use the script, simply select a group of messages and then choose the script from the AppleScript menu. The OE Many to Word script will copy the text from all the messages and paste that text into a single Microsoft Word document.

Speed Up Startup

If you'd like your Mac to get the lead out when it starts up, try these techniques:

- If you have a lot of RAM, you might try disabling the Mac's memory test. To do so, hold down the Command and Option keys while launching the Memory control panel. When you do, a new Memory Test option appears. Disabling this option tells the Mac to skip RAM tests as the Mac starts up.
- Make sure that you have a valid startup disk selected in the Startup Disk control panel.
- The Multiple Users option can introduce delays as well. If you don't need Multiple Users, disable it.

Sherlock Folder Search

You don't have to search your entire drive with Sherlock. Instead, you can search just one folder. To do so, drag the folder from the Mac's Desktop to Sherlock's main window. That folder will appear as a searchable item.

Reset and Programmer's Buttons

The Reset and Programmer's buttons on recent Mac models—the resting-in-peace Cube and iMac, for example—are located in places that are difficult to see. Fortunately, Apple provides a tactile clue to the identity of each button. Should your Cube freeze, slip your hand under the back of the Cube and feel around for a button that bulges out; that's the Reset button. The Programmer's button is indented. You'll find this same bulginess/indentation on recent versions of the iMac as well. On these iMacs, the Reset and Programmer's buttons are located near the ports on the right side of the computer.

Escape the Repair Warning

If you've failed to turn off the Warn Me If Computer Was Shut Down Improperly option in the General Controls control panel, and the repair window appears every time you restart your Mac after it crashes, you can get out of this repair window by pressing the Escape key on your Mac's keyboard. Because it's hard to tell exactly when pressing this key will do the most good, try pressing it repeatedly when the repair window first appears. This technique not only removes the window as quickly as possible but also provides an avenue for you to take out your frustrations on the Mac for crashing in the first place.

Note that the repair procedure may actually be doing some good. If you choose to escape this window (or disable it from the General Controls control panel), it might be a good idea to run Disk First Aid every so often to confirm that your Mac is hunky-dory.

Mass Delete

If your email account is like mine, you get a lot of unsolicited junk mail (also known as *spam*). You generally can tell what this crud is by its subject—you know, "Find Out Anything About Anyone," "Free Money!," "Be Your Own Boss," that kind of nonsense—so there's no need to actually open or read these messages.

To get rid of them in one fell swoop in Outlook Express, just Command-click each junky message to select it; then press the Delete key.

Window Screen Shot

If you hold down Shift-Command-CapsLock-4, you can take a picture of any open window. When you invoke this command, the mouse pointer turns into a darkened circle (a bull's-eye?). Place this bull's-eye in any open window, and click the mouse button. A picture of that window (marked Picture 1) appears at the root level of your hard drive.

Microsoft Word Annoyances

Microsoft Word tries to make your work easier by formatting certain types of text for you automatically, but sometimes, its help is intrusive. To hold many of Word's auto-formatting horses, choose the AutoCorrect command in the Tools menu. In the AutoFormat and AutoFormat As You Type tabs, uncheck the Ordinals with Superscript, Symbol Characters with Symbols, and Internet Paths with Hyperlinks checkboxes. To keep bulleted and numbered lists from appearing automatically, turn off these options as well. If you're likewise tired of Word 98 automatically inserting a capital *I* at the beginning of the word *iMac* when *iMac* is the first word of a sentence, turn off the Capitalize First Letter of Sentences option in the AutoCorrect tab.

Word 2001 Disk Full Error

If you have File Sharing enabled and attempt to save a Word 2001 document more than 60 times in a single session, you'll receive a Disk Full error and won't be able to save your document to a local disk. If File Sharing is disabled, you can save 250 times before you receive this error.

Should you be stuck in such a situation, you can quit Word, relaunch it, and begin saving, but you'll lose any changes made since the last save. If you're on a network, however, you can use the Save As command to save the document to another volume on the network.

Mac OS X

Using Apple's new operating system? These tips are for you.

Mac OS X Toolbar

You probably know that to customize the Mac OS X toolbar, you can simply click the Toolbar button (that clear button up there in the right corner of a window) while holding down the Shift key.

But you may not know that to pull this same kind of customization trick with Mac OS X applications (those that support Mac OS X toolbars, natch), you hold down the Command and Option keys while clicking this button.

The Slow-Motion Dock Trick

If you've witnessed just about any demo of Mac OS X, you've seen the minimize-in-slo-mo trick in which a window is ever so slowly sucked into the Dock. To perform this same trick with your copy of Mac OS X, just hold down the Shift key while clicking a window's Minimize button.

Re-Creating Desktop Alias

If Mac OS 9.x and Mac OS X are installed on the same disk, and you delete the Desktop alias (Mac OS 9), you can't get that alias back by the normal means—navigating to the OS Desktop folder and creating an alias. Instead, you must open Mac OS X's Terminal application and type the following:

```
ln -s /"Desktop Folder" ~/Desktop/"Desktop (Mac OS 9)"
```

Press Return after this line. Now when you click the Desktop, you should see the Desktop (Mac OS 9) alias.

Sherlock Mac OS X Error

Apple reports that if you have a graphic file in Mac OS X's Clipboard when you open Sherlock (or make it the active application), you may receive an error that reads:

"An unexpected error occurred. If you continue to encounter problems, quit and start again."

The solution to this problem is to place something other than a graphic file in the Clipboard. Select a block of text and copy it, for example.

Disable Auto-Dial in Mac OS X

If you'd prefer that the modem on your Mac running Mac OS X not dial your ISP automatically when you initiate an Internet-based action, here's how to disable the auto-dial feature:

1. Open System Preferences.
2. Click the Network preference.
3. Click the Modem tab, and choose your modem from the Modem pop-up menu.
4. Click the PPP tab and then click the PPP Options button at the bottom of the window.
5. Deselect the Connect Automatically When Starting TCP/IP Applications option.
6. Click OK and save.

Be Careful When Renaming Items

Unlike Mac OS 9.2 and earlier, Mac OS X is particular about where certain folders (directories) are located and what they're called. If you rename Mac OS X's Utilities folder, for example, you alter the path to that folder and therefore interrupt any processes that require that pathname. So if you rename the Utilities folder, you can't print, because Mac OS X expects Print Center to be inside a folder called Utilities. When Mac OS X finds that Print Center isn't in that folder, the process gives up and refuses to print.

Add Mac OS X Alert Sounds

To add new alert sounds to Mac OS X, try this:

1. Open the Sounds folder inside the Library folder inside your Users folder.

    You can navigate to your Users folder quickly by clicking the Home button in a Finder window.

2. Drag an AIFF sound file from another Finder window or from the Desktop into your Sounds folder.
3. Choose System Preferences from the Apple menu.
4. Click the Sound system preference.
5. Select your new sound in the Alert Sound list.

The sound file must bear the .AIFF suffix; .AIF won't work. Also, if System Preferences was open before you moved the sound file to the Sounds folder, you might have to quit and relaunch System Preferences before the file is recognized.

PC-Formatted Zip Disks and Mac OS X

If you've mounted a PC-formatted Zip disk on your Mac running Mac OS X, you cannot save directly to that disk from an open Classic application. In other words, you can't use the Save dialog box within a Classic application to save that file to Zip disks formatted in this way. Instead, you must save the file to your hard disk and then copy the file to the Zip by dragging and dropping.

Likewise, you can't use a Classic application's Open dialog box to open files on PC-formatted Zip disks. Again, you must copy these files to your hard drive before opening them.

Desktop Files

If you switch back and forth between Mac OS X and Mac OS 9 and routinely save files to the Desktop, you may wonder where the files that once resided on your Desktop have gone. Under Mac OS X, you can find your Mac OS 9 Desktop files in a folder called (aptly enough) Desktop Folder, at the root level of the drive on which your Mac OS 9 System Folder lives.

When you're running Mac OS 9, you'll find Mac OS X's Desktop files inside the Desktop folder inside your user folder (Chris, for example) inside the Users folder at the root level of the drive that holds Mac OS X.

Mailbox Locked Warning

If, like me, you've opened Mac OS X's Mail application only to be greeted by a message indicating that such-and-such mailbox is locked, there's a reason. The Mail application will produce this error message if Mail was not shut down properly (if you force-quit the application, for example), if you've changed the Mac's network connection with Mail open, or if two or more accounts are configured to place messages in the Personal Mailboxes Inbox.

You usually can work around this error by selecting the Open Anyway option and silently cursing the application for not just opening the darned thing without this kind of intervention.

10 Surefire Ways to Become Wildly Unpopular on the Web

If you're new to the Web, you're undoubtedly there because you've heard so many glowing reports about the online world: email transmitted in a micro-moment, vast reserves of information just waiting to be mined, terabytes of downloadable software...a veritable silver lining with nary a cloud in sight. Web veterans realize, of course, that this utopian notion is pure hokum. The e-world is, if anything, less forgiving than this mortal coil. (If you doubt me, try making the mistake of posting the same message twice to a newsgroup. The flaming responses you receive would make a hockey player blush.)

In such a potentially churlish and unforgiving place, it helps to know the rules of the road, and that's exactly what I propose to provide. Join me as I reveal 10 Surefire Ways to Become Wildly Unpopular on the Web.

1. Type in ALL CAPS

Every computer keyboard has a Caps Lock key, and although it's a handy "always run" key for Quake, it's appropriate for use in online communications only when you really want to torque someone off. But you must all-cap correctly. A single all-capped word is used for emphasis, as in "The coffee you spilled in my lap is HOT!" Whose feathers would be ruffled by that? Ah, but watch what happens when you capitalize the entire sentence: "THE COFFEE YOU SPILLED IN MY LAP IS HOT!" Now you're cooking! That stream of capital letters hint that you're *thiiisss* close to delivering the electronic equivalent of a poke in the snoot.

2. Spam

You've probably heard this term used to describe the electronic junk mail stuffed into every mailbox in computerdom (and stuffed six or seven times into mailboxes belonging to AOL members). The term also applies to a message posted multiple times across bulletin boards and newsgroups. More often than not, people post messages to multiple groups because they can't determine the appropriate place to post; therefore, they go for the scattershot approach. If you enjoy having your character impugned by all comers, spam at will (and if Will's not available, spam everyone else).

3. Don't Read the FAQ/Manual/Previous Posts

Care to demonstrate what a lazy sod you are? Impatiently demand information without bothering to research the answer on your own. FAQs (frequently asked questions), manuals, and previous posts may—and probably do—contain the answer you're seeking. Avoid documentation at all costs if you want to inspire ire.

4. Respond Immediately

If you want to join the ranks of the hotheaded, it's always a good idea to fire off a huffy response instantly to messages you disagree with. When you do, you're likely to get just as good as you gave—affording you the opportunity to demonstrate the principle of perpetual motion by starting the cycle again with yet another immediate, testy response.

5. Post Inappropriately

This tip is a great one for people who feel that the universe reveres their every burp and chortle. The truly intolerable will find a cozy newsgroup devoted to the serious discussion of Subject X, Y, or Z and take an unreasonably opposing viewpoint. To rise to the top of the class, sprinkle the subject heading of your inappropriate posts with such adolescent terms as *suck* (as in "PCs Suck!") and *rules* (as in "Apple Rules!"). Then sit back and watch in smug satisfaction as the quality of the discussion plummets!

6. Send Long Email Messages with Huge Attachments without Asking Permission

This technique works best if the email and attachment are sent to a person you barely know or, better yet, a total stranger. Just imagine the questioning consternation of your victims ("Should I accept this file? Who is this guy!?") as they watch a 2.2 MB file that contains nothing more than an uncompressed picture of your dog wearing sunglasses and a fedora trickle across their 28.8 connection. This trick is particularly exasperating thanks to the existence of computer viruses. Nearly everyone is aware that viruses can be transmitted via email attachments, and sending just such an attachment forces your recipients to strip precious moments from their day to run your file through a virus-scanning program.

7. Be as Esoteric, Techy, and Condescending as Possible

Look up the term *blowhard* in the dictionary, and if your name appears as the colloquial definition, this one's for you. After all, what good are the dozens of dollars spent on technical publications if you can't talk the talk in all the wrong places? To make this tip work, enter a newsgroup, and look for an innocent post along the lines of "I'm not a very savvy computer user, and my Mac (I think it's a beige G3 of some kind) seems to have slowed down recently. Any ideas?" Then respond:

"A beige G3!? Hello! Welcome to the 21st century! If you're gonna stick with this pile, you're gonna have to overclock your processor and upgrade your hard drive. You know what THOSE are, don't you?" After that, drift into line after line of obscure and possibly dangerous instructions without bothering to explain one syllable of it.

Bonus points if your advice is completely off the mark.

8. Be as Clueless and Vague as Possible

To invite the kind of response outlined in tip 7, when you ask for help, be unspecific about your problems—particularly when someone politely asks for clarification. This model may help:

You: "My Mac is broken."

Them: "Broken in what way? Will it start up?"

You: "I don't know; it's just kind of broken."

Them: "Is it plugged in? Does the screen light up when you turn it on?"

You: "How should I know? It's got ALL KINDS of plugs in it. It's just BROKEN! HELP ME!!"

This technique is also a jim-dandy when you're calling tech support.

9. Send Chain Mail

You can do your part to help strangle what little remains of the Net's bandwidth by creating or passing along electronic chain mail. You know what I mean—messages that begin this way: "DON'T BREAK THE CHAIN! A resident of Delaware neglected to send 27 copies of this message to his unsuspecting friends and developed a short-lived but very nasty itch."

You may think that passing along messages that might actually do some good—raise awareness for one cause or another, for example—won't incur the kind of wrath you seek. Fear not. Regardless of the content of the message, no one, but *no one*, really likes to get chain mail.

A just-for-fun project: Test the faith of chain-mailers by sending the mail right back to those who helped push it along. No chain mail I've ever seen has a "no back-sies" clause.

10. Disrupt Others' Leisure Activities

Finally, the surefire, can't-be-beat method for becoming wildly unpopular on the Internet: Intentionally wreck other people's fun. Try popping in and out of a lively chat room like a jack-in-the-box while using inappropriate language, or entering a peaceful online game and killing anyone who crosses your path. It's possible that some people may chalk up the previous nine offenses to ignorance, but nary a soul will forgive such willfully destructive acts.

And there you have it—10 simple steps to becoming an Internet outcast. May those of you who practice these methods earn the rewards you so richly deserve.

Index

A

AAUI (Apple Attachment Unit Interface) Ethernet ports, 207
Accelerate Your Mac Web site, 284
Adaptec's PCI SCSI card adapters, 203
ADB devices, upgrading Macs, 201
Adobe's ATM Deluxe, 68
AGP cards, startup process troubleshooting, 27
AIFF sound files, 266
AirPort, 217–218
   basics, 208
   configuring, 218–220
AirPort Base Station
   basics, 209
   configuring, 218–220
      Macs, 221–222
Aladdin Systems' Spring Cleaning
   uninstalling applications, 90
Aladdin Systems' Stuffit, 114
   features in Mac OS X, 145
Alsoft's Disk Warrior, 60
   Ask Al Web site, 285
   booting Macs, 30
   diagnosis and repair basics, 70–71
   emergency startup CDs, 105
   Mac OS 9.2 and earlier, 106–109
   Mac OS X troubleshooting/repairs, 149, 152
   System Folder corruption, 38
annotations, QuickTime Player Pro, 275–276
antivirus utilities
   characteristics of future utilities, 135–137
   Norton AntiVirus, 137–138
   Virex, 137
   virus basics, 133–135
   VirusBarrier, 137, 138

Apple
   Apple Attachment Unit Interface (AAUI) Ethernet ports, 207
   Apple Authorized Dealers
      hard drive repair, 42
      startup process troubleshooting, 25
   AppleCare Knowledge Base, 278–279
      software bugs, 74
   Disk Burner, 105
   Disk Copy, 105
   Disk First Aid
      diagnosis and repair basics, 69–70
      hard drive appears missing, 40
      Mac OS 9.2 and earlier, 102–104
      Mac OS X, 150–151, 152
      System Folder corruption, 37–38
   Drive Setup
      Mac OS X, 150–151
      troubleshooting appearance of missing hard drive, 40–41
   Extended Keyboard II, 201
   iDVD, 253
   iMovie
      editing techniques, 265–266
      exporting movies, 267
      image settings, 268
      shooting techniques, 264–265
      sound settings, 270–271
      video settings, 268–269
   purchasing RAM, 173
   slide shows
      AppleWorks, 256–258
      iMovie, 258–260
   software downloads, 280
   specifications database, 280
   System Profiler, 180–181

Apple *(continued)*
  technical support, 281–282
    startup process, 25
  Web site discussions, 279
AppleShare, network logon, 230–231
AppleTalk networking
  configuration, 211
  history, 206–207
  Mac OS X, 225–226
  troubleshooting printing, 92, 93
AppleWorks, slide shows, 256–258
applications
  bug handling, 73–75, 80–81
    Mac OS X, 165
  conflict handling, 81
  corruption
    basics, 65
    Desktop rebuilding, 66–67
    Finder, 68
    Finder, Preferences file, 67
    font files, 68
    preferences files, susceptibility, 67
    uninstalling applications, 88–89
  memory allocation
    browsers, 85
    insufficient memory, 82–83
    Mac OS X, 144–145
    virtual memory, 83–85
Arboretum Systems' Ray Gun sound filters, 247, 250
Asante's EtherTalk-to-LocalTalk Bridge, 202, 208
Ask Al Web site, 285
ATI Radeon graphics card, 198
ATM Deluxe (Adobe), 68
audio cards. *See* sound cards
Avid Cinema, movie recording, 266

B

backups
  backup server projects, 233–240
  basics, 43
  Copy Agent, 131–132
  Mac OS X installation, preparation, 147–148
  restoring hard drives, 42
  Retrospect Desktop and Retrospect Express, 132–133
batteries
  specifications from Technical Information Library, 21
  startup process troubleshooting, 20–21
Belkin's serial-port adapters, 202
Bias's Peak LE, 250–251
booting Macs
  from System software CD, 30
  OS X
    creating bootable discs, 154

inability to boot, 149–154
Breeden, Max; Accelerate Your Mac Web site, 284
browsers
  memory allocation, 85
  networking configuration, 216–217
bugs (software)
  basics, 73–74
  handling, 80–81
  handling bugs, 74–75
  Mac OS X, 165

C

cable connections
  modem problems, 93–95
  networking
    types, 207–208
  printing problems, 91
  SCSI, 29
  startup process troubleshooting, 19–20
cards. *See* graphics cards; sound cards; video cards
Casady & Greene
  Chaos Master, uninstalling applications, 90
  Conflict Catcher
    extensions management, 50, 53–54, 59–60
    file corruption scans, 68
    Mac OS 9.2 and earlier, 128–130
cassettes and LPs, recording
  basics, 244
  burning CDs, 251–253
  hardware, 244–246
  software
    CD Spin Doctor, 246–248
    Peak LE, 250–251
    Sound Studio, 248–250
Category 5 network cable connections, 207
CD-ROM drives, 4
CD-RW media drives, backups, 43
central processing units. *See* processors
Chaos Master (Casady & Greene), uninstalling applications, 90
Chimes of Doom, troubleshooting startup
  add-on cards, 27
  bad RAM modules, 26
  Cuda button, 23, 26
  SCSI devices, 27–29
  startup disk confusion, 30–31
Chooser
  networking configuration, 215–216
  printing problems, 91
Chou Ming, Teng. *See* Teng Chou Ming
Cinepak video codecs, 268–269
clean installs, System Folder, 38–39
  Conflict Catcher, 77–78, 128–129
Cleaner utility (Discreet), 271
codecs, sound and video, 268–271

color depth settings, performance enhancement, 99-100
compressing databases, email application performance, 96-98
compressors/decompressors. *See* codecs
Conflict Catcher (Casady & Greene)
  extensions management, 50, 53-54, 59-60
  file corruption scans, 68
  Mac OS 9.2 and earlier, 128-130
Connectix's Copy Agent, 131-132
control panels. *See also* extensions
  deleting for performance enhancement, 96
  Mac OS 9.2 and earlier, 8
  Mac OS X, lack of, 145
Copy Agent (Connectix), 131-132
CPUs (central processing units). *See* processors
crashes and freezes
  checklist, 76
  diagnostic and repair utilities
    Disk First Aid, 69-70
    Disk Warrior, 70-71
    Norton Utilities, 70, 72-73
    TechTool Pro, 70, 71-72
  extensions
    conflicts, 47-49
    conflicts, preventing, 49-50
    Extensions Manager, 50-54
    origin, 46, 47-49
    troubleshooting, 55-61
  file or application corruption
    basics, 65
    Desktop rebuilding, 66-67
    Finder, 68
    Finder, Preferences file, 67
    font files, 68
    preferences files, susceptibility, 67
  hardware conflicts, 46
    RAM modules, 64
    SCSI devices, 61
    USB devices, 61-63
  Mac OS X, 11, 158-161
  repairing problems
    clean install of System Folder, 77-78
    reformatting hard drives, 78
    reinstalling applications, 77
  software bugs
    basics, 73-74
    handling bugs, 74-75
Creative Technology's SoundBlaster Live! sound card, 201, 245
crossover Ethernet cables, 208
CubePort (Griffin Technology) adapters, 201, 202
Cuda button, startup process troubleshooting, 23
  Sad Mac icon, 26

D

Dantz
  backups
    Retrospect Desktop, 233-238
    Retrospect Express, 43
  backups, Mac OS 9.2 and earlier
    Retrospect Desktop and Express, 132-133
Degidesign, sound cards and input devices, 245
Deniz, Tuncer; Inside Mac Games Web site, 286
Desktop
  invisible files, 65-66
  Mac OS 9.2 and earlier, basics, 6
  Mac OS X, 10
    startup problems, 14, 15
  rebuilding, 65-67
    performance enhancement, 100
  TechTool Lite, 66-67
DiamondSoft's Font Reserve, scanning for font corruption, 68
digital camcorders and cameras, 4
digital tape media drives, backups, 43
Discreet's Cleaner utility, 271
Disk Burner (Apple), 105
disk caching, performance enhancement, 98, 99
Disk Copy (Apple), emergency startup CDs, 105
Disk Doctor (Symantec's Norton Utilities), 72-73, 118-119
Disk First Aid (Apple)
  diagnosis and repair basics, 69-70
  hard drive appears missing, 40
  Mac OS 9.2 and earlier, 102-104
  Mac OS X, 150-151, 152
  System Folder corruption, 37-38
Disk Light (Symantec's Norton Utilities), 72, 122
Disk Shield (Alsoft's Disk Warrior), 108
Disk Utility, Mac OS X, 150-151
Disk Warrior (Alsoft), 60
  Ask Al Web site, 285
  booting Macs, 30
  diagnosis and repair basics, 70-71
  emergency startup CDs, 105
  Mac OS 9.2 and earlier, 106-109
  Mac OS X troubleshooting/repairs, 149, 152
  System Folder corruption, 38
Drive Setup (Apple)
  Mac OS X, 150-151
  troubleshooting appearance of missing hard drive, 40-41
drives. *See* specific types of drives
DriveSavers, restoring hard drives, 42
dynamic IP addresses, 224

E

EasyScript (Dantz's Retrospect), 239-240
EMagic, sound cards and input devices, 245
email applications, compressing databases for
    performance enhancement, 96-98
Engst, Adam and Tonya; TidBITS Web site, 284
Entourage (Microsoft)
    compressing email databases, 97
    preferences files, 86
EtherMac iPrint Adapter LT (Proxim), 202
Ethernet
    hubs, 207-208
    ports
        AAUI (Apple Attachment Unit Interface), 207
        networking history, 206-207
        transceivers, 207
Ethernet-to-LocalTalk adapters, 208
EtherTalk-to-LocalTalk Bridge (Asante), 202
Eudora (Qualcomm)
    compressing email databases, 97-98
    preferences files, 86
Extension Overload (Teng Chou Ming and Peter
    Hardman)
    extensions management, 50, 53, 54
extensions. *See also* control panels
    conflicts, 47-49
        preventing, 49-50
        troubleshooting, 55-58, 81
        troubleshooting by halving, 56-57, 59, 60
    control panel uses, 52-54
    deleting for performance enhancement, 96
    lack of in Mac OS X, 145
    Mac OS 9.2 and earlier
        Conflict Catcher, 128-130
        defined, 8
        TechTool Pro, 114-115
    Mac OS X, lack of, 10
    origin, 46, 47-49
    printing troubleshooting, 92
    startup process problems, 13-14
    third-party management
        Conflict Catcher, 50, 53-54, 59-60, 128-130
        Extension Overload, 50, 53, 54
Extensions Manager (Apple)
    conflict handling, 50-54, 81
    Mac OS 9.2 and earlier, 124-127
Extensis's Suitcase, scanning for font corruption, 68

F

Fast Find (Symantec's Norton Utilities), 122-123
Felt Tip Software's Sound Studio, 248-250
file or application corruption
    basics, 65
    Desktop rebuilding, 66-67
    Finder, 68
    Finder, Preferences file, 67
    font files, 68
    preferences files, susceptibility, 67
    reinstalling applications, 77
    testing with TechTool Pro, 115-116
file recovery, TechTool Pro, 110-112
File Sharing control panel
    networking, 214
File Sharing control panel, security, 140
file sharing, networking, 211-214
    Mac OS X, 224-225
files and folders
    Desktop organization, 6
    Mac OS X placement, 10
    suitcases, 7
FileSaver (Symantec's Norton Utilities), 120-121
filter effects, QuickTime Player Pro, 274-275
Finder
    Preference files, 8, 67
    susceptibility to corruption, 67-68
    System Folder, 7
        corruption, 35-36
firewall utilities, Mac OS 9.2 and earlier
    File Sharing control panel, 140
    firewall basics, 139-140
    hardware firewalls and routers, 140-141
    NetBarrier, 142
    Norton Personal Firewall, 142
FireWire devices, startup process troubleshooting,
    32-34
folders and files
    Desktop organization, 6
    Mac OS X placement, 10
    suitcases, 7
Font Doctor (Morrison FontDesign), scanning for
    font corruption, 68
font files, susceptibility to corruption, 68
Font Reserve (DiamondSoft), scanning for font
    corruption, 68
Ford, Ric; MacInTouch Web site, 284
formatting hard drives, 40-42
forums
    general troubleshooting, 76
    Macworld, 283
    software bugs, 80
FreeBSD 3.2, basis for Mac OS X, 10
freezes. *See* crashes and freezes
FWB's Hard Disk Toolkit, formatting hard drive, 41

G

gain adjustments, sound input devices, 249
Game Ranger Web site, 286
gap settings, sound input devices, 251-253
GeForce 3 (nVidia) graphics card, 199

GHz (gigahertz), 3
Gigabit Ethernet ports, 206-207
gPort and g4Port (Griffin Technology) adapters, 201
graphical user interfaces (GUIs), 6
graphics card upgrades, 170-171
   basics, 198
   configuring monitors, 199-200
   purchasing recommendations, 198-199
Griffin Technology
   gPort, g4Port, and Cube Port adapters, 201
   iMate adapters, 201
   iMic and PowerWave sound input devices, 245, 299
   iPort adapters, 201
Griffith, Rob; Mac OS X Hints Web site, 285
grounding straps, installing RAM, 174
GUIs (graphical user interfaces), 6

H

halving extensions and control panels, troubleshooting conflicts, 56-57, 59, 60
Hard Disk SpeedTools (Intech), formatting hard drives, 41
Hard Disk Toolkit (FWB), formatting hard drives, 41
hard drives
   backups, basics, 43
   data recovery, TechTool Pro, 110-112
   defined, 4
   optimizing, 100
      Disk Warrior, 107-108
      Speed Disk, 119-120
      TechTool Pro, 112-114
   recovering/restoring, 40-42, 121
   reformatting, 78
   upgrading, 168-169
      installing, 182-193
      jumpers, 178- 180
      purchasing tips, 181-182
Hardman, Peter and Teng Chou Ming's Extension Overload, 50, 53, 54
hot-pluggable devices, 33
hot-swapping, 28
hubs, USB devices, 62-63

I

IDE (Integrated Drive Electronics) drives, addresses, 178-180
iDVD (Apple), 253
IEEE 1394. *See* FireWire devices
IEEE 802.11 standard, AirPort, 208
ihnatko, Andy; Temporary Waste of Bandwidth Web site, 286

iLink. *See* FireWire devices
IMA 4:1 sound codec, 270-271
iMate adapters (Griffin Technology), 201
iMic and PowerWave (Griffin Technology) sound input devices, 245, 299
iMovie (Apple)
   movies
      editing, 265-266
      exporting, 267
      image settings, 268
      shooting, 264-265
      sound settings, 270-271
      video settings, 268-269
   slide shows, 258-260
Inside Mac Games Web site, 286
Intech's Hard Disk SpeedTools, formatting hard drives, 41
Intego
   NetBarrier, 142
   VirusBarrier, 137, 138
   versus TechTool Pro, 115
Integrated Drive Electronics. *See* IDE (Integrated Drive Electronics)
internal batteries, startup process troubleshooting, 20-21
IP addresses, networking configuration, 224
iPort adapters (Griffin Technology), 201
iTools iDisk, backups, 43
iTunes player/encoder, 240-241
   gap settings, 251-252
iView Media Pro (iView Multimedia) slide shows, 261-262

J

Jaz removable media drives, backups, 43
joysticks, 4
jumpers, hard drives, 178- 180

K

kernel panics, Mac OS X, 162-163
Kevill, Scott; Game Ranger Web site, 286
keyboards
   peripheral type, 4
   startup process troubleshooting, 19-20
Keyspan's serial-port adapters, 202

L

Landau, Ted; *Sad Macs, Bombs, and Other Disasters*, 76
LC cards, startup process troubleshooting, 27
LinkSys
    Ethernet hubs, 208
    router/firewall combinations, 141
    routers, 208
The Little Mac Book, 2
LiveUpdate (Symantec's Norton Utilities), 72, 117
LocalTalk, networking history, 206
LPs and cassettes, recording
    basics, 244
    burning CDs, 251-253
    hardware, 244-246
    software
        CD Spin Doctor, 246-248
        Peak LE, 250-251
        Sound Studio, 248-250

M

Mac OS 9.2 and earlier
    antivirus utilities
        characteristics of future utilities, 135-137
        Norton AntiVirus, 137- 138
        TechTool Pro, 115
        Virex, 137
        virus basics, 133-135
        VirusBarrier, 137, 138
    backup utilities
        Copy Agent, 131-132
        Retrospect Desktop and Retrospect Express, 132-133
    control panels, 8
    Desktop, 6
    diagnostic tools
        Disk First Aid, 102-104
        Disk Warrior, 106-109
        Norton Utilities, 117-123
        TechTool Pro, 109-116
    extensions, 8
    extensions management
        Conflict Catcher, 128-130
        Extensions Manager, 124-127
    features similar in OS X, 146
    firewall utilities
        firewall basics, 139-140
        hardware firewalls and routers, 140-141
        NetBarrier, 142
        Norton Personal Firewall, 142
    hard drive installation, 183
    preference files
        Finder, 8
        System Folder, 8
    startup process problems, 13-16
    Startup/Shutdown Items folder, 9
    System Folder, 7
    tips and tricks
        AOL, common errors, 290
        AOL, killing sounds, 290
        AppleWorks buttons, 293
        calculating with Netscape, 291
        creator code changes, 289
        escaping repair warnings, 295
        hiding PowerPoint's innards, 291
        mass deletes, 295
        Microsoft Word 2001 Disk Full error, 296
        Microsoft Word keyboard commands, list, 292
        Microsoft Word preference files, resetting, 296
        opening multiple Web pages, 293
        opening SuperDrive media drives, 288-289
        remote printing, 292
        renaming hard drives, 292
        Reset and Programmer's buttons, 294-295
        restoring hard drives from Software Restore discs, 288
        saving Outlook Express messages to Word, 294
        Sherlock folder searches, 294
        speeding up startup, 294
        TCP/IP, remote access settings, 293
        title-bar folder icons, 291-292
        USB Overdrive package, 291
        window screen shots, 296
Mac OS X
    applications
        bugs, 165
        Mail, 165
    crashes, lack of, 11
    creating bootable discs, 154
    Desktop, 10
    features, 9-10, 144-145
    features similar to OS 9.2 and earlier, 146
    files and folders, placement, 10
    hard drive installation, 183
    installation preparations
        backups, 147-148
        creating OS 9.2 volume, 148-149
        separate hard drive or hard drive partition, 148
    preferences files, 11, 87
    printer drivers, 91
    protected memory, 11
    screen savers, 262-263
    startup process, 12
    startup process problems, 13-16
    tips and tricks
        adding alert sounds, 298-299
        customizing application toolbars, 297
        Desktop aliases, 297
        Desktop files, 299
        disabling Auto-Dial, 298

file/folder renaming cautions, 298
Mail application, locked mailbox, 299
Sherlock errors, 297
slow-motion Dock, 297
using PC-formatted Zip disks, 299
troubleshooting problems
crashes and freezes, 158–161
inability to boot, 149–154
incompatibility of peripherals, 164
kernel panics, 162–163
password loss, 163–164
username, lack of, 154–157
virtual memory, 85–86
virus targets, 134
weaknesses, 146–147
Mac OS X Hints Web site, 285
MacConnection, purchasing RAM, 173
MacFixIt Web site, 283–284
extensions conflicts, 60–61
general troubleshooting, 76
software bugs, 74, 80
Mach, basis for Mac OS X, 10
MacInTouch Web site, 284
MacSense, Ethernet transceivers, 207
MacWarehouse, purchasing RAM, 173
MacWindows Web site, 285
Macworld
Conflict Catcher rating, 130
forums
advice on purchasing RAM, 173
troubleshooting, 76
software bugs, 80
modem script testing, 95
processor upgrades, 195
MacZone, purchasing RAM, 173
magneto-optical media drives, backups, 43
Mail application, Mac OS X, 165
Mark of the Unicorn
Moto sound input devices, 201
sound cards and input devices, 245
media drives. *See* removable media drives
memory. *See also* RAM; ROM; virtual memory
allocating for applications
browsers, 85
insufficient memory, 82–83
Mac OS X, 144–145
virtual memory, 83–85
disabling startup memory tests, 98
protected memory, Mac OS X, 144
MHz (megahertz), 3
Micromac, processor upgrades, 195
Micromat
TechTool Lite, rebuilding Desktop, 66–67
TechTool Pro, 60
booting Macs, 30
diagnosis and repair basics, 70, 71–72
emergency startup CDs, 106

Mac OS 9.2 and earlier, 109–116
Mac OS X troubleshooting/repairs, 149, 152
System Folder corruption, 38
virus testing, 115
Microsoft
Entourage
compressing email databases, 97
preferences files, 86
Outlook Express
compressing email databases, 97, 98
preferences files, 86
Word preferences files, 87–88
MIDI (Music Instrument Digital Interface) format, 272
MidiMan, sound cards and input devices, 245
Ming, Teng Chou. *See* Teng Chou Ming
modem problems
cable connections, 93–94
slow or dropped connections, 94–95
modem scripts, 95
monitors, 4
Morrison FontDesign's Font Doctor
scanning for font corruption, 68
Moto (Mark of the Unicorn) sound input devices, 201
MP3 audio files, 299
MP3 wireless jukebox project, 240–241
players, 4
Music Library, iTunes, 241
Musical Instruments (QuickTime Player Pro), 272

N

NetBarrier (Intego), 142
NetGear's Ethernet hubs, 208
Network Associates' Virex, 137
versus TechTool Pro, 115
networking
connections, 207
physical, 208–209
history, 206–207
logging on
Mac OS 9.2 and earlier, 230–231
Mac OS X, 231–232
practical projects
backup server, 233–240
wireless MP3 jukebox, 240–241
sharing USB printers, 209, 210
terminology, 207–209
networking software
Mac OS 9.2 and earlier
AirPort, 217–218
AirPort Base Station, 218
AirPort Base Station, configuration, 218–220
Airport Base Station, Mac configuration, 221–222

networking software *(continued)*
    AirPort, configuration, 218-220
    AppleTalk configuration, 211
    browsers, 216-217
    Chooser selections, 215-216
    file sharing, 211-213, 214
    IP addresses, 224
    routers, 222-223
    user access, 211-212
    user access, passwords and privileges, 212-213
    volume sharing, 211-213
  Mac OS X
    AppleTalk, enabling, 225-226
    file sharing, 224-225
    user access, 226-227
    user access, passwords, 227-228
    user access, passwords and privileges, 227-230
    user access, privileges, 229-230
newsgroups for Macs, software bugs, 74
NewWorld Mac architecture, ROM, 3
Norton Utilities (Symantec), 60
  booting Macs, 30
  diagnosis and repair basics, 70, 72-73
  emergency startup CDs, 105
  Mac OS 9.2 and earlier, 117-123
  Mac OS X features, 145
  Mac OS X troubleshooting/repairs, 149, 152
  Norton AntiVirus, 137-138
    versus TechTool Pro, 115
  Norton Personal Firewall, 142
  System Folder corruption, 38
Now Up-to-Date, features in Mac OS X, 145
NuBus cards, startup process troubleshooting, 27
nVidia GeForce 3 graphics card, 199

O

Orange Micro's PCI SCSI card adapters, 203
Orb removable media drives, backups, 43
Outlook Express (Microsoft)
  compressing email databases, 97, 98
  preferences files, 86

P

packages, extensions and control panels, 53
parameter RAM. *See* PRAM
partitions, 6
passwords
  Mac OS 9.2 and earlier, 212-213
  Mac OS X, 163-164
    networking, 227-228
PCI cards, startup process troubleshooting, 27
PCI IDE adapter cards, 180
PDS cards, startup process troubleshooting, 27

Peak LE (Bias), 250-251
performance enhancement
  choosing startup disk, 100
  compressing email databases, 96-98
  decreasing color depth, 99-100
  deleting control panels and extensions, 96
  increasing disk caching, 98, 99
  optimizing hard drives, 100
  purchasing new Macs, 100
  RAM module additions instead of virtual memory, 98
  rebuilding Desktop, 100
  upgrading Macs, 100
Power Manager, startup process troubleshooting, 21-22
power problems, startup process, 13
power supply, startup process troubleshooting, 23-24
power transmission, startup process troubleshooting, 18-19
  checklist, 24
PowerLogix, processor-upgrade companies, 195, 196
PowerWave and iMic (Griffin Technology) sound input devices, 245, 299
PRAM
  repair with TechTool Lite, 66-67
  System Folder corruption, 36-37
preemptive multitasking, Mac OS X, 144
preferences files
  applications, 86-87
  Finder, System Folder corruption, 35-36
  Mac OS 9.2 and earlier
    Finder, 8
    System Folder, 8
  Mac OS X, 11
  Microsoft Word, 87-88
  susceptibility to corruption, 67
print queues, printer troubleshooting, 92
printers
  network upgrades, 202
  networking, 209, 210
printing problems
  basics, 90-91
  cable connections, 91
  Chooser selections, 91
  troubleshooting, 92-93
Process Viewer utility, Mac OS X, 160-161
processors
  defined, 2-3
  speed ratings, 3
  startup process, 5
  upgrading, 169-170
    basics, 194
    installing, 196-198
    purchasing recommendations, 195
    types of upgrades, 194-195

ProMax's TurboMax adapter cards, 180
protected memory, Mac OS X, 11, 144
Proxim
    EtherMac iPrint Adapter LT, 202
    Ethernet transceivers, 207
    Ethernet-to-LocalTalk adapters, 208
publishing resources, *Macworld* and *Macworld Weekly Newsletter*, 283

Q

QDesign Music sound codec, 270-271
Qualcomm's Eudora
    compressing email databases, 97-98
    preferences files, 86
questioning Mac logo, no startup disk with valid System Folder, 31
QuicKeys, features in Mac OS X, 145
QuicKTime iMovies
    exporting, 267
    image settings, 268
    sound and video codecs, 268-271
    sound settings, 270-271
    video settings, 268-269
QuickTime Player Pro
    annotations, 275-276
    filter effects, 274-275
    multiple audio tracks, 272-273
    Musical Instruments, 272

R

Radeon (ATI) graphics card, 198
RAM (random-access memory)
    defined, 3
    modules
        damaged, 26, 64
        recommendations for purchasing, 64
    startup process, 4-5
        problems, 12
    upgrading, 168
        installing, 174-177
        purchasing recommendations, 172-173
        steps, 171
    versus virtual memory, 83-85
        performance enhancement, 98
RAMSeeker Web site, tracking RAM module prices, 64, 172, 173
random-access memory. *See* RAM
Ray Gun (Arboretum Systems) sound filters, 247, 250
read-only memory. *See* ROM
rebuilding Desktop, 65-66
    performance enhancement, 100

recording LPs and cassettes
    basics, 244
    burning CDs, 251-253
    hardware, 244-246
    software
        CD Spin Doctor, 246-248
        Peak LE, 250-251
        Sound Studio, 248-250
removable media drives
    backups, 43
    peripheral types, 4
resources
    Apple
        AppleCare Knowledge Base, 278-279
        software downloads, 280
        specifications database, 280
        Technical support line, 281-282
        Web site discussions, 279
    publishing
        Macworld, 282
        Macworld Weekly Newsletter, 283
    Web sites
        Accelerate Your Mac, 284
        Andy Ihnatko's Temporary Waste of Bandwidth, 286
        Ask Al, 285
        Game Ranger, 286
        Inside Mac Games, 286
        Mac OS X Hints, 285
        MacFixit, 283-284
        MacInTouch, 284
        MacWindows, 285
        Macworld, 283
        TidBITS, 284
        Version Tracker, 285
restoring hard drives, 41-42
Retrospect Desktop (Dantz), backups, 233-238
    Mac OS 9.2 and earlier, 132-133
Retrospect Express (Dantz), backups, 43
    Mac OS 9.2 and earlier, 132-133
RJ-45 Ethernet connectors, 206
Roland, sound cards and input devices, 245
ROM (read-only memory)
    defined, 3
    startup process, 4-5
        problems, 12
root level, System Folder, 7
routers, 208
    hardware firewalls, 140-141
    networking configuration, 222-223
Roxio's Toast and Toast Titanium
    CD Spin Doctor, 246-248
    emergency startup CDs, 105-106
    gap settings, 252-253
    Video CDs, 254-255

S

Sad Mac, troubleshooting startup
   add-on cards, 27
   bad RAM modules, 26
   Cuda button, 23, 26
   SCSI devices, 27-29
   startup disk confusion, 30-31
Sad Macs, Bombs, and Other Disasters, 76
safety precautions, installing RAM, 174
Scan for Damage (Conflict Catcher), 129
scanners, SCSI, 29
screen savers, Mac OS X, 262-263
SCSI devices
   addresses, 178-180
   hardware conflicts, 61
   startup process troubleshooting, 27-29, 32
   upgrading Macs, 203
serial ports, upgrading Macs, 201-202
Shutdown Items folder, Mac OS 9.2 and earlier, 9
slide show creation
   basics, 255
   with AppleWorks, 256-258
   with iMovie, 258-260
   with iView Media Pro, 261-262
Small Computer System Interface. *See* SCSI
software bugs
   basics, 73-74
   handling bugs, 74-75, 80-81
   Mac OS X, 165
Sonnet Technology, processor-upgrade companies, 195, 196
Sonnet Technology, upgrading with CPUs, 169
Sorenson Video codecs, 268-269
sound cards
   startup process troubleshooting, 27
   upgrading Macs, 200-201
sound filters, 247, 250
sound input devices, 245
   gain adjustments, 249
sound recordings
   basics, 244
   burning CDs, 251-253
   hardware, 244-246
   software
      CD Spin Doctor, 246-248
      Peak LE, 250-251
      Sound Studio, 248-250
   tips, 266
Sound Studio (Felt Tip Software), 248-250
SoundBlaster Live! (Creative Technology) sound card, 201, 245
specifications database, Apple, 280
Speed Disk (Symantec's Norton Utilities), 72, 119-120
Spring Cleaning (Aladdin Systems), uninstalling applications, 90

startup disks
   emergency startup CDs, 104-106
   performance enhancement, 100
   questioning Mac logo, 31
   Sad Mac or Chimes of Doom icons, 30-31
Startup Items folder, Mac OS 9.2 and earlier, 9
startup process
   Mac OS X, 12
   roles of RAM and ROM, 4-5
startup process troubleshooting
   batteries, 20-21
   cable connections, 19-20, 40
   contacting Apple Authorized Dealers, 25
   hard drive appears missing, checklist, 40-41
   hardware, 13, 15-16
   last-ditch efforts, checklist, 41-42
   peripheral devices, 40
      FireWire, 32-34
      SCSI, 32
      USB, 32-34
   Power Manager, 21-22, 40
   power supply, 23-24
   power transmission, 18-19
      checklist, 24
   pressing Cuda button, 23, 26
   questioning Mac logo, no startup disk with valid System Folder, 31
   Sad Mac or Chimes of Doom icons
      add-on cards, 27
      bad RAM modules, 26
      SCSI devices, 27-29
      startup disk confusion, 30-31
   software, 13-16
   System Folder corruption, causes and solutions, 34-39
static IP addresses, 224
straight-through Ethernet cables, 208
Stuffit (Aladdin Systems), 114
   features in Mac OS X, 145
Suitcase (Extensis), scanning for font corruption, 68
Surface Scan (Micromat's TechTool Pro), 115
Symantec's Norton Utilities, 60
   booting Macs, 30
   diagnosis and repair basics, 70, 72-73
   emergency startup CDs, 105
   Mac OS 9.2 and earlier, 117-123
   Mac OS X features, 145
   Mac OS X troubleshooting/repairs, 149, 152
   Norton AntiVirus, 137-138
   versus TechTool Pro, 115
   Norton Personal Firewall, 142
   System Folder corruption, 38
System files
   suitcases, 7
   System Folder corruption, 35

System Folder
  clean installs, 38–39
    Conflict Catcher, 77–78, 128–129
  Font folder corruption, 68
  Mac OS 9.2 and earlier, 7
  preferences file, 86–87
  startup process troubleshooting
    corrupt folder, causes and solutions, 34–39
    questioning Mac logo, 31
System Profiler (Apple), 180–181
System software CDs, booting Macs, 20

T

TCP/IP, networking history, 207
technical support (Apple), 281–282
  troubleshooting startup process, 25
TechTool Lite (Micromat)
  Mac OS X troubleshooting/repairs, 149, 152
  rebuilding Desktop, 66–67
TechTool Pro (Micromat), 60
  booting Macs, 30
  diagnosis and repair basics, 70, 71–72
  Mac OS 9.2 and earlier, 109–116
  System Folder corruption, 38
  virus testing, 115
TechTools Pro (Micromat), emergency startup CDs, 106
TechWorks, purchasing RAM modules, 64, 172–173
Temporary Waste of Bandwidth Web site, 286
10Base-T and 100Base-T Ethernet ports, 206–207
Teng Chou Ming and Peter Hardman's Extension Overload, 50, 53, 54
TidBITS Web site, 284
tips and tricks
  Mac OS 9.2 and earlier
    AOL, common errors, 290
    AOL, killing sounds, 290
    AppleWorks buttons, 293
    calculating with Netscape, 291
    creator code changes, 289
    escaping repair warnings, 295
    hiding PowerPoint's innards, 291
    mass deletes, 295
    Microsoft Word 2001 Disk Full error, 296
    Microsoft Word keyboard commands, list, 292
    Microsoft Word preference files, resetting, 296
    opening multiple Web pages, 293
    opening SuperDrive media drives, 288–289
    remote printing, 292
    renaming hard drives, 292
    Reset and Programmer's buttons, 294–295
    restoring hard drives from Software Restore discs, 288
    saving Outlook Express messages to Word, 294
    Sherlock folder searches, 294
    speeding up startup, 294
    TCP/IP, remote access settings, 293
    title-bar folder icons, 291–292
    USB Overdirve package, 291
    window screen shots, 296
  Mac OS X
    adding alert sounds, 298–299
    customizing application toolbars, 297
    Desktop aliases, 297
    Desktop files, 299
    disabling Auto-Dial, 298
    file/folder renaming cautions, 298
    Mail application, locked mailbox, 299
    Sherlock errors, 297
    slow-motion Dock, 297
    using PC-formatted Zip disks, 299
Toast and Toast Titanium (Roxio)
  CD Spin Doctor, 246–248
  emergency startup CDs, 105–106
  gap settings, 252–253
  Video CDs, 254–255
transceivers (Ethernet), 207
Transmission Control Protocol/Internet Protocol. *See* TCP/IP
TurboMax (ProMax) adapter cards, 180

U

UnErase (Symantec's Norton Utilities), 120, 121
uninstalling applications, 88–89
  utilities, 90
Universal Serial Bus. *See* USB
Unix, version basis for Mac OS X, 10
upgrading Macs
  ADB devices, 201
  checklist, 168
  CPUs, 169–170
    basics, 194
    installing, 196–198
    purchasing recommendations, 195
    types of upgrades, 194–195
  graphics cards, 170–171
    basics, 198
    configuring monitors, 199–200
    purchasing recommendations, 198–199
  hard drives, 168–169
    installing, 182–193
    jumpers, 178–180
    purchasing tips, 181–182
  network printers, 202
  performance enhancement, 100
  RAM, 168
    installing, 174–177
    purchasing recommendations, 172–173
    steps, 171
  SCSI devices, 203

upgrading Macs *(continued)*
   serial ports, 201-202
   sound cards, 200-201
USB devices
   hardware conflicts, 61-63
   network printers, 209, 210
   printing troubleshooting, 92
   startup process troubleshooting, 32-34

V

VersionTracker Web site, 285
   software bugs, 75
video cards, startup process troubleshooting, 27. *See also* movies; slide shows
Video CDs, 253-255
video game, hidden in Conflict Catcher, 129
Virex (Network Associates), 137
   versus TechTool Pro, 115
virtual memory
   Mac OS X, 85-86
   memory allocation for applications, 83-85
   startup process, 5
   versus RAM, performance enhancement, 98
VirusBarrier (Intego), 137, 138
   versus TechTool Pro, 115
viruses
   antivirus utilities
      Norton AntiVirus, 137-138
      Virex, 137
      VirusBarrier, 137, 138
   basics, 133-135
   characteristics of future utilities, 135-137
Volume Recover (Symantec's Norton Utilities), 120, 121
volumes, defined, 6

W

Web etiquette
   displaying tact, 303-304
   disrupting other's fun with inappropriate actions or language, 305
   failing to read FAQs, manuals, and previous posts, 302
   inappropriate language, 303
   responding hotheadedly to messages, 302
   responding with vagueness, 304
   sending chain mail, 304
   sending messages/attachments without permission, 303
   spam, 302
   typing in ALL CAPS, 302
WiFi devices, 208
Williams, Robin; *The Little Mac Book*, 2

Wipe Data (Micromat's TechTool Pro), 116
Wipe Info (Symantec's Norton Utilities), 122
wireless MP3 jukebox project, 240-241
Word (Microsoft), preferences files, 87-88

X-Z

XLR8, processor-upgrade companies, 195, 197
Yamaha, sound cards and input devices, 245
ZIF (Zero Insertion Force) socket design, 194, 196
Zip removable media drives, backups, 43

Take Your Mac to the Max!

Macworld magazine is *the* indispensable guide to Macintosh computing. In every issue you'll find the technical information you need to get the most from your Mac.

Features that objectively cover emerging technologies and issues

Reviews of the latest hardware and software

Buying tips you should know before you make any important purchase

How-to's, pointers, and shortcuts the manuals don't give you

Ratings from our Macworld Lab, the industry's foremost product-comparison lab

And don't forget your FREE Double Bonus!

Two digital image libraries—CD-ROMs filled with an incredible selection of exclusive clip art images, digital stock photos, and other graphic applications and software—FREE with your order.

Go online now! http://www.macworld-freetrial.com

CLIP HERE

Macworld® SUBSCRIPTION BENEFITS

- **79% Savings Off the Cover Price**

- **Two FREE CD-ROMs**
  Loaded with clip art images, digital photos, graphics, and more.

- **Money-Back Guarantee**
  If you're ever dissatisfied with your subscription, we'll send you a full refund for all unmailed issues.

- **Guaranteed Savings**
  Your subscription will continue for as long as you wish, unless you instruct us otherwise. We will notify and bill you at the discounted renewal rate then in effect prior to each new subscription term.

Mail this form to: Macworld • P.O. Box 54500 • Boulder, CO 80322-4500

FREE TRIAL!
TWO FREE CDs!